Taste of Home

SIMPLE, EASY, FAST
SLOW COOKER

TASTE OF HOME BOOKS • RDA ENTHUSIAST BRANDS, LLC • MILWAUKEE WI

Taste of Home

Reader's digest

A TASTE OF HOME/READER'S DIGEST BOOK

© 2016 RDA Enthusiast Brands, LLC 1610 N. 2nd St., Suite 102, Milwaukee WI 53212 All rights reserved.
Taste of Home and Reader's Digest are registered trademarks of The Reader's Digest Association, Inc.

EDITORIAL

Editor-in-Chief: Catherine Cassidy
Creative Director: Howard Greenberg
Editorial Operations Director: Kerri Balliet

Managing Editor, Print & Digital Books: Mark Hagen
Associate Creative Director: Edwin Robles Jr.

Layout Designer: Courtney Lovetere
Editorial Production Manager: Dena Ahlers
Editorial Production Coordinator: Jill Banks
Copy Chief: Deb Warlaumont Mulvey
Copy Editor: Mary-Liz Shaw
Contributing Copy Editor: Valerie Phillips
Editorial Intern: Michael Welch
Business Analyst, Content Tools: Amanda Harmatys
Content Operations Assistant: Shannon Stroud
Editorial Services Administrator: Marie Brannon

Food Editors: Gina Nistico; James Schend; Peggy Woodward, RD
Recipe Editors: Mary King; Jenni Sharp, RD; Irene Yeh

Test Kitchen & Food Styling Manager: Sarah Thompson
Test Cooks: Nicholas Iverson (lead), Matthew Hass, Lauren Knoelke
Food Stylists: Kathryn Conrad (lead), Leah Rekau, Shannon Roum
Prep Cooks: Bethany Van Jacobson (lead), Megumi Garcia, Melissa Hansen
Culinary Team Assistant: Megan Behr

Photography Director: Stephanie Marchese
Photographers: Dan Roberts, Jim Wieland
Photographer/Set Stylist: Grace Natoli Sheldon
Set Stylists: Melissa Franco, Stacey Genaw, Dee Dee Jacq
Photo Studio Assistant: Ester Robards

Editorial Business Manager: Kristy Martin
Editorial Business Associate: Samantha Lea Stoeger

BUSINESS

Vice President, Group Publisher: Kirsten Marchioli
Publisher: Donna Lindskog
General Manager, Taste of Home Cooking School: Erin Puariea
Executive Producer, Taste of Home Online Cooking School: Karen Berner

THE READER'S DIGEST ASSOCIATION, INC.

President & Chief Executive Officer: Bonnie Kintzer
Vice President, Chief Financial Officer/ Chief Operating Officer, North America: Howard Halligan
Chief Revenue Officer: Richard Sutton
Chief Marketing Officer: Leslie Dukker Doty
Senior Vice President, Global HR & Communications: Phyllis E. Gebhardt, SPHR; SHRM–SCP
Vice President, Digital Content & Audience Development: Diane Dragan
Vice President, Brand Marketing: Beth Gorry
Vice President, Financial Planning & Analysis: William Houston
Publishing Director, Books: Debra Polansky
Vice President, Chief Technology Officer: Aneel Tejwaney
Vice President, Consumer Marketing Planning: Jim Woods

For other Taste of Home books and products, visit us at **tasteofhome.com.**

For more Reader's Digest products and information, visit **rd.com** (in the United States) or see **rd.ca** (in Canada).

International Standard Book Number: 978-1-61765-506-7
Library of Congress Control Number: 2015948969

Cover Photographer: Dan Roberts
Set Stylist: Melissa Franco
Food Stylist: Kathryn Conrad

Pictured on front cover:
Greek Pasta Salad, page 222;
Chipotle Carne Guisada, page 80

Pictured on back cover:
Meat-Lover's Pizza Hot Dish, page 79; Chile Colorado Burritos, page 74; Molten Mocha Cake, page 193

Printed in USA
1 3 5 7 9 10 8 6 4 2

LIKE US
facebook.com/tasteofhome

TWEET US
@tasteofhome

FOLLOW US
pinterest.com/taste_of_home

SHOP WITH US
shoptasteofhome.com

SHARE A RECIPE
tasteofhome.com/submit

GOOEY PEANUT BUTTER-CHOCOLATE CAKE, 197

SHOEPEG CORN SIDE DISH, 70

SLOW COOKER CHICKEN & BLACK BEAN SOFT TACOS, 107

CONTENTS

8
Effortless Appetizers & Beverages

26
Simple Soups

52
Speedy Side Dishes & More

72
Easy Entrees
    BEEF 74
    POULTRY 100
    PORK. 130
    OTHER ENTREES 158

184
Swift Sweets

212
BONUS: No-Fuss Salads & Sides

230
BONUS: Quick Breads

246
Indexes

BUFFALO WING DIP, 18

Making the most of your slow cooker is **simple, easy and *FAST!***

WELCOME HOME! Let the savory aroma of a hot meal fill your house even on your busiest nights. For years family cooks relied on their slow cookers to do just that, but now *Taste of Home Simple, Easy, Fast Slow Cooker* cookbook makes it even easier to whip up those simmering specialties.

Like no other slow-cooker book, this collection of 390 recipes offers quick prep times, speedy cook times and short ingredient lists to help you set hearty meals on the table...regardless of your schedule!

See the icons at right to find the fastest and easiest recipes this book has to offer. Don't miss the two bonus chapters that round out slow-cooked entrees perfectly, and visit the Cook Time Index on page 255 for effortless menu planning. Then dish out the goodness with *Simple, Easy, Fast Slow Cooker!*

At-a-Glance Icons

READY IN 4
These recipes are ready, start to finish, **in just 4 hours** or less!

5 INGREDIENTS
Not including water, salt, pepper and oil, these dishes need only **five items.**

EXPRESS PREP
You only need **10 minutes of preparation time** for these delicious family favorites.

ADVANTAGES OF **SLOW COOKING**

CONVENIENCE. Slow cookers provide families the ease of safely preparing meals while away from home. With this book, they can create those meals in 2, 4 or 8 hours!

HEALTH. As more people turn to nutritious food choices to improve health, slow cooking has gained popularity. Low-temperature cooking retains more vitamins in foods, and leaner cuts of meat become tender in the slow cooker without added fats. Lower-sodium and lower-fat versions of many canned goods are available, which can help you create even lighter, healthier meals.

And, for many family cooks, knowing that a healthy meal is waiting at home helps them avoid the temptation of the drive-thru after work.

FINANCIAL SAVINGS. A slow cooker uses very little electricity because of its low wattage. Also, slow cookers do not heat up the kitchen like ovens do, which saves on summertime cooling costs. In addition, many slow-cooked entrees freeze well. See the freezer directions at the end of particular recipes and save money by serving comfort favorites stashed away in the freezer for particularly busy evenings.

TIPS FOR **TASTY OUTCOMES**

- Be sure the lid is well-placed over the ceramic insert, not tilted or askew. The steam during cooking creates a seal.

- Refrain from lifting the lid while using the slow cooker, unless the recipe instructs you to stir or add ingredients. The loss of steam each time you lift the lid can mean an extra 20 to 30 minutes of cooking time.

- Remember that slow cooking may take longer at higher altitudes.

- When food is finished cooking, remove it from the slow cooker within an hour. Promptly refrigerate any leftovers.

- Use a slow cooker on a buffet table to keep soup, stew, savory dips or mashed potatoes hot.

- Heat cooked food on the stovetop or in the microwave and then put it into a slow cooker to keep it hot for serving. Reheating food in a slow cooker isn't recommended.

- Don't forget your slow cooker when you go camping, if electricity will be available. When space is limited and you want effortless meals, the slow cooker is a handy appliance.

MAPLE-WALNUT SWEET POTATOES, 54

PREPARING FOOD **FOR THE SLOW COOKER**

BEANS. Dried beans can be tricky to cook in a slow cooker. Minerals in the water and variations in voltage affect various types of beans in different ways. Always soak dried beans prior to cooking. Soak them overnight or

place them in a Dutch oven and add enough water to cover by 2 inches. Bring to a boil and boil for 2 minutes. Remove from the heat, cover and let stand for 1 to 4 hours or until softened. Drain and rinse beans, discarding liquid. Sugar, salt and acidic ingredients, such as vinegar, interfere with the beans' ability to cook and become tender. Add these ingredients only after the beans are fully cooked. Lentils and split peas do not need soaking.

COUSCOUS. Couscous is best cooked on the stovetop rather than in the slow cooker.

DAIRY. Milk-based products tend to break down during slow cooking. Items like milk, cream,

sour cream or cream cheese are best added during the last hour of cooking. Cheeses don't generally hold up during the slow cooker's extended cooking time and should be added near the end of cooking. Condensed cream soups generally hold up well in the slow cooker.

SEAFOOD & FISH. Seafood and fish cook quickly and can break down if cooked too long. They are generally added to the slow cooker toward the end of the cooking time to keep them at optimal quality.

MEATS. To cut prep time, few of the recipes in this book call for browning meat before placing it in the slow cooker. While browning is not necessary, it generally adds to the flavor and appearance of the meat and allows you to drain off the fat. Cut roasts of more than 3 pounds in half before placing in the slow cooker to ensure even cooking. Trim off any excess fat, as large amounts of fat could raise the temperature of the cooking liquid in the slow cooker, causing the meat to overcook.

OATS. Quick-cooking and old-fashioned oats are often interchangeable in recipes. However, old-fashioned oats hold up better in the slow cooker.

PASTA. If added to a slow cooker when dry, pasta tends to become very sticky. It's better to cook it according to the package directions and stir it into the slow cooker just before serving. Small pastas such as orzo and ditalini may be cooked in the slow cooker, however. To keep them from becoming mushy, add during the last hour of cooking.

RICE. Converted rice is ideal for all-day cooking. If using instant rice, add it during the last 30 minutes of cooking.

VEGETABLES. Firm vegetables like potatoes and carrots tend to cook more slowly than meat. Cut these foods into uniform pieces and place on the bottom and around the sides of the slow cooker. Place the meat over the vegetables. During the last 15 to 60 minutes of cooking, add tender vegetables, like peas and zucchini, or ones you'd prefer to be crisp-tender.

145°F

- Medium-rare beef and lamb roasts
- Fish

160°F

- Medium beef and lamb roasts
- Pork
- Egg dishes

165°F

- Ground chicken and turkey

170°F

- Well-done beef and lamb roasts
- Chicken and turkey that is whole or in pieces

COOKING **BASICS**

- While slow cooker models vary, they usually have at least two settings, low (about 180°) and high (about 280°). Some models also have a keep-warm setting.
- The keep-warm setting is useful if you plan to use the slow cooker to serve hot food while entertaining. Some slow cookers will automatically switch to a keep-warm setting after cooking. This provides added convenience and helps you avoid overcooking the food while you're away from home.
- A range in cooking time is provided to account for variables such as thickness of meat, fullness of the slow cooker and desired finished temperature of the food being cooked. As you grow familiar with your slow cooker, you'll be able to judge which end of the range to use.
- New slow cookers tend to heat up more quickly than older models. If you have an older appliance and your recipe directs to cook on low, you may wish to cook on high for the first hour to ensure food safety temperatures are successfully met.
- Old slow cookers can lose their efficiency and may not achieve proper cooking temperatures. To confirm safe cooking temperatures, use a meat thermometer to verify temperatures as noted at left.
- To learn more about specific models, check online or in reputable consumer magazines for product reviews.

AUTUMN
PUMPKIN CHILI,
180

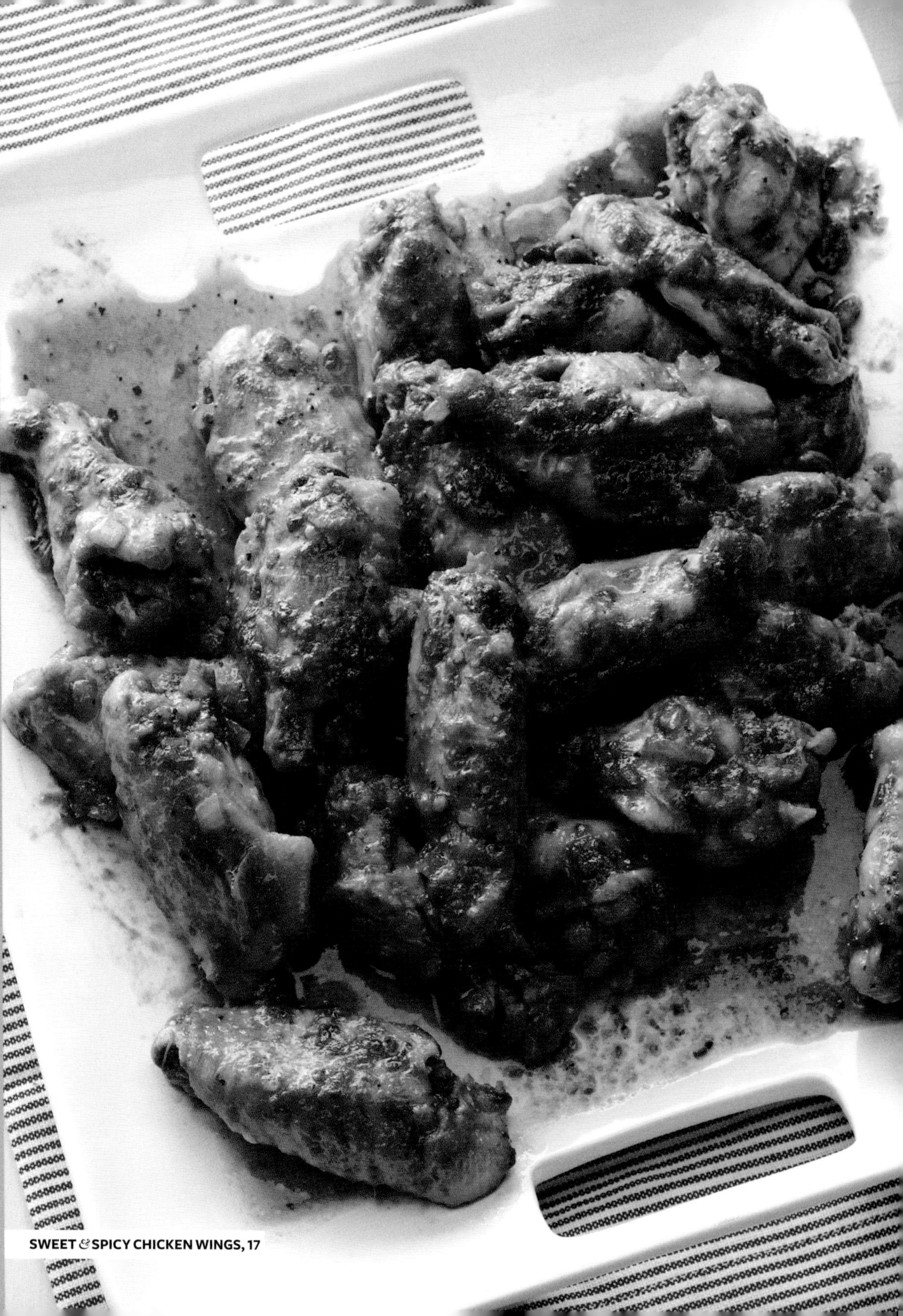

SWEET & SPICY CHICKEN WINGS, 17

18

19

20

Effortless Appetizers
& Beverages

Whether served as party starters, late-night snacks or after-school treats, these recipes always hit the spot. They come together easily with a slow cooker, giving you more time to get in on the fun!

TACO JOE DIP, 24

PEPPERONI EXTREME DIP

**PORKY PICADILLO
LETTUCE WRAPS**

Porky Picadillo Lettuce Wraps

Warm pork and cool, crisp lettuce are a combination born in culinary heaven. My spin on a lettuce wrap is chock-full of scrumptious flavor and unique spices.

—JANICE ELDER CHARLOTTE, NC

PREP: 30 MIN. • **COOK:** 2½ HOURS
MAKES: 2 DOZEN

- 3 garlic cloves, minced
- 1 tablespoon chili powder
- 1 teaspoon salt
- ½ teaspoon pumpkin pie spice
- ½ teaspoon ground cumin
- ½ teaspoon pepper
- 2 pork tenderloins (1 pound each)
- 1 large onion, chopped
- 1 small Granny Smith apple, peeled and chopped
- 1 small sweet red pepper, chopped
- 1 can (10 ounces) diced tomatoes and green chilies, undrained
- ½ cup golden raisins
- ½ cup chopped pimiento-stuffed olives
- 24 Bibb or Boston lettuce leaves
- ¼ cup slivered almonds, toasted

1. Mix garlic and seasonings; rub over pork. Transfer to a 5-qt. slow cooker. Add onion, apple, sweet pepper and tomatoes. Cook, covered, on low 2½-3 hours or until meat is tender.

2. Remove pork; cool slightly. Shred meat into bite-size pieces; return to slow cooker. Stir in the raisins and olives; heat through. Serve in lettuce leaves; sprinkle with almonds.

Pepperoni Extreme Dip

With just 10 minutes of prep time and assistance from a slow cooker, this truly is a no-fuss dip.

—LAURA MAGEE HOULTON, WI

PREP: 10 MIN. • **COOK:** 3 HOURS
MAKES: 2¼ QUARTS

- 4 cups (16 ounces) shredded cheddar cheese
- 3½ cups spaghetti sauce
- 2 cups mayonnaise
- 1 package (8 ounces) sliced pepperoni, chopped
- 1 can (6 ounces) pitted ripe olives, chopped
- 1 jar (5¾ ounces) sliced green olives with pimientos, drained and chopped
  Tortilla chips

Combine the first six ingredients in a 4-qt. slow cooker coated with cooking spray. Cover and cook on low for 1½ hours; stir. Cover and cook 1½ hours longer or until the cheese is melted. Serve with tortilla chips.

Beer Cheese Fondue

This thick fondue originated in my kitchen when I didn't have all of the ingredients I needed to make the recipe I initially planned to prepare. Served with bread cubes, it has since become a staple, particularly while we watch football games on television.

—CHRYSTIE WEAR OAK RIDGE, NC

START TO FINISH: 15 MIN.
MAKES: ABOUT 3 CUPS

- 1 loaf (1 pound) French bread, cubed
- ¼ cup chopped onion
- 1 tablespoon butter
- 1 teaspoon minced garlic
- 1 cup beer or nonalcoholic beer
- 4 cups (16 ounces) shredded cheddar cheese
- 1 tablespoon all-purpose flour
- 2 to 4 tablespoons half-and-half cream

1. Place bread cubes in a single layer in an ungreased 15x10x1-in. baking pan. Bake at 450° for 5-7 minutes or until lightly crisp, stirring twice.

2. Meanwhile, in a small saucepan, saute onion in butter until tender. Add garlic; cook 1 minute longer. Stir in beer. Bring to a boil; reduce heat to medium-low. Toss cheese with flour; stir into saucepan until melted. Stir in 2 tablespoons of the cream.

3. Transfer to a 1½-qt. slow cooker. Keep warm; add additional cream if fondue thickens. Serve with toasted bread cubes.

Chunky Applesauce

My mother gave me the recipe for this cinnamony apple delight, which fills the house with a wonderful aroma as it simmers in a slow cooker. I like to serve the warm dish with ice cream for dessert.

—LISA ROESSNER FORT RECOVERY, OH

PREP: 5 MIN. • **COOK:** 6 HOURS
MAKES: 5 CUPS

- 8 to 10 large tart apples, peeled and cut into chunks
  Sugar substitute equivalent to ½ to 1 cup sugar
- ½ cup water
- 1 teaspoon ground cinnamon

Combine apples, sugar substitute, water and cinnamon in a 3-qt. slow cooker; stir gently. Cover and cook on low for 6-8 hours or until apples are tender.

Butterscotch Dip

If you like the sweetness of butterscotch chips, you'll enjoy this rum-flavored fruit dip. I serve it with apple and pear wedges. It holds up nicely for up to 2 hours in the slow cooker.

—JEAUNE HADL VAN METER
LEXINGTON, KY

PREP: 5 MIN. • **COOK:** 45 MIN.
MAKES: ABOUT 3 CUPS

- 2   packages (10 to 11 ounces each) butterscotch chips
- ⅔   cup evaporated milk
- ⅔   cup chopped pecans
- 1   tablespoon rum extract
     Apple and pear wedges

In a 1½-qt. slow cooker, combine butterscotch chips and milk. Cover and cook on low for 45-50 minutes or until chips are softened; stir until smooth. Stir in pecans and extract. Serve warm with fruit.

Spiced Apricot Cider

You'll need just a few ingredients to simmer together for this hot spiced beverage. Each delicious serving is rich with apricot flavor, making a great sipper any time of year.

—CONNIE CUMMINGS
GLOUCESTER, NJ

PREP: 5 MIN. • **COOK:** 2 HOURS
MAKES: 6 SERVINGS

- 2   cans (12 ounces each) apricot nectar
- 2   cups water
- ¼   cup lemon juice
- ¼   cup sugar
- 2   whole cloves
- 2   cinnamon sticks (3 inches)

In a 3-qt. slow cooker, combine all ingredients. Cover and cook on low for 2 hours or until cider reaches desired temperature. Discard cloves and cinnamon sticks.

REUBEN SPREAD

Reuben Spread

My daughter shared this recipe for a hearty spread that tastes just like a Reuben sandwich. Serve it from a slow cooker set to low so that it stays warm and gooey!

—ROSALIE FUCHS PAYNESVILLE, MN

PREP: 5 MIN. • **COOK:** 2 HOURS
MAKES: 3½ CUPS

- 1   can (14 ounces) sauerkraut, rinsed and well drained
- 1   package (8 ounces) cream cheese, cubed
- 2   cups (8 ounces) shredded Swiss cheese
- 1   package (3 ounces) deli corned beef, chopped
- 3   tablespoons prepared Thousand Island salad dressing
     Snack rye bread or crackers

In a 1½-qt. slow cooker, combine the first five ingredients. Cover and cook on low for 2-3 hours or until cheeses are melted; stir to blend. Serve warm with bread or crackers.

BUTTERSCOTCH DIP

MARINATED CHICKEN WINGS

Marinated Chicken Wings

I've made these nicely flavored chicken wings many times for get-togethers. They're so moist and tender. I always get compliments and requests for the recipe.

—JANIE BOTTING SULTAN, WA

PREP: 5 MIN. + MARINATING
COOK: 3 HOURS
MAKES: 20 SERVINGS

- 20 **whole chicken wings (about 4 pounds)**
- 1 **cup reduced-sodium soy sauce**
- ¼ **cup white wine or reduced-sodium chicken broth**
- ¼ **cup canola oil**
- 3 **tablespoons sugar**
- 2 **garlic cloves, minced**
- 1 **teaspoon ground ginger**

1. Cut chicken wings into three sections; discard wing tips. Place in a large resealable plastic bag. In a small bowl, whisk the remaining ingredients until blended. Add to chicken; seal bag and turn to coat. Refrigerate overnight.

2. Transfer chicken and marinade to a 5-qt. slow cooker. Cook, covered, on low 3-4 hours or until chicken is tender. Using tongs, remove wings to a serving plate.

NOTE *To brown wings before serving, preheat broiler. Using tongs, remove wings from slow cooker to a foil-lined baking sheet. Broil 3-4 in. from heat for 3-5 minutes or until lightly browned.*

BARBECUE SAUSAGE BITES

SLOW-COOKER CANDIED NUTS

EXPRESS PREP READY IN ④

Barbecue Sausage Bites

This sweet-and-tangy appetizer pairs pineapple chunks with barbecue sauce and three kinds of sausage. It'll tide over even the biggest appetites until dinner.

—**REBEKAH RANDOLPH** GREER, SC

PREP: 10 MIN. • **COOK:** 2½ HOURS
MAKES: 12-14 SERVINGS

- 1 package (16 ounces) miniature smoked sausages
- ¾ pound fully cooked bratwurst links, cut into ½-inch slices
- ¾ pound smoked kielbasa or Polish sausage, cut into ½-inch slices
- 1 bottle (18 ounces) barbecue sauce
- ⅔ cup orange marmalade
- ½ teaspoon ground mustard
- ⅛ teaspoon ground allspice
- 1 can (20 ounces) pineapple chunks, drained

1. In a 3-qt. slow cooker, combine the sausages. In a small bowl, whisk the barbecue sauce, marmalade, mustard and allspice. Pour over sausage mixture; stir to coat.

2. Cover and cook on high for 2½-3 hours or until heated through. Stir in pineapple. Serve with toothpicks.

EXPRESS PREP READY IN ④

Slow-Cooker Candied Nuts

I like giving spiced nuts as holiday gifts. This slow-cooker recipe with ginger and cinnamon is so good, you just might use it all year long.

—**YVONNE STARLIN** HERMITAGE, TN

PREP: 10 MIN. • **COOK:** 2 HOURS
MAKES: 4 CUPS

- ½ cup butter, melted
- ½ cup confectioners' sugar
- 1½ teaspoons ground cinnamon
- ¼ teaspoon ground ginger
- ¼ teaspoon ground allspice
- 1½ cups pecan halves
- 1½ cups walnut halves
- 1 cup unblanched almonds

1. In a greased 3-qt. slow cooker, mix butter, confectioners' sugar and spices. Add nuts; toss to coat. Cook, covered, on low 2-3 hours or until nuts are crisp, stirring once.

2. Transfer nuts to waxed paper to cool completely. Store in an airtight container.

TOP TIP

Slow-Cooker Candied Nuts are a great way to take advantage of your slow cooker. Mix up the recipe by adding cashews or dry roasted peanuts. You can also adjust the seasonings a bit to best suit your tastes.

Championship Bean Dip

My friends and neighbors expect me to bring this irresistible dip to every gathering. When I arrive, they ask, "You brought your bean dip, didn't you?" If there are any leftovers, we use them to make bean and cheese burritos the next day. I've given out this recipe a hundred times.

—**WENDI WAVRIN LAW** OMAHA, NE

PREP: 10 MIN. • **COOK:** 2 HOURS
MAKES: 4½ CUPS

- 1 can (16 ounces) refried beans
- 1 cup picante sauce
- 1 cup (4 ounces) shredded Monterey Jack cheese
- 1 cup (4 ounces) shredded cheddar cheese
- ¾ cup sour cream
- 1 package (3 ounces) cream cheese, softened
- 1 tablespoon chili powder
- ¼ teaspoon ground cumin
  Tortilla chips and salsa

In a large bowl, combine the first eight ingredients; transfer to a 1½-qt. slow cooker. Cover and cook on high for 2 hours or until heated through, stirring once or twice. Serve with tortilla chips and salsa.

Party-Pleasing Beef Dish

Mild and saucy, this mixture is served over tortilla chips and topped with popular taco ingredients. Consider it a nacho platter kicked up a bit! My guests can't get enough of it.

—**GLEE WITZKE** CRETE, NE

PREP: 15 MIN. • **COOK:** 4¼ HOURS
MAKES: 6-8 SERVINGS

- 1 pound ground beef
- 1 medium onion, chopped
- ¾ cup water
- 1 can (8 ounces) tomato sauce
- 1 can (6 ounces) tomato paste
- 2 teaspoons sugar
- 1 garlic clove, minced
- 1 teaspoon chili powder
- 1 teaspoon ground cumin
- 1 teaspoon dried oregano
- 1 cup cooked rice
  Tortilla chips
  Optional toppings: shredded cheddar cheese, chopped green onions, sliced ripe olives, sour cream, chopped tomatoes and taco sauce

1. In a large skillet, cook beef and onion over medium heat until meat is no longer pink; drain. Transfer to a 3-qt. slow cooker. Stir in the water, tomato sauce, tomato paste, sugar, garlic and seasonings.

2. Cover and cook on low for 4-5 hours or until heated through. Add the rice; cover and cook 10 minutes longer.

3. Before serving, dollop beef mixture over tortilla chips with toppings of your choice.

CHAMPIONSHIP BEAN DIP

BACON-RANCH SPINACH DIP

SWEET & SPICY CHICKEN WINGS

SPICED FRUIT PUNCH

Bacon-Ranch Spinach Dip

During the hectic holiday season, my slow cooker works overtime. I fill it with a savory bacon dip and watch everyone line up for a helping. Keep the recipe in mind for tailgating, too.
—CRYSTAL SCHLUETER
NORTHGLENN, CO

PREP: 15 MIN. • **COOK:** 2 HOURS
MAKES: 24 SERVINGS (¼ CUP EACH)

- 2 packages (8 ounces each) cream cheese, softened
- 1½ cups bacon ranch salad dressing
- ¼ cup 2% milk
- 2 cups (8 ounces) shredded sharp cheddar cheese
- 1 can (14 ounces) water-packed artichoke hearts, rinsed, drained and chopped
- 1 package (10 ounces) frozen chopped spinach, thawed and squeezed dry
- 2 plum tomatoes, seeded and finely chopped
- ½ cup crumbled cooked bacon
- 4 green onions, thinly sliced Assorted crackers and fresh vegetables

1. In a large bowl, beat the cream cheese, salad dressing and milk until blended. Stir in the cheese, artichokes, spinach, tomatoes, bacon and green onions. Transfer to a 4- or 5-qt. slow cooker.
2. Cook, covered, on low 2-3 hours or until heated through. Serve with crackers and vegetables.

Sweet & Spicy Chicken Wings

The meat literally falls off the bones of these wings! Spice lovers will get a kick out of the big sprinkling of red pepper flakes.
—SUE BAYLESS PRIOR LAKE, MN

PREP: 25 MIN. • **COOK:** 5 HOURS
MAKES: ABOUT 2½ DOZEN

- 3 pounds chicken wings
- 1½ cups ketchup
- 1 cup packed brown sugar
- 1 small onion, finely chopped
- ¼ cup finely chopped sweet red pepper
- 2 tablespoons chili powder
- 2 tablespoons Worcestershire sauce
- 1½ teaspoons crushed red pepper flakes
- 1 teaspoon ground mustard
- 1 teaspoon dried basil
- 1 teaspoon dried thyme
- 1 teaspoon pepper

Cut wings into three sections; discard wing tip sections. Place chicken in a 4-qt. slow cooker. In a small bowl, combine the remaining ingredients. Pour over chicken; stir until coated. Cover and cook on low for 5-6 hours or until chicken juices run clear.
NOTE *Uncooked chicken wing sections (wingettes) may be substituted for whole chicken wings.*

Spiced Fruit Punch

Red-hot candies add rich color and spiciness to this festive punch.
—JULIE STERCHI CAMPBELLSVILLE, KY

PREP: 5 MIN. • **COOK:** 2 HOURS
MAKES: 8 SERVINGS (2 QUARTS)

- 1 bottle (32 ounces) cranberry juice
- 5 cans (6 ounces each) unsweetened pineapple juice
- ⅓ cup Red Hots
- 1 cinnamon stick (3½ inches) Additional cinnamon sticks, optional

1. In a 3-qt. slow cooker, combine the juices, Red Hots and cinnamon stick. Cover and cook on low for 2-4 hours or until heated through and candies are dissolved.
2. Discard cinnamon stick before serving. Use additional cinnamon sticks as stirrers if desired.

Creamy Artichoke Dip

This creamy dip is a family favorite. My sister, Teresa, got this recipe from a friend and she passed it along. It's loaded with cheese, artichokes and just the right amount of spice for a crowd-pleasing flavor.
—MARY SPENCER GREENDALE, WI

PREP: 20 MIN. • **COOK:** 1 HOUR
MAKES: 5 CUPS

- 2 cans (14 ounces each) water-packed artichoke hearts, rinsed, drained and coarsely chopped
- 2 cups (8 ounces) shredded part-skim mozzarella cheese
- 1 package (8 ounces) cream cheese, cubed
- 1 cup shredded Parmesan cheese
- ½ cup mayonnaise
- ½ cup shredded Swiss cheese
- 2 tablespoons lemon juice
- 2 tablespoons plain yogurt
- 1 tablespoon seasoned salt
- 1 tablespoon chopped seeded jalapeno pepper
- 1 teaspoon garlic powder Tortilla chips

In a 3-qt. slow cooker, combine the first 11 ingredients. Cover and cook on low for 1 hour or until heated through. Serve with tortilla chips.
NOTE *Wear disposable gloves when cutting hot peppers; the oils can burn skin. Avoid touching your face.*

PEACHY SPICED CIDER

READY IN 4

Buffalo Wing Dip

If you love spicy wings, you'll love this dip. It's super cheesy, ready to serve in no time and offers the taste of Buffalo wings everyone craves!
—*TASTE OF HOME* TEST KITCHEN

PREP: 20 MIN. • **COOK:** 2 HOURS
MAKES: 6 CUPS

- 2 **packages (8 ounces each) cream cheese, softened**
- ½ **cup ranch salad dressing**
- ½ **cup sour cream**
- 5 **tablespoons crumbled blue cheese**
- 2 **cups shredded cooked chicken**
- ½ **cup Buffalo wing sauce**
- 2 **cups (8 ounces) shredded cheddar cheese, divided**
- 1 **green onion, sliced Tortilla chips**

1. In a small bowl, combine the cream cheese, dressing, sour cream and blue cheese. Transfer to a 3-qt. slow cooker. Layer with chicken, wing sauce and 1 cup of cheese. Cover and cook on low for 2-3 hours or until heated through.
2. Sprinkle with the remaining cheese and onion. Serve with the tortilla chips.

DID YOU KNOW?

Reduced-fat cheeses work well in slow-cooker recipes. It's true! Because slow-cooked dishes simmer up with the cover tightly in place, low-fat cheeses melt nicely, offering all the ooey-gooey appeal people love. Consider making the switch if you're trying to trim down a bit or cut a few fat grams.

EXPRESS *PREP*

Peachy Spiced Cider

I served this spiced cider at a party and received so many compliments. Everyone enjoys the subtle peach flavor and warm blend of spices.
—**ROSE HARMAN** HAYS, KS

PREP: 5 MIN. • **COOK:** 4 HOURS
MAKES: ABOUT 1 QUART

- 4 **cans (5½ ounces each) peach nectar or apricot nectar**
- 2 **cups apple juice**
- ¼ to ½ **teaspoon ground ginger**
- ¼ **teaspoon ground cinnamon**
- ¼ **teaspoon ground nutmeg**
- 4 **fresh orange slices (¼-inch thick), halved**

In a 1½-qt. slow cooker, combine the first five ingredients. Top with the orange slices. Cover and cook on low for 4-6 hours or until heated through. Stir before serving.

---

(5) INGREDIENTS **EXPRESS** *PREP*

Simmered Smoked Links

No one can resist the sweet 'n' spicy glaze on these bite-size sausages. They're effortless to prepare, and they make the perfect party nibbler for any occasion any time of year. Serve them on toothpicks.
—**MAXINE CENKER** WEIRTON, WV

PREP: 5 MIN. • **COOK:** 4 HOURS
MAKES: 16-20 SERVINGS

- 2 **packages (16 ounces each) miniature smoked sausage links**
- 1 **cup packed brown sugar**
- ½ **cup ketchup**
- ¼ **cup prepared horseradish**

Place sausages in a 3-qt. slow cooker. Combine the brown sugar, ketchup and horseradish; pour over sausages. Cover and cook on low for 4 hours.

Slow-Cooker Spiced Mixed Nuts

What slow cookers do for soups and stews, they do for nuts, too. Just add, stir and enjoy the heartwarming scent of all the cooking spices.

—STEPHANIE LOAIZA LAYTON, UT

PREP: 15 MIN.
COOK: 1 HOUR 50 MIN. + COOLING
MAKES: 6 CUPS

- 1 **large egg white**
- 2 **teaspoons vanilla extract**
- 1 **cup unblanched almonds**
- 1 **cup pecan halves**
- 1 **cup shelled walnuts**
- 1 **cup unsalted cashews**
- 1 **cup sugar**
- 1 **cup packed brown sugar**
- 4 **teaspoons ground cinnamon**
- 2 **teaspoons ground ginger**
- 1 **teaspoon ground nutmeg**
- ½ **teaspoon ground cloves**
- ⅛ **teaspoon salt**
- 2 **tablespoons water**

1. In a large bowl, whisk egg white and vanilla until blended; stir in nuts. In a small bowl, mix sugars, spices and salt. Add to nut mixture and toss to coat.

2. Transfer to a greased 3-qt. slow cooker. Cook, covered, on high for 1½ hours, stirring nuts every 15 minutes. Gradually stir in water. Cook, covered, on low 20 minutes.

3. Spread nuts onto waxed paper; cool completely. Store in airtight containers up to 1 week.

BUFFALO WING DIP

SLOW-COOKER SPICED MIXED NUTS

EXPRESS PREP READY IN ④

Creamy Chipped Beef Fondue

My mother often served fondue at parties, and I've since followed in that tradition. It's nice to offer a hearty appetizer that requires very little work.
—**BETH FOX** LAWRENCE, KS

START TO FINISH: 15 MIN.
MAKES: ABOUT 4 CUPS

- 1⅓ to 1½ **cups milk**
- 2 **packages (8 ounces each) cream cheese, softened**
- 1 **package (2½ ounces) thinly sliced dried beef, chopped**
- ¼ **cup chopped green onions**
- 2 **teaspoons ground mustard**
- 1 **loaf (1 pound) French bread, cubed**

In a large saucepan, heat milk and cream cheese over medium heat; stir until smooth. Stir in the beef, onions and mustard; heat through. Transfer to a fondue pot or 1½-qt. slow cooker; keep warm. Serve with bread cubes.

EXPRESS PREP READY IN ④

Hot Cider with Orange Twists

I first tasted a steaming mug of this comforting beverage on a frigid evening. It's still a family favorite on a wintry day.
—**CATHERINE ALLAN** TWIN FALLS, ID

PREP: 10 MIN. • **COOK:** 2 HOURS
MAKES: 2½ QUARTS

- 2 **quarts apple cider or juice**
- 1 **cup pineapple juice**
- 1 **cup orange juice**
- 1 **tablespoon brown sugar**
- 1 **tablespoon lemon juice**
- ⅛ **teaspoon salt**
- 8 **whole cloves**
- 4 **unpeeled fresh orange slices (¼-inch thick)**
- 4 **cinnamon sticks (3 inches)**
   Additional orange slices and cinnamon sticks

1. In a 5-qt. slow cooker, combine the first six ingredients. Push two cloves through each orange slice. Push a cinnamon stick through the center of each orange slice; add to cider mixture.

2. Cover and cook on low for 2-4 hours or until heated through. Discard the oranges, cloves and cinnamon sticks. Stir cider before serving. Use additional oranges and cinnamon sticks to make orange twist garnishes.

READY IN ④

Jalapeno Popper & Sausage Dip

My workplace had an appetizer contest, and I won it with my hearty jalapeno and cheese dip. Whenever I take this dip somewhere, folks empty the slow cooker.
—**BEV SLABIK** DILWORTH, MN

PREP: 15 MIN. • **COOK:** 3 HOURS
MAKES: 24 SERVINGS (¼ CUP EACH)

- 1 **pound bulk spicy pork sausage**
- 2 **packages (8 ounces each) cream cheese, cubed**
- 4 **cups shredded Parmesan cheese (about 12 ounces)**
- 1 **cup (8 ounces) sour cream**
- 1 **can (4 ounces) chopped green chilies**
- 1 **can (4 ounces) diced jalapeno peppers**
   Assorted fresh vegetables

1. In a large skillet, cook sausage over medium heat 6-8 minutes or until no longer pink, breaking into crumbles. Using a slotted spoon, transfer the sausage to a 3-qt. slow cooker.

2. Stir in cream cheese, Parmesan cheese, sour cream, chilies and peppers. Cook, covered, on low for 3-3½ hours or until heated through. Stir before serving. Serve with vegetables.

⑤ INGREDIENTS *EXPRESS PREP*
READY IN ④

Creamy Cranberry Meatballs

Meatballs are always a hit on appetizer buffets, but they are particularly successful when they come together as quickly and easily as these do!
—**AMY WARREN** MAINEVILLE, OH

PREP: 10 MIN. • **COOK:** 3 HOURS
MAKES: ABOUT 5 DOZEN

- 2 **envelopes brown gravy mix**
- 1 **package (32 ounces) frozen fully cooked Swedish meatballs**
- ⅔ **cup jellied cranberry sauce**
- 2 **teaspoons Dijon mustard**
- ¼ **cup heavy whipping cream**

Prepare gravy mix according to package directions. In a 4-qt. slow cooker, combine the meatballs, cranberry sauce, mustard and gravy. Cover and cook on low for 3-4 hours or until heated through, adding cream during the final 30 minutes of cooking.

TOP TIP

Need a quick dinner? Extras from rich and juicy Creamy Cranberry Meatballs easily turn into a hearty entree. Simply reheat leftover meatballs and sauce in the microwave. Then serve them over a bed of white rice or noodles. Add a salad or a loaf of crusty bread, and dinner is ready!

CREAMY CRANBERRY
MEATBALLS

JALAPENO POPPER
& SAUSAGE DIP

EXPRESS PREP **READY IN ④**

Garlic Swiss Fondue

I've been making this fondue recipe for years—everyone flips over the wonderful flavors. When cooled, this cheesy appetizer is also fantastic as a cracker spread.

—CLEO GONSKE REDDING, CA

PREP: 10 MIN. • **COOK:** 2 HOURS
MAKES: 3 CUPS

- 4 **cups (16 ounces) shredded Swiss cheese**
- 1 **can (10¾ ounces) condensed cheddar cheese soup, undiluted**
- 2 **tablespoons sherry or chicken broth**
- 1 **tablespoon Dijon mustard**
- 2 **garlic cloves, minced**
- 2 **teaspoons hot pepper sauce Cubed French bread baguette, sliced apples and seedless red grapes**

In a 1½-qt. slow cooker, mix the first six ingredients. Cook, covered, on low for 2-2½ hours or until the cheese is melted, stirring every 30 minutes. Serve warm with bread cubes and fruit.

READY IN ④

Slow-Cooked Crab Dip

Slow-cooked dips are ideal for entertaining since they free up the oven. Plus, leftovers are great served over a baked potato the next day.

—SUSAN D'AMORE WEST CHESTER, PA

PREP: 20 MIN. • **COOK:** 2 HOURS
MAKES: 2⅓ CUPS

- 1 **package (8 ounces) cream cheese, softened**
- 2 **green onions, chopped**
- ¼ **cup chopped sweet red pepper**
- 2 **tablespoons minced fresh parsley**
- 2 **tablespoons mayonnaise**
- 1 **tablespoon Dijon mustard**
- 1 **teaspoon Worcestershire sauce**
- ¼ **teaspoon salt**
- ¼ **teaspoon pepper**
- 2 **cans (6 ounces each) lump crabmeat, drained**
- 2 **tablespoons capers, drained Dash hot pepper sauce Assorted crackers**

1. In a 1½-qt. slow cooker, combine the first nine ingredients; stir in crab.

2. Cover and cook on low for 1-2 hours. Stir in capers and pepper sauce; cook 30 minutes longer to allow flavors to blend. Serve with crackers.

EXPRESS PREP **READY IN ④**

Cranberry Apple Cider

I love to start this soothing cider in the slow cooker on nights before my husband goes hunting. Then he can fill his thermos and take it with him out into the cold. The cider has a terrific flavor we both enjoy.

—JENNIFER NABOKA
NORTH PLAINFIELD, NJ

PREP: 10 MIN. • **COOK:** 2 HOURS
MAKES: 10 SERVINGS
(ABOUT 2½ QUARTS)

- 4 **cups water**
- 4 **cups apple juice**
- 1 **can (12 ounces) frozen apple juice concentrate, thawed**
- 1 **medium apple, peeled and sliced**
- 1 **cup fresh or frozen cranberries**
- 1 **medium orange, peeled and sectioned**
- 1 **cinnamon stick**

In a 5-qt. slow cooker, combine all ingredients. Cover and cook on low for 2 hours or until cider reaches desired temperature. Discard the cinnamon stick. If desired, remove the fruit with a slotted spoon before serving.

GARLIC SWISS FONDUE

SWEET & SALTY PARTY MIX

JALAPENO SPINACH DIP

READY IN ④
Sweet & Salty Party Mix

My husband doesn't like traditional party mixes because he thinks they're too salty or sweet. He calls this one his favorite because it's just right.
—**JACKIE BURNS** KETTLE FALLS, WA

PREP: 20 MIN. • **COOK:** 1 HOUR
MAKES: 16 SERVINGS (¾ CUP EACH)

- 3 **cups each Corn Chex, Rice Chex and Wheat Chex**
- 3 **cups miniature pretzels**
- 1 **cup dried cranberries**
- 1 **cup sliced almonds**
- ½ **cup butter, cubed**
- 1 **cup packed brown sugar**
- ¼ **cup corn syrup**
- ¼ **teaspoon baking soda**

1. Place the cereal, pretzels, cranberries and almonds in a greased 6-qt. slow cooker; toss to combine. In a small saucepan, melt butter over medium heat; stir in the brown sugar and corn syrup. Bring to a boil; cook and stir for 5 minutes. Remove from heat; stir in baking soda. Drizzle over cereal mixture and toss to coat.

2. Cook, covered, on low 1 hour, stirring halfway. Spread mix onto waxed paper; cool completely. Store in airtight containers.

EXPRESS PREP READY IN ④
Jalapeno Spinach Dip

Everyone loves spinach dip, and this version is as easy as it is delicious. Just mix the ingredients together in the slow cooker for a savory and creamy appetizer.
—**MICHAELA DEBELIUS** WADDELL, AZ

PREP: 10 MIN. • **COOK:** 2 HOURS
MAKES: 16 SERVINGS (¼ CUP EACH)

- 2 **packages (10 ounces each) frozen chopped spinach, thawed and squeezed dry**
- 2 **packages (8 ounces each) cream cheese, softened**
- 1 **cup grated Parmesan cheese**
- 1 **cup half-and-half cream**
- ½ **cup finely chopped onion**
- ¼ **cup chopped seeded jalapeno peppers**
- 2 **teaspoons Worcestershire sauce**
- 2 **teaspoons hot pepper sauce**
- 1 **teaspoon garlic powder**
- 1 **teaspoon dill weed**
  Tortilla chips

In a 1½-qt. slow cooker, combine the first 10 ingredients. Cover and cook on low for 2-3 hours or until heated through. Serve with chips.
NOTE *Wear disposable gloves when cutting hot peppers; the oils can burn skin. Avoid touching your face.*

READY IN ④

Warm Broccoli Cheese Dip

When my family gathers for a party, this flavorful, creamy dip is the guest of honor. Everyone loves its zip from the jalapeno pepper and the crunch from the broccoli.

—**BARBARA MAIOL** CONYERS, GA

PREP: 15 MIN. • **COOK:** 2½ HOURS
MAKES: 5½ CUPS

- 2 jars (8 ounces each) process cheese sauce
- 1 can (10¾ ounces) condensed cream of chicken soup, undiluted
- 3 cups frozen chopped broccoli, thawed and drained
- ½ pound fresh mushrooms, chopped
- 2 tablespoons chopped seeded jalapeno pepper
  Assorted fresh vegetables

In a 1½-qt. slow cooker, combine cheese sauce and soup. Cover and cook on low for 30 minutes or until cheese mixture is melted and well combined, stirring occasionally. Stir in the broccoli, mushrooms and jalapeno. Cover and cook on low for 2-3 hours or until the vegetables are tender. Serve with assorted fresh vegetables.

NOTE *Wear disposable gloves when cutting hot peppers; the oils can burn skin. Avoid touching your face.*

EXPRESS PREP

Cheesy Pizza Fondue

I keep these dip ingredients on hand for spur-of-the-moment gatherings. Folks can't resist the savory sauce.

—**NEL CARVER** MOSCOW, ID

PREP: 10 MIN. • **COOK:** 4 HOURS
MAKES: 4 CUPS

- 1 jar (29 ounces) meatless spaghetti sauce
- 2 cups (8 ounces) shredded part-skim mozzarella cheese
- ¼ cup shredded Parmesan cheese
- 2 teaspoons dried oregano
- 1 teaspoon dried minced onion
- ¼ teaspoon garlic powder
  Cubed Italian bread

1. In a 1½-qt. slow cooker, combine the spaghetti sauce, cheeses, oregano, onion and garlic powder.
2. Cover and cook on low for 4-6 hours or until heated through and cheese is melted. Serve with bread.

EXPRESS PREP

Taco Joe Dip

My daughter was the first to try this recipe, and thought it was so good she passed it on to me. My husband and I think it's terrific. Because it's made in a slow cooker, it's great for parties or busy days.

—**LANG SECREST** SIERRA VISTA, AZ

PREP: 5 MIN. • **COOK:** 5 HOURS
MAKES: ABOUT 7 CUPS

- 1 can (16 ounces) kidney beans, rinsed and drained
- 1 can (15¼ ounces) whole kernel corn, drained
- 1 can (15 ounces) black beans, rinsed and drained
- 1 can (14½ ounces) stewed tomatoes, undrained
- 1 can (8 ounces) tomato sauce
- 1 can (4 ounces) chopped green chilies, drained
- 1 envelope taco seasoning
- ½ cup chopped onion
  Tortilla chips

In a 5-qt. slow cooker, combine the first eight ingredients. Cover and cook on low for 5-6 hours. Serve with tortilla chips.

NOTE *To make Taco Joe Soup, add a 29-ounce can of tomato sauce to the slow cooker. It will serve 6-8.*

⑤ INGREDIENTS EXPRESS PREP
READY IN ④

Viennese Coffee

This isn't your regular cup of joe! I dress it up with chocolate and whipped cream, making it a drink to truly savor.

—**SHARON DELANEY-CHRONIS**
SOUTH MILWAUKEE, WI

PREP: 10 MIN. • **COOK:** 3 HOURS
MAKES: 4 SERVINGS

- 3 cups strong brewed coffee
- 3 tablespoons chocolate syrup
- 1 teaspoon sugar
- ⅓ cup heavy whipping cream
- ¼ cup creme de cacao or Irish cream liqueur
  Whipped cream and chocolate curls, optional

1. In a 1½-qt. slow cooker, combine the coffee, chocolate syrup and sugar. Cover and cook on low for 2½ hours.
2. Stir in the heavy cream and creme de cacao. Cover and cook 30 minutes longer or until heated through.
3. Ladle coffee into mugs. Garnish with whipped cream and chocolate curls if desired.

TOP TIP

To make chocolate curls for garnishes, set a 4-ounce semisweet or bittersweet chocolate bar in a warm place (80° to 85°) until thoroughly warm but not melted. With a vegetable peeler, draw along the flat side of the chocolate bar, making a curl.

CHEESY PIZZA FONDUE

TACO JOE DIP

VIENNESE COFFEE

PORK & RICE NOODLE SOUP, 31

40

51

39

Simple Soups

Nothing soothes the soul like a bowl of soup. Let these savory specialties simmer in the slow cooker while you get on with your day. Served on their own or alongside a sandwich, these recipes promise to become new favorites.

BEEF & BLACK BEAN SOUP, 30

COCONUT-LIME CHICKEN CURRY SOUP

Coconut-Lime Chicken Curry Soup

I created this recipe to replicate the flavors of my favorite curry dish—slightly sweet with just the right amount of spicy heat. When served with a garnish of green onions and toasted coconut, the soup makes the perfect cold-weather meal.
—**LISA RENSHAW** KANSAS CITY, MO

PREP: 15 MIN. • **COOK:** 4¼ HOURS
MAKES: 8 SERVINGS (2½ QUARTS)

- 2 **cans (13.66 ounces each) light coconut milk**
- 2 **cans (4 ounces each) chopped green chilies**
- 8 **green onions, sliced**
- 2 **teaspoons grated lime peel**
- ½ **cup lime juice**
- ¼ **cup sweet chili sauce**
- 6 **garlic cloves, minced**
- 4 **teaspoons curry powder**
- ½ **teaspoon salt**
- 2 **pounds boneless skinless chicken thighs, cut into ½-inch pieces**
- 3 **cups cooked basmati rice**
  Minced fresh cilantro

1. Place the first nine ingredients in a 4- or 5-qt. slow cooker; stir in chicken. Cook, covered, on low for 4-5 hours or until the chicken is tender.
2. Skim fat; stir in the cooked rice. Cook, covered, on low for 15-30 minutes or until heated through. Sprinkle servings with cilantro.

Pepperoni Pizza Soup

My husband and I used to own a pizzeria, where this dish was always popular. We've since sold the restaurant, but I still make this slow-cooked specialty.

—ESTELLA PETERSON MADRAS, OR

PREP: 20 MIN. • **COOK:** 8¼ HOURS
MAKES: 6 SERVINGS (2¼ QUARTS)

- 2 cans (14½ ounces each) Italian stewed tomatoes, undrained
- 2 cans (14½ ounces each) reduced-sodium beef broth
- 1 small onion, chopped
- 1 small green pepper, chopped
- ½ cup sliced fresh mushrooms
- ½ cup sliced pepperoni, halved
- 1½ teaspoons dried oregano
- ⅛ teaspoon pepper
- 1 package (9 ounces) refrigerated cheese ravioli
  Shredded part-skim mozzarella cheese and sliced ripe olives

1. In a 4-qt. slow cooker, combine the first eight ingredients. Cook, covered, on low 8-9 hours.

2. Stir in ravioli; cook, covered, on low 15-30 minutes or until pasta is tender. Top servings with cheese and olives.

Minestrone Soup

When this hearty minestrone has about 30 minutes left to cook, I add the macaroni. Then there's time to toss together a salad and slice some French bread.

—KARA DE LA VEGA SANTA ROSA, CA

PREP: 15 MIN. • **COOK:** 7 HOURS
MAKES: 10 SERVINGS

- 6 cups chicken broth
- 1 can (15 ounces) garbanzo beans or chickpeas, rinsed and drained
- 1 medium potato, peeled and cubed
- 1 cup cubed deli ham
- ⅓ cup chopped onion
- 1 small carrot, chopped
- 1 celery rib, chopped
- 2 tablespoons minced fresh parsley
- ½ teaspoon minced garlic
- ½ cup uncooked elbow macaroni
- 1 can (14½ ounces) diced tomatoes, undrained
- 1 package (10 ounces) frozen chopped spinach, thawed and squeezed dry

1. In a 5-qt. slow cooker, combine the first nine ingredients. Cover and cook on high for 1 hour. Reduce heat to low; cook for 6-8 hours or until vegetables are almost tender.

2. During the last 30 minutes of cooking, stir in the macaroni. Cover and cook until macaroni is tender. Stir in the tomatoes and spinach; heat through.

PEPPERONI PIZZA SOUP

Hearty Veggie Meatball Soup

EXPRESS *PREP*

It's a snap to put together this satisfying soup before I leave for work. I just add the cooked pasta when I get home, and then I have a few minutes to relax before supper is ready.

—**CHARLA TINNEY** TYRONE, OK

PREP: 10 MIN. • **COOK:** 4 HOURS
MAKES: 6 SERVINGS

- 3 cups beef broth
- 2 cups frozen mixed vegetables, thawed
- 1 can (14½ ounces) stewed tomatoes
- 12 frozen fully cooked Italian meatballs (½ ounce each), thawed
- 3 bay leaves
- ¼ teaspoon pepper
- 1 cup spiral pasta, cooked and drained

In a 3-qt. slow cooker, combine the first six ingredients. Cover and cook on low for 4-5 hours. Just before serving, stir in pasta; heat through. Discard bay leaves.

Slow-Cooker Vegetable Soup

What a treat to come home from work and have this savory soup ready to eat. It's a nice traditional beef soup with old-fashioned goodness. We pair it with crusty rolls topped with melted mozzarella cheese.

—**HEATHER THURMEIER** PENSE, SK

PREP: 15 MIN. • **COOK:** 8 HOURS
MAKES: 8-10 SERVINGS (ABOUT 2½ QUARTS)

- 1 pound beef top round steak, cut into ½-inch cubes
- 1 can (14½ ounces) diced tomatoes, undrained
- 2 medium potatoes, peeled and cubed
- 2 medium onions, diced
- 3 celery ribs, sliced
- 2 carrots, sliced
- 3 beef bouillon cubes
- ½ teaspoon salt
- ½ teaspoon dried basil
- ½ teaspoon dried oregano
- ¼ teaspoon pepper
- 3 cups water
- 1½ cups frozen mixed vegetables

In a 3-qt. slow cooker, combine the first 12 ingredients. Cover and cook on high for 6-8 hours. Add the mixed vegetables; cover and cook 2 hours longer or until meat and vegetables are tender.

Beef & Black Bean Soup

EXPRESS *PREP*

I lead a busy life, so I'm always trying to come up with time-saving recipes. This zippy and colorful soup is one of my husband's favorites. It has been a hit at family gatherings, too.

—**VICKIE GIBSON** GARDENDALE, AL

PREP: 10 MIN. • **COOK:** 6 HOURS
MAKES: 10 SERVINGS (2½ QUARTS)

- 1 pound lean ground beef (90% lean)
- 2 cans (14½ ounces each) chicken broth
- 1 can (14½ ounces) diced tomatoes, undrained
- 8 green onions, thinly sliced
- 3 medium carrots, thinly sliced
- 2 celery ribs, thinly sliced
- 2 garlic cloves, minced
- 1 tablespoon sugar
- 1½ teaspoons dried basil
- ½ teaspoon salt
- ½ teaspoon dried oregano
- ½ teaspoon ground cumin
- ½ teaspoon chili powder
- 2 cans (15 ounces each) black beans, rinsed and drained
- 1½ cups cooked rice

In a skillet over medium heat, cook beef until no longer pink; drain. Transfer to a 5-qt. slow cooker. Add the next 12 ingredients. Cover and cook on high for 1 hour. Reduce heat to low; cook for 4-5 hours or until vegetables are tender. Add the beans and rice; cook 1 hour longer or until heated through.

Pork & Rice Noodle Soup

My husband and I are crazy over the Korean noodle bowls at our favorite restaurant. I created this recipe to enjoy the same flavors in a quick and easy meal. You can find rice noodles in the Asian section of just about any grocery store.

—**LISA RENSHAW** KANSAS CITY, MO

PREP: 15 MIN. • **COOK:** 6½ HOURS
MAKES: 8 SERVINGS (3 QUARTS)

- 1½ **pounds boneless country-style pork ribs, cut into 1-inch cubes**
- 6 **garlic cloves, minced**
- 2 **tablespoons minced fresh gingerroot**
- 2 **cans (14½ ounces each) reduced-sodium chicken broth**
- 2 **cans (13.66 ounces each) coconut milk**
- ¼ **cup reduced-sodium soy sauce**
- 4 **ounces uncooked thin rice noodles**
- 2 **cups frozen pepper strips, thawed**
- 1 **can (8 ounces) sliced water chestnuts, drained**
- ¼ **cup minced fresh cilantro**
- 2 **tablespoons lime juice**

1. In a 5-qt. slow cooker, combine the first six ingredients. Cook, covered, on low 6-8 hours or until meat is tender.

2. Add the rice noodles, pepper strips and water chestnuts; cook 30-35 minutes longer or until noodles are tender. If desired, skim soup. Just before serving, stir in cilantro and lime juice.

BEEF & BLACK BEAN SOUP

PORK & RICE NOODLE SOUP

POTATO
MINESTRONE

CHICKEN
VEGETABLE SOUP

BEEF BARLEY SOUP

Potato Minestrone

When I prepare this savory soup, I only have to slice some bread and toss a salad and dinner is ready! For a thicker soup, simply mash half of the garbanzo beans before adding them to the slow cooker.
—**PAULA ZSIRAY** LOGAN, UT

PREP: 10 MIN. • **COOK:** 8½ HOURS
MAKES: 12 SERVINGS (ABOUT 3 QUARTS)

- 2 cans (14½ ounces each) chicken or vegetable broth
- 1 can (28 ounces) crushed tomatoes
- 1 can (16 ounces) kidney beans, rinsed and drained
- 1 can (15 ounces) garbanzo beans or chickpeas, rinsed and drained
- 1 can (14½ ounces) beef broth
- 2 cups frozen cubed hash brown potatoes, thawed
- 1 tablespoon dried minced onion
- 1 tablespoon dried parsley flakes
- 1 teaspoon salt
- 1 teaspoon dried oregano
- ½ teaspoon garlic powder
- ½ teaspoon dried basil
- ½ teaspoon dried marjoram
- 1 package (10 ounces) frozen chopped spinach, thawed and drained
- 2 cups frozen peas and carrots, thawed

In a 5-qt. slow cooker, combine the first 13 ingredients. Cover and cook on low for 8 hours. Stir in the spinach, peas and carrots; cook for 30 minutes or until heated through.

Chicken Vegetable Soup

This healthy chicken soup gets a special twist from tomato paste, lentils and Worcestershire sauce.
—**CONNIE THOMAS** JENSEN, UT

PREP: 5 MIN. • **COOK:** 6 HOURS
MAKES: 8 SERVINGS (2 QUARTS)

- 1 can (28 ounces) diced tomatoes, undrained
- 2 cups reduced-fat reduced-sodium chicken broth
- 2 cups cubed cooked chicken breast
- 1 cup frozen corn
- 2 celery ribs with leaves, chopped
- 1 can (6 ounces) tomato paste
- ¼ cup dried lentils, rinsed
- 1 tablespoon sugar
- 1 tablespoon Worcestershire sauce
- 2 teaspoons dried parsley flakes
- 1 teaspoon dried marjoram

In a 3-qt. slow cooker, combine all ingredients. Cover and cook on low for 6-8 hours or until vegetables are tender.

Beef Barley Soup

My hungry clan doesn't usually consider a bowl of soup "dinner," but after one taste of my comforting beef barley, they declared it a keeper!
—**GINNY PERKINS** COLUMBIANA, OH

PREP: 15 MIN. • **COOK:** 9 HOURS
MAKES: 8 SERVINGS (2½ QUARTS)

- 1½ pounds beef stew meat
- 1 tablespoon canola oil
- 1 can (14½ ounces) diced tomatoes
- 1 cup chopped onion
- 1 cup diced celery
- 1 cup sliced fresh carrots
- ½ cup chopped green pepper
- 4 cups beef broth
- 2 cups water
- 1 cup spaghetti sauce
- ⅔ cup medium pearl barley
- 1 tablespoon dried parsley flakes
- 2 teaspoons salt
- 1½ teaspoons dried basil
- ¾ teaspoon pepper

1. In a large skillet, brown meat in oil over medium heat; drain.
2. Meanwhile, in a 5-qt. slow cooker, combine the vegetables, broth, water, spaghetti sauce, barley and seasonings.
3. Stir in beef. Cover and cook on low for 9-10 hours or until meat is tender. Skim fat.

TOP TIP

Can't finish all of that soup? Freeze it for a future meal! Simply mark your freezer-proof containers with the date, the name of your dish and any significant reheating instructions. Most soups can be stored in the freezer for 2 to 3 months.

Slow Cooker Chicken Vegetable Soup

As a mom to four busy children, I find this recipe convenient. All I have to do is throw everything into the slow cooker and relax while it simmers.
—**AMANDA WEST** SIBLEY, LA

PREP: 15 MIN. • **COOK:** 8 HOURS
MAKES: 8 SERVINGS (2½ QUARTS)

- 2 cups chicken broth
- 1 can (14½ ounces) diced tomatoes, undrained
- 1 package (10 ounces) frozen corn
- 1½ cups cubed red potatoes
- 1 medium onion, chopped
- 1 medium sweet red or yellow pepper, chopped
- 1 medium green pepper, chopped
- 1 can (4 ounces) chopped green chilies
- 1 teaspoon ground cumin
- ½ teaspoon garlic powder
- ¼ teaspoon freshly ground pepper
- 1 package (22 ounces) fully cooked frozen grilled chicken breast strips
- 1½ cups fresh baby spinach

1. In a 4- or 5-qt. slow cooker, combine the first 11 ingredients.
2. If desired, cut larger chicken strips into bite-size pieces; add to slow cooker.
3. Cook, covered, on low for 8-10 hours or until potatoes are tender. Stir in spinach.

Southwest Vegetarian Lentil Soup

There may be a lot of ingredients here, but the recipe comes together easily. It's a variation of a chicken and lentil soup that I make for my vegan friends, but everyone seems to like it. The addition of tofu, which is packed with protein, adds satisfying bulk.
—**LAURIE STOUT-LETZ** BOUNTIFUL, UT

PREP: 25 MIN. • **COOK:** 7 HOURS
MAKES: 6 SERVINGS (ABOUT 2 QUARTS)

- 3 cups vegetable broth
- 1 large onion, chopped
- 1 can (10 ounces) mild diced tomatoes and green chilies, undrained
- 1 cup mild salsa
- 1 cup dried lentils, rinsed
- 1 cup frozen corn
- 1 can (8 ounces) tomato sauce
- 1 can (4 ounces) chopped green chilies
- 3 garlic cloves, minced
- 1½ teaspoons chili powder
- 1 teaspoon ground cumin
- ½ teaspoon celery salt
- ½ teaspoon paprika
- ⅛ teaspoon cayenne pepper
- 1 package (16 ounces) firm tofu, drained and cut into ¼-inch cubes
- 1 can (4¼ ounces) chopped ripe olives
- 3 green onions, sliced

In a 3- or 4-qt. slow cooker, combine the first 14 ingredients. Cover and cook on low for 8-10 hours or until lentils are tender. Sprinkle with tofu, olives and green onions.

Chicken Bean Soup

This easy soup is tasty and nutritious. I like to top individual bowls with a few sprigs of fresh parsley. Home-baked rolls are an added treat.
—**PHYLLIS SHAUGHNESSY** LIVONIA, NY

PREP: 10 MIN. • **COOK:** 4 HOURS
MAKES: 12 SERVINGS (3 QUARTS)

- 1 pound boneless skinless chicken breasts, cubed
- 2 cans (14½ ounces each) chicken broth
- 2 cans (14½ ounces each) Italian diced tomatoes, undrained
- 1 can (16 ounces) kidney beans, rinsed and drained
- 1 can (15¼ ounces) whole kernel corn, drained, or 1½ cups frozen corn
- 1 can (15 ounces) lima beans, rinsed and drained, or 1½ cups frozen lima beans
- 1 cup frozen peas and pearl onions
- 1 tablespoon snipped fresh dill or 1 teaspoon dill weed
- ½ teaspoon ground ginger, optional

In a 5-qt. slow cooker, combine all ingredients. Cover and cook on low for 4-5 hours or until chicken is no longer pink.

SOUTHWEST VEGETARIAN LENTIL SOUP

CHICKEN BEAN SOUP

**FRENCH ONION SOUP
WITH MEATBALLS**

French Onion Soup with Meatballs

I got the idea for this soup after I went to a restaurant that put ale in its gravy. I make this every time the weather starts to cool down in the fall. It's comfort food at its best.
—**CRYSTAL HOLSINGER** SURRISE, AZ

PREP: 15 MIN. • **COOK:** 8 HOURS
MAKES: 6 SERVINGS

- 1 **package (12 ounces) frozen fully cooked Italian meatballs**
- 2 **large sweet onions, sliced**
- 2 **garlic cloves, minced**
- 1 **teaspoon beef bouillon granules**
- ½ **teaspoon dried thyme**
- ¼ **teaspoon salt**
- ¼ **teaspoon pepper**
- 5 **cups beef broth**
- 1 **bottle (12 ounces) pale ale or additional beef broth**
- 18 **slices French bread baguette (¼-inch thick)**
- 12 **slices Muenster or cheddar cheese**

1. In a 4-qt. slow cooker, combine the first nine ingredients. Cook, covered, on low 8-10 hours or until onions are tender.
2. Ladle soup into six broiler-safe 16-oz. ramekins. Top each with three slices of bread and two slices of cheese. Broil 4-6 in. from heat 2-3 minutes or until the cheese is melted. Serve immediately.

Spicy Chicken Chili

This easy chili is loaded with chicken and beans. If you want, the spicy heat can be tamed a bit with sour cream.
—**FRED LOCKWOOD** PLANO, TX

PREP: 25 MIN. • **COOK:** 5 HOURS
MAKES: 10 SERVINGS (3½ QUARTS)

- 4 bone-in chicken breast halves (14 ounces each)
- 2 medium onions, chopped
- 2 medium green peppers, chopped
- 1 cup pickled jalapeno slices
- 1 can (4 ounces) chopped green chilies
- 2 jars (16 ounces each) salsa verde
- 2 cans (15½ ounces each) navy beans, rinsed and drained
- 1 cup (8 ounces) sour cream
- ½ cup minced fresh cilantro
  Optional toppings: shredded Colby-Monterey Jack cheese, sour cream and crushed tortilla chips

1. Place the chicken, onions, peppers, jalapenos and chilies in a 5- or 6-qt. slow cooker. Pour salsa over the top. Cover and cook on low for 5-6 hours or until the chicken is tender.

2. Remove chicken; cool slightly. Shred chicken with two forks, discarding skin and bones; return meat to slow cooker. Stir in the beans, sour cream and cilantro; heat through. Serve with toppings of your choice.

FREEZE OPTION *Before adding sour cream, cilantro and toppings, cool chili. Freeze chili in freezer containers. To use, partially thaw in refrigerator overnight. Heat through in a saucepan, stirring occasionally and adding a little water if necessary. Stir in sour cream and cilantro. Serve with toppings if desired.*

NOTE *Wear disposable gloves when cutting hot peppers; the oils can burn skin. Avoid touching your face.*

Smoked Sausage Soup

This rich soup is packed with vegetables, sausage and more. I guarantee it's unlike any other soup you've ever tasted.
—**RACHEL LYN GRASMICK** ROCKY FORD, CO

PREP: 10 MIN. • **COOK:** 5 HOURS
MAKES: 6-8 SERVINGS (2½ QUARTS)

- 2 cups chopped onions
- 2 tablespoons butter
- 2 cups cubed cooked chicken
- 1 pound smoked sausage, cut into bite-size pieces
- 3 cups sliced celery
- 3 cups sliced summer squash
- 2 cups chicken broth
- 1 can (8 ounces) tomato sauce
- ¼ cup minced fresh parsley
- 2 tablespoons cornstarch
- 2 tablespoons poultry seasoning
- 1 teaspoon dried oregano
- 1 teaspoon ground cumin
- 1 teaspoon liquid smoke, optional
- ½ teaspoon pepper

In a small skillet, saute onions in butter until tender. Transfer to a 4- or 5-qt. slow cooker. Stir in the remaining ingredients. Cook on high for 5-6 hours or until vegetables are tender.

NOTE *The stew may also be cooked in a Dutch oven on the stovetop. Cover and simmer for 1½ hours.*

SPICY CHICKEN CHILI

HEARTY
SPLIT PEA SOUP

SLOW COOKER CHEESY
BROCCOLI SOUP

READY IN ④

Slow Cooker Cheesy Broccoli Soup

Whenever I order soup at a restaurant, I go for broccoli-cheese. I finally put my slow cooker to the test and made my own. It took a few tries, but now the soup is exactly how I like it.

—**KRISTEN HILLS** LAYTON, UT

PREP: 15 MIN. • **COOK:** 3 HOURS
MAKES: 4 SERVINGS

- 2 **tablespoons butter**
- 1 **small onion, finely chopped**
- 2 **cups finely chopped fresh broccoli**
- 3 **cups reduced-sodium chicken broth**
- 1 **can (12 ounces) evaporated milk**
- ½ **teaspoon pepper**
- 1 **package (8 ounces) process cheese (Velveeta), cubed**
- 1½ **cups (6 ounces) shredded extra-sharp cheddar cheese**
- 1 **cup shredded Parmesan cheese**
  Additional shredded extra-sharp cheddar cheese

1. In a small skillet, heat butter over medium-high heat. Add onion; cook and stir 3-4 minutes or until tender. Transfer to a 3- or 4-qt. slow cooker. Add broccoli, broth, milk and pepper.

2. Cook, covered, on low 3-4 hours or until broccoli is tender. Stir in process cheese until melted. Add the shredded cheeses; stir until melted. Just before serving, stir soup to combine. Top servings with additional cheddar cheese.

EXPRESS *PREP*

Hearty Split Pea Soup

This slow-cooker soup is one of my favorite meals to make during a busy workweek. When I get home, I just add the milk...and supper is served!

—**DEANNA WAGGY** SOUTH BEND, IN

PREP: 5 MIN. • **COOK:** 4 HOURS
MAKES: 9 SERVINGS

- 1 **package (16 ounces) dried split peas**
- 2 **cups cubed fully cooked ham**
- 1 **cup diced carrots**
- 1 **medium onion, chopped**
- 2 **garlic cloves, minced**
- 2 **bay leaves**
- ½ **teaspoon salt**
- ½ **teaspoon pepper**
- 5 **cups boiling water**
- 1 **cup hot milk**

In a 5-qt. slow cooker, layer the first nine ingredients in order listed (do not stir). Cover and cook on high for 4-5 hours or until the vegetables are tender. Stir in milk. Discard bay leaves before serving.

TOP TIP

I like to make split pea soup in my slow cooker. The last time I prepared it, I stirred an envelope of onion soup mix into the ingredients before setting the slow cooker to simmer. The results were delicious.

—**ALICE KOMIC** WARREN, MI

Big Red Soup

We're Nebraska football fans, and on game day I make up a big pot of this soup, which boasts a dash of Mexican flavor. The whole family gathers around the TV to eat while we watch the game and cheer on our team.

—SHELLY KORELL BAYARD, NE

PREP: 20 MIN. • **COOK:** 8 HOURS
MAKES: 12 SERVINGS (3 QUARTS)

- 2 **pounds beef stew meat, cut into 1-inch cubes**
- 2 **tablespoons canola oil**
- ¾ **cup chopped onion**
- 2 **cloves garlic, minced**
- 2 **cans (14½ ounces each) diced tomatoes in sauce**
- 1 **can (10½ ounces) condensed beef broth, undiluted**
- 1 **can (10½ ounces) condensed chicken broth, undiluted**
- 1 **can (10¾ ounces) condensed tomato soup, undiluted**
- ¼ **cup water**
- 1 **teaspoon ground cumin**
- 1 **teaspoon chili powder**
- 1 **teaspoon salt**
- ½ **teaspoon lemon-pepper seasoning**
- 2 **teaspoons Worcestershire sauce**
- ⅓ **cup picante sauce**
- 8 **corn tortillas, cut into quarters**
- 1 **cup (4 ounces) shredded cheddar cheese**

1. In a large skillet, brown beef in oil. Transfer to a 5-qt. slow cooker; add the remaining ingredients except for tortillas and cheese. Cover and cook on low for 8-10 hours or until meat is tender.

2. To serve, place enough tortilla quarters to cover bottom of each bowl. Pour the soup over tortilla pieces; sprinkle with cheese.

Sauerkraut Sausage Soup

My husband and I make our own sauerkraut and grow many of the vegetables in this simple soup. It cooks all day and smells delicious when we come home from work.

—YVONNE KETT APPLETON, WI

PREP: 20 MIN. • **COOK:** 5 HOURS
MAKES: 10 SERVINGS

- 4 **cups chicken broth**
- 1 **pound smoked Polish sausage, cut into ½-inch slices**
- 1 **can (16 ounces) sauerkraut, rinsed and well drained**
- 2 **cups sliced fresh mushrooms**
- 1½ **cups cubed peeled potatoes**
- 1 **can (10¾ ounces) condensed cream of mushroom soup, undiluted**
- 1¼ **cups chopped onions**
- 2 **large carrots, sliced**
- 2 **celery ribs, chopped**
- 2 **tablespoons white vinegar**
- 2 **teaspoons dill weed**
- 1 **teaspoon sugar**
- ¼ **teaspoon pepper**

In a 5-qt. slow cooker, combine all ingredients. Cover and cook on low for 5-6 hours or until vegetables are tender.

BIG RED SOUP

Hearty Hash Brown Soup

Here's the perfect recipe to chase away chills on a cool night. Best of all, turkey bacon and reduced-fat canned soup keep things on the lighter side.
—**JUDITH WEBB** BLUE SPRINGS, MO

PREP: 15 MIN. • **COOK:** 6 HOURS
MAKES: 8 SERVINGS

- 2 green onions, chopped
- 2 teaspoons canola oil
- 1 package (28 ounces) frozen O'Brien potatoes, thawed
- 2 cups 2% milk
- 1 can (10¾ ounces) reduced-fat reduced-sodium condensed cream of chicken soup, undiluted
- 6 turkey bacon strips, diced and cooked
- ½ cup shredded cheddar cheese

1. In a small skillet, saute onions in oil until tender. In a 5-qt. slow cooker, combine the potatoes, milk, soup and onions.
2. Cover and cook on low for 6-7 hours or until heated through. Top each serving with 2 tablespoons bacon and 1 tablespoon cheese.

Vegetable Barley Soup

You'll love this delicious vegetarian soup brimming with veggies and barley. And the great news is, it's good for you, too!
—**MARY TALLMAN** ARBOR VITAE, WI

PREP: 25 MIN. • **COOK:** 8¼ HOURS
MAKES: 12 SERVINGS (ABOUT 3½ QUARTS)

- 1 large sweet potato, peeled and cubed
- 1½ cups fresh baby carrots, halved
- 1½ cups frozen cut green beans
- 1½ cups frozen corn
- 3 celery ribs, thinly sliced
- 1 small onion, chopped
- ½ cup chopped green pepper
- 2 garlic cloves, minced
- 6 cups water
- 2 cans (14½ ounces each) vegetable broth
- 1 cup medium pearl barley
- 1 bay leaf
- 1¾ teaspoons salt
- ½ teaspoon fennel seed, crushed
- ¼ teaspoon pepper
- 1 can (14½ ounces) Italian diced tomatoes, undrained

1. In a 5-qt. slow cooker, combine the first eight ingredients. Stir in the water, broth, barley, bay leaf and seasonings. Cover and cook on low for 8-10 hours or until barley and vegetables are tender.
2. Stir in tomatoes; cover and cook on high for 10-20 minutes or until heated through. Discard bay leaf.

Beefy Cabbage Bean Stew

While on one of our small group quilting retreats, one of my friends made this wonderful recipe for dinner. We all loved it and have since passed it around for others to enjoy.
—**MELISSA GLANCY** LA GRANGE, KY

PREP: 20 MIN. • **COOK:** 6 HOURS
MAKES: 6 SERVINGS

- ½ pound lean ground beef (90% lean)
- 3 cups shredded cabbage or angel hair coleslaw mix
- 1 can (16 ounces) red beans, rinsed and drained
- 1 can (14½ ounces) diced tomatoes, undrained
- 1 can (8 ounces) tomato sauce
- ¾ cup salsa or picante sauce
- 1 medium green pepper, chopped
- 1 small onion, chopped
- 3 garlic cloves, minced
- 1 teaspoon ground cumin
- ½ teaspoon pepper

1. In a large skillet, cook beef over medium heat for 4-6 minutes or until no longer pink, breaking into crumbles; drain.
2. Transfer meat to a 4-qt. slow cooker. Stir in the remaining ingredients. Cook, covered, on low for 6-8 hours or until the cabbage is tender.

TOP TIP

Looking to jazz up your slow-cooked soup? Add a garnish before serving for extra color, flavor and texture. Easy ideas include: finely chopped green onions or chives, minced fresh parsley, shredded cheese, diced cooked bacon, sesame seeds, a dollop of sour cream or even crushed tortilla chips.

Herbed Chicken & Spinach Soup

To create a hearty meal, I serve this substantial soup with a side of rustic bread slathered in butter.

—TANYA MACDONALD
ANTIGONISH COUNTY, NS

PREP: 20 MIN. • **COOK:** 4½ HOURS
MAKES: 4 SERVINGS

- 1 **pound boneless skinless chicken thighs, cut into ½-inch pieces**
- 1 **can (16 ounces) kidney beans, rinsed and drained**
- 1 **can (14½ ounces) chicken broth**
- 1 **medium onion, chopped**
- 1 **medium sweet red pepper, chopped**
- 1 **celery rib, chopped**
- 2 **tablespoons tomato paste**
- 3 **garlic cloves, minced**
- ½ **teaspoon minced fresh rosemary or ¼ teaspoon dried rosemary, crushed**
- ½ **teaspoon minced fresh thyme or ¼ teaspoon dried thyme**
- ½ **teaspoon dried oregano**
- ¼ **teaspoon salt**
- ¼ **teaspoon pepper**
- 3 **cups fresh baby spinach**
- ¼ **cup shredded Parmesan cheese**

In a 3-qt. slow cooker, combine the first 13 ingredients. Cover and cook on low for 4-5 hours or until chicken is tender. Stir in spinach; cook 30 minutes longer or until spinach is wilted. Top with cheese.

BEEFY CABBAGE BEAN STEW

HERBED CHICKEN & SPINACH SOUP

**POTATO AND
LEEK SOUP**

**SLOW-COOKED
SPLIT PEA SOUP**

Slow-Cooked Split Pea Soup

I've been making this soup for years. After every holiday event when ham is served, the hostess sends me home with the ham bone and a bag of peas so I can cook up this family favorite.
—**SUSAN SIMONS** EATONVILLE, WA

PREP: 15 MIN. • **COOK:** 7 HOURS
MAKES: 8 SERVINGS (ABOUT 3 QUARTS)

- 1 meaty ham bone or 2 pounds smoked ham hocks
- 1 package (16 ounces) dried green split peas
- 1 pound potatoes, peeled and cubed (about 3 cups)
- 1 large onion, chopped
- 2 medium carrots, chopped
- 1 tablespoon dried celery flakes
- ½ teaspoon garlic powder
- ½ teaspoon dried thyme
- ½ teaspoon dried basil
- ¼ teaspoon lemon-pepper seasoning
- ⅛ teaspoon dried marjoram
- 1 bay leaf
- 6 cups reduced-sodium chicken broth

1. In a 4- or 5-qt. slow cooker, combine all ingredients. Cook, covered, on low 7-9 hours or until peas are tender.
2. Remove ham bone from soup. When cool enough to handle, remove meat from bone; discard bone. Cut meat into cubes and return to soup or save meat for another use. Remove bay leaf.
FREEZE OPTION *Freeze cooled soup in freezer containers. To use, partially thaw in the refrigerator overnight. Heat through in a saucepan, stirring occasionally and adding a little broth if necessary.*

Potato and Leek Soup

Sour cream adds just a little tang to this chowder that's packed with vegetables and bacon. I like to serve it with a sandwich and crackers.
—**MELANIE WOODEN** RENO, NV

PREP: 20 MIN. • **COOK:** 8 HOURS
MAKES: 8 SERVINGS (2 QUARTS)

- 4 cups chicken broth
- 3 medium potatoes, peeled and cubed
- 1½ cups chopped cabbage
- 2 medium carrots, chopped
- 1 medium leek (white portion only), chopped
- 1 medium onion, chopped
- ¼ cup minced fresh parsley
- ½ teaspoon salt
- ½ teaspoon caraway seeds
- ½ teaspoon pepper
- 1 bay leaf
- ½ cup sour cream
- 1 pound bacon strips, cooked and crumbled

1. Combine the first 11 ingredients in a 4- or 5-qt. slow cooker. Cover and cook on low for 8-10 hours or until vegetables are tender.
2. Before serving, combine sour cream with 1 cup soup; return all to the slow cooker. Stir in bacon and discard bay leaf.

Beef Barley Lentil Soup

I serve this soup often to family and friends on cold nights, along with homemade rolls and a green salad. For variety, you can substitute jicama for the potatoes.
—**JUDY METZENTINE** THE DALLES, OR

PREP: 5 MIN. • **COOK:** 8 HOURS
MAKES: 10 SERVINGS

- 1 pound lean ground beef (90% lean)
- 1 medium onion, chopped
- 2 cups cubed red potatoes (¼-inch pieces)
- 1 cup chopped celery
- 1 cup chopped carrot
- 1 cup dried lentils, rinsed
- ½ cup medium pearl barley
- 8 cups water
- 2 teaspoons beef bouillon granules
- 1 teaspoon salt
- ½ teaspoon lemon-pepper seasoning
- 2 cans (14½ ounces each) stewed tomatoes

1. In a nonstick skillet, cook beef and onion over medium heat until meat is no longer pink; drain.
2. Transfer to a 5-qt. slow cooker. Layer with the potatoes, celery, carrots, lentils and barley. Combine the water, bouillon, salt and lemon-pepper; pour over the vegetables. Cover and cook on low for 6 hours or until vegetables and barley are tender.
3. Add the stewed tomatoes; cook 2 hours longer.

Healthy Tomato Soup

To trim the sodium in my slow-cooked soup, I season it with herbs and spices instead of salt. The soup is especially good served with fresh bread for dipping.
—**HEATHER CAMPBELL** LAWRENCE, KS

PREP: 10 MIN. • **COOK:** 5 HOURS
MAKES: 6 SERVINGS

- 1 can (46 ounces) tomato juice
- 1 can (8 ounces) tomato sauce
- ½ cup water
- ½ cup chopped onion
- 1 celery rib with leaves, chopped
- 2 tablespoons sugar
- ½ teaspoon dried basil
- 3 to 5 whole cloves
- 1 bay leaf

In a 3-qt. slow cooker, combine all ingredients. Cover and cook on low for 5-6 hours or until heated through. Discard the cloves and bay leaf.

NAVY BEAN VEGETABLE SOUP

SHRIMP CHOWDER

Navy Bean Vegetable Soup

My family really likes bean soup, so I came up with this enticing version. The leftovers are, dare I say, even better the next day!

—**ELEANOR MIELKE** MITCHELL, SD

PREP: 15 MIN. • **COOK:** 9 HOURS
MAKES: 12 SERVINGS (3 QUARTS)

- 4 **medium carrots, thinly sliced**
- 2 **celery ribs, chopped**
- 1 **medium onion, chopped**
- 2 **cups cubed fully cooked ham**
- 1½ **cups dried navy beans**
- 1 **envelope vegetable recipe mix**
- 1 **envelope onion soup mix**
- 1 **bay leaf**
- ½ **teaspoon pepper**
- 8 **cups water**

In a 5-qt. slow cooker, combine the first nine ingredients. Stir in water. Cover and cook on low for 9-10 hours or until beans are tender. Discard bay leaf.

Shrimp Chowder

READY IN 4

I simmer this rich and creamy dish in the slow cooker for hands-off convenience. Best of all, it's ready in less than four hours, so it can be prepared in the afternoon and then served to dinner guests the very same night.

—**WILL ZUNIO** GRETNA, LA

PREP: 15 MIN. • **COOK:** 3½ HOURS
MAKES: 12 SERVINGS (3 QUARTS)

- ½ **cup chopped onion**
- 2 **teaspoons butter**
- 2 **cans (12 ounces each) evaporated milk**
- 2 **cans (10¾ ounces each) condensed cream of potato soup, undiluted**
- 2 **cans (10¾ ounces each) condensed cream of chicken soup, undiluted**
- 1 **can (7 ounces) white or shoepeg corn, drained**
- 1 **teaspoon Creole seasoning**
- ½ **teaspoon garlic powder**
- 2 **pounds peeled and deveined cooked small shrimp**
- 1 **package (3 ounces) cream cheese, cubed**

1. In a small skillet, saute onion in butter until tender. In a 5-qt. slow cooker, combine the onion, milk, soups, corn, Creole seasoning and garlic powder.

2. Cover and cook on low for 3 hours. Stir in shrimp and cream cheese. Cook 30 minutes longer or until shrimp are heated through and cheese is melted. Stir to blend.

NOTE *The following spices may be substituted for 1 teaspoon Creole seasoning: ¼ teaspoon each salt, garlic powder and paprika; and a pinch each of dried thyme, ground cumin and cayenne pepper.*

Savory Beef Soup

Here's a real stick-to-your-ribs soup. I've also substituted chuck roast, rump roast and London broil cut into bite-size pieces, all with tremendous success.

—JANE WHITTAKER PENSACOLA, FL

PREP: 20 MIN. • **COOK:** 8½ HOURS
MAKES: 8 SERVINGS (2 QUARTS)

- 1½ pounds beef stew meat, cut into ½-inch cubes
- 1 tablespoon canola oil
- 1 carton (32 ounces) beef broth
- 1 bottle (12 ounces) beer or nonalcoholic beer
- 1 small onion, chopped
- ½ cup medium pearl barley
- 3 garlic cloves, minced
- 1 teaspoon dried oregano
- 1 teaspoon dried parsley flakes
- 1 teaspoon Worcestershire sauce
- ½ teaspoon crushed red pepper flakes
- ½ teaspoon pepper
- ¼ teaspoon salt
- 1 bay leaf
- 2 cups frozen mixed vegetables, thawed

1. In a large skillet, brown beef in oil; drain. Transfer to a 3-qt. slow cooker.

2. Add the broth, beer, onion, barley, garlic, oregano, parsley, Worcestershire sauce, crushed red pepper flakes, pepper, salt and bay leaf. Cover and cook on low for 8-10 hours.

3. Stir in vegetables; cover and cook 30 minutes longer or until meat is tender and vegetables are heated through. Discard bay leaf.

Hearty Minestrone

I picked up this recipe in California in the '80s and have been making it ever since. I love it partly because it's simple to put together and partly because the flavor is so wonderful!

—BONNIE HOSMAN YOUNG, AZ

PREP: 25 MIN. • **COOK:** 6¼ HOURS
MAKES: 7 SERVINGS (ABOUT 2½ QUARTS)

- 2 cans (one 28 ounces, one 14½ ounces) diced tomatoes, undrained
- 2 cups water
- 2 medium carrots, sliced
- 1 medium onion, chopped
- 1 medium zucchini, chopped
- 1 package (3½ ounces) sliced pepperoni
- 2 teaspoons minced garlic
- 2 teaspoons chicken bouillon granules
- ½ teaspoon dried basil
- ½ teaspoon dried oregano
- 2 cans (16 ounces each) kidney beans, rinsed and drained
- 1 package (10 ounces) frozen chopped spinach, thawed and squeezed dry
- 1¼ cups cooked elbow macaroni
  Shredded Parmesan cheese

1. In a 5-qt. slow cooker, combine the first 10 ingredients. Cover and cook on low for 6-8 hours or until vegetables are tender.

2. Stir in the beans, spinach and macaroni. Cover and cook for 15 minutes longer or until heated through. Sprinkle with cheese.

FREEZE OPTION *Cool soup and transfer to freezer containers. Freeze for up to 3 months. To use frozen soup, thaw in the refrigerator overnight. Transfer to a saucepan. Cover and cook over medium heat until heated through. Sprinkle with Parmesan cheese.*

SAVORY BEEF SOUP

Corn Chowder

I combine and refrigerate the ingredients for this easy chowder the night before. In the morning, I start the slow cooker before I leave for work. When I come home, a hot, tasty meal awaits.

—**MARY HOGUE** ROCHESTER, PA

PREP: 10 MIN. • **COOK:** 6 HOURS
MAKES: 8 SERVINGS (2 QUARTS)

- 2½ cups 2% milk
- 1 can (14¾ ounces) cream-style corn
- 1 can (10¾ ounces) condensed cream of mushroom soup, undiluted
- 1¾ cups frozen corn
- 1 cup frozen shredded hash brown potatoes
- 1 cup cubed fully cooked ham
- 1 large onion, chopped
- 2 teaspoons dried parsley flakes
- 2 tablespoons butter
  Salt and pepper to taste

In a 3-qt. slow cooker, combine all ingredients. Cover and cook on low for 6 hours.

Ginger Chicken Noodle Soup

READY IN ④

This is one of my favorite soup recipes to serve in the wintertime because it's super easy to make and fills the entire house with a wonderful aroma. My whole family loves it!

—**BRANDY STANSBURY** EDNA, TX

PREP: 15 MIN. • **COOK:** 3½ HOURS
MAKES: 8 SERVINGS (2½ QUARTS)

- 1 pound boneless skinless chicken breasts, cubed
- 2 medium carrots, shredded
- 3 tablespoons sherry or reduced-sodium chicken broth
- 2 tablespoons rice vinegar
- 1 tablespoon reduced-sodium soy sauce
- 2 to 3 teaspoons minced fresh gingerroot
- ¼ teaspoon pepper
- 6 cups reduced-sodium chicken broth
- 1 cup water
- 2 cups fresh snow peas, halved
- 2 ounces uncooked angel hair pasta, broken into thirds

1. In a 5-qt. slow cooker, combine the first seven ingredients; stir in broth and water. Cook, covered, on low 3-4 hours or until chicken is tender.

2. Stir in snow peas and pasta. Cook, covered, on low 30 minutes longer or until snow peas and pasta are tender.

Slow-Cooked Cannellini Turkey Soup

All you have to do is add these ingredients to a slow cooker and let them cook! Nothing could be simpler.

—**GARY FENSKI** HURON, SD

PREP: 20 MIN. • **COOK:** 5 HOURS
MAKES: 4 SERVINGS

- 2 cans (15 ounces each) white kidney or cannellini beans, rinsed and drained
- 2 cups cubed cooked turkey
- 1 can (14½ ounces) chicken broth
- 1 can (10 ounces) diced tomatoes and green chilies, undrained
- 1 cup salsa
- ½ teaspoon ground cumin
- ¼ teaspoon curry powder
- ¼ teaspoon ground ginger
- ¼ teaspoon paprika

In a 3-qt. slow cooker, combine all ingredients. Cover and cook on low for 5-6 hours or until heated through.

Slow-Cooker Potato & Ham Soup

In our house, this recipe is a win-win. It's easy for me to whip up and easy for my family to devour. Crusty bread for dipping doesn't hurt, either.

—**LINDA HAGLUND** BUFFALO, MN

PREP: 10 MIN. • **COOK:** 6¼ HOURS
MAKES: 8 SERVINGS (2½ QUARTS)

- 1 carton (32 ounces) chicken broth
- 1 package (30 ounces) frozen shredded hash brown potatoes, thawed
- 1 small onion, finely chopped
- ¼ teaspoon pepper
- 4 ounces cream cheese, softened and cubed
- 1 cup cubed deli ham
- 1 can (5 ounces) evaporated milk
  Sour cream and chopped green onions, optional

1. In a 4- or 5-qt. slow cooker, combine broth, potatoes, onion and pepper. Cook, covered, on low 6-8 hours or until the vegetables are tender.

2. Mash potatoes to desired consistency. Whisk in cream cheese until melted. Stir in ham and milk. Cook, covered, 15-20 minutes longer or until heated through. Serve with sour cream and green onions if desired.

GINGER CHICKEN NOODLE SOUP

SLOW-COOKED CANNELLINI TURKEY SOUP

SLOW-COOKER POTATO & HAM SOUP

ITALIAN CABBAGE SOUP

Italian Cabbage Soup

After doing yard work all day, we love to come in for a light but hearty soup like this one. It's brimming with fresh cabbage, veggies and white beans. Pass the bread!

—**JENNIFER STOWELL** SMITHVILLE, MO

PREP: 15 MIN. • **COOK:** 6 HOURS
MAKES: 8 SERVINGS (2 QUARTS)

- 4 **cups chicken stock**
- 1 **can (6 ounces) tomato paste**
- 1 **small head cabbage (about 1½ pounds), shredded**
- 1 **can (15½ ounces) great northern beans, rinsed and drained**
- 4 **celery ribs, chopped**
- 2 **large carrots, chopped**
- 1 **small onion, chopped**
- 2 **fresh thyme sprigs**
- 1 **bay leaf**
- 2 **garlic cloves, minced**
- ½ **teaspoon salt**
  Shredded Parmesan cheese, optional

1. In a 5- or 6-qt. slow cooker, whisk stock and tomato paste until blended; add cabbage, beans, celery, carrots, onion, thyme, bay leaf, garlic and salt. Cook, covered, on low 6-8 hours or until vegetables are tender.

2. Remove thyme sprigs and bay leaf. If desired, top each serving with cheese.

Vegetable Chicken Soup

This satisfying veggie soup hits the spot at lunch or dinner. Add a few slices of whole grain bread for a filling and nutritious meal.

—AMY CHEATHAM SANDUSKY, OH

PREP: 25 MIN. • **COOK:** 5 HOURS
MAKES: 7 SERVINGS (2¾ QUARTS)

- 1 large sweet onion, chopped
- 1 cup sliced baby portobello mushrooms
- ½ cup chopped green pepper
- ½ cup chopped sweet red pepper
- 1 tablespoon butter
- 1 tablespoon olive oil
- 5 garlic cloves, minced
- ¾ pound boneless skinless chicken breasts, cut into ½-in. cubes
- 1 can (49½ ounces) chicken broth
- 1 can (28 ounces) crushed tomatoes, undrained
- 2 medium carrots, cut into ¼-inch slices
- ½ cup medium pearl barley
- 1¾ teaspoons Italian seasoning
- 1½ teaspoons pepper
- ½ teaspoon salt

1. In a large skillet, saute the onion, mushrooms and peppers in butter and oil until tender. Add garlic; cook 1 minute longer.

2. Transfer to a 5-qt. slow cooker. Add the remaining ingredients. Cover and cook on low for 5-6 hours or until chicken and barley are tender.

VEGETABLE CHICKEN SOUP

FREEZE OPTION *Freeze cooled soup in freezer containers. To use, partially thaw in the refrigerator overnight. Heat through in a saucepan, stirring occasionally and adding a little broth if necessary.*

EXPRESS *PREP*

Texas Black Bean Soup

This stew-like dish, made with convenient canned items, is perfect for spicing up a family gathering on a cool day. It tastes great and requires little time and attention.

—PAMELA SCOTT GARLAND, TX

PREP: 5 MIN. • **COOK:** 4 HOURS
MAKES: 8-10 SERVINGS (ABOUT 2½ QUARTS)

- 2 cans (15 ounces each) black beans, rinsed and drained
- 1 can (14½ ounces) stewed tomatoes or Mexican stewed tomatoes, cut up
- 1 can (14½ ounces) diced tomatoes or diced tomatoes with green chilies
- 1 can (14½ ounces) chicken broth
- 1 can (11 ounces) Mexicorn, drained
- 2 cans (4 ounces each) chopped green chilies
- 4 green onions, thinly sliced
- 2 to 3 tablespoons chili powder
- 1 teaspoon ground cumin
- ½ teaspoon dried minced garlic

In a 3-qt. slow cooker, combine all ingredients. Cover and cook on high for 4-6 hours or until heated through.

Southwestern Chicken Soup

This slow-cooker recipe brings people back for seconds. Chock-full of chicken, corn, tomatoes, peppers and chilies, each sip puts a little zip into mealtime.

—HAROLD TARTAR
WEST PALM BEACH, FL

PREP: 10 MIN. • **COOK:** 6 HOURS
MAKES: 10 SERVINGS

- 1¼ pounds boneless skinless chicken breasts, cut into thin strips
- 1 to 2 tablespoons canola oil
- 2 cans (14½ ounces each) chicken broth
- 1 package (16 ounces) frozen corn, thawed
- 1 can (14½ ounces) diced tomatoes, undrained
- 1 medium onion, chopped
- 1 medium green pepper, chopped
- 1 medium sweet red pepper, chopped
- 1 can (4 ounces) chopped green chilies
- 1½ teaspoons seasoned salt, optional
- 1 teaspoon ground cumin
- ½ teaspoon garlic powder

In a large skillet, saute chicken in oil until lightly browned. Transfer to a 5-qt. slow cooker with a slotted spoon. Stir in the remaining ingredients. Cover and cook on low for 6-8 hours or until the chicken and vegetables are tender. Stir before serving.

Savory Beef & Veggie Soup

Here's a meal-in-one just perfect for chilly winter nights. It's nice to come home to a hearty soup that's ready to eat. Try serving it alongside fruit salad for a fun change of pace.

—COLLEEN JUBL DAYTON, OH

PREP: 10 MIN. • **COOK:** 8 HOURS
MAKES: 9 SERVINGS (2¼ QUARTS)

- 1 pound lean ground beef (90% lean)
- 1 medium onion, chopped
- 2 garlic cloves, minced
- 4 cups spicy hot V8 juice
- 2 cups coleslaw mix
- 1 can (14½ ounces) Italian stewed tomatoes
- 1 package (10 ounces) frozen corn
- 1 package (9 ounces) frozen cut green beans
- 2 tablespoons Worcestershire sauce
- 1 teaspoon dried basil
- ¼ teaspoon pepper

1. In a large nonstick skillet, cook beef and onion over medium heat until meat is no longer pink. Add garlic; cook 1 minute longer. Drain.
2. Transfer to a 5-qt. slow cooker. Stir in the remaining ingredients. Cover and cook on low for 8-10 hours or until heated through.

Curried Lentil Soup

Curry gives a tasty sensation to this hearty vegetarian specialty. It's delicious with a dollop of sour cream. My family gets so excited every time I make it.

—CHRISTINA TILL SOUTH HAVEN, MI

PREP: 15 MIN. • **COOK:** 8 HOURS
MAKES: 10 SERVINGS (2½ QUARTS)

- 4 cups water
- 1 can (28 ounces) crushed tomatoes
- 3 medium potatoes, peeled and diced
- 3 medium carrots, thinly sliced
- 1 cup dried lentils, rinsed
- 1 large onion, chopped
- 1 celery rib, chopped
- 4 teaspoons curry powder
- 2 bay leaves
- 2 garlic cloves, minced
- 1½ teaspoons salt, optional

In a 4- or 5-qt. slow cooker, combine the first 10 ingredients. Cover and cook on low for 8 hours or until vegetables and lentils are tender. Season with salt if desired. Discard bay leaves.

DID YOU KNOW?

Jarred spaghetti sauce makes a terrific replacement for tomato sauce. Try it in your favorite soup or stew recipes where tomato sauce is called for. You might also be able to eliminate or decrease some of the spices called for in the recipe, depending on the flavor of the sauce you use.

Maryland-Style Crab Soup

Try this hearty soup that incorporates the best of vegetable soup and flavorful crab. Whole crabs and claws can be broken into pieces and dropped into the soup, which is my personal preference.

—FREELOVE KNOTT PALM BAY, FL

PREP: 20 MIN. • **COOK:** 6¼ HOURS
MAKES: 8 SERVINGS (3 QUARTS)

- 2 **cans (14½ ounces each) diced tomatoes with green peppers and onions, undrained**
- 2 **cups water**
- 1½ **pounds potatoes, cut into ½-inch cubes (about 5 cups)**
- 2 **cups cubed peeled rutabaga**
- 2 **cups chopped cabbage**
- 1 **medium onion, finely chopped**
- 1 **medium carrot, sliced**
- ½ **cup frozen corn, thawed**
- ½ **cup frozen lima beans, thawed**
- ½ **cup frozen peas, thawed**
- ½ **cup cut fresh green beans (1-inch pieces)**
- 4 **teaspoons seafood seasoning**
- 1 **teaspoon celery seed**
- 1 **vegetable bouillon cube**
- ¼ **teaspoon salt**
- ¼ **teaspoon pepper**
- 1 **pound fresh or lump crabmeat, drained**

1. In a 6-qt. slow cooker, combine the first 16 ingredients. Cook, covered, on low 6-8 hours or until vegetables are tender.
2. Stir in crab. Cook, covered, on low 15 minutes longer or until heated through.

CURRIED LENTIL SOUP

MARYLAND-STYLE
CRAB SOUP

SAVORY SAUSAGE STUFFING, 60

 **68**

 **63**

 **55**

Speedy Side Dishes & More

If you're looking to round out a meal, why not turn to a slow-cooked classic? Great additions to dinner as well as potlucks and parties, these flavorful sides are all a snap to prepare.

PECAN-COCONUT SWEET POTATOES, 64

MAPLE-WALNUT SWEET POTATOES

READY IN ④

Rich & Creamy Mashed Potatoes

It's a cinch to jazz up instant mashed potatoes with sour cream and cream cheese, then cook and serve them from a slow cooker. For a special touch, sprinkle the potatoes with chopped fresh chives, canned French-fried onions or freshly grated Parmesan cheese.

—**DONNA BARDOCZ** HOWELL, MI

PREP: 15 MIN. • **COOK:** 2 HOURS
MAKES: 10 SERVINGS

- 3¾ **cups boiling water**
- 1½ **cups 2% milk**
- 1 **package (8 ounces) cream cheese, softened**
- ½ **cup butter, cubed**
- ½ **cup sour cream**
- 4 **cups mashed potato flakes**
- 1 **teaspoon garlic salt**
- ¼ **teaspoon pepper**
  Minced fresh parsley, optional

In a greased 4-qt. slow cooker, whisk the boiling water, milk, cream cheese, butter and sour cream until smooth. Stir in the potato flakes, garlic salt and pepper. Cover and cook on low for 2-3 hours or until heated through. Sprinkle with parsley if desired.

Maple-Walnut Sweet Potatoes

Sweet potatoes with dried cherries and walnuts make this a classy and delectable side!

—**SARAH HERSE** BROOKLYN, NY

PREP: 15 MIN. • **COOK:** 5 HOURS
MAKES: 12 SERVINGS (¾ CUP EACH)

- 4 **pounds sweet potatoes (about 8 medium)**
- ¾ **cup coarsely chopped walnuts, divided**
- ½ **cup packed light brown sugar**
- ½ **cup dried cherries, coarsely chopped**
- ½ **cup maple syrup**
- ¼ **cup apple cider or juice**
- ¼ **teaspoon salt**

1. Peel and cut sweet potatoes lengthwise in half; cut crosswise into ½-in. slices. Place in a 5-qt. slow cooker. Add ½ cup walnuts, brown sugar, cherries, syrup, cider and salt; toss to combine.
2. Cook, covered, on low 5-6 hours or until potatoes are tender. Sprinkle with remaining walnuts.

DID YOU KNOW?

Sweet potatoes and yams are similar in many ways, so they're often confused with one another. To add to the confusion, canned sweet potatoes are often labeled yams. Yams have dark skin with a dark orange flesh and cook to a moist texture. Fresh yams are not readily available in the US.

Slow Cooker Mushroom Rice Pilaf

A few modifications to our dear Great-Aunt Bernice's mushroom rice pilaf recipe have made this a popular dish for potlucks, barbecues and family get-togethers. It'll become a slow cooker favorite of yours, too!

—AMY WILLIAMS RIALTO, CA

PREP: 20 MIN. • **COOK:** 3 HOURS
MAKES: 6 SERVINGS

- 1   **cup medium grain rice**
- ¼   **cup butter**
- 6   **green onions, chopped**
- 2   **garlic cloves, minced**
- ½   **pound sliced baby portobello mushrooms**
- 2   **cups warm water**
- 4   **teaspoons beef base**

1. In a large skillet, saute rice in butter until lightly browned. Add the green onions and garlic; cook and stir until tender. Stir in the mushrooms.

2. Transfer to a 1½-qt. slow cooker. In a small bowl, whisk water and beef base; pour over rice mixture. Cover and cook on low for 3 to 3½ hours or until the rice is tender and liquid is absorbed. Fluff with a fork.

NOTE *Look for beef base near the broth and bouillon.*

RICH & CREAMY MASHED POTATOES

SLOW COOKER MUSHROOM RICE PILAF

COMFORTING CHEESY POTATOES

GARLIC GREEN BEANS WITH GORGONZOLA

EXPRESS *PREP*

Comforting Cheesy Potatoes

As a four-generation Idaho family, we love our potatoes and cook with them in every way possible. I have served this dish for weddings, family dinners and more. It has become a favorite for my whole gang!

—**KARLA KIMBALL** EMMETT, ID

PREP: 10 MIN. • **COOK:** 4 HOURS
MAKES: 8 SERVINGS

- 1 can (10¾ ounces) condensed cream of chicken soup, undiluted
- 1 cup (8 ounces) sour cream
- 1 small onion, finely chopped
- ¼ cup butter, melted
- ¾ teaspoon salt
- ¼ teaspoon pepper
- 1 package (32 ounces) frozen cubed hash brown potatoes, thawed
- 2 cups (8 ounces) shredded cheddar cheese, divided

In a 4-qt. slow cooker, combine the first six ingredients. Stir in hash browns and 1½ cups cheese. Cook, covered, on low 4-5 hours or until potatoes are tender, sprinkling with remaining cheese during the last 5 minutes.

READY IN ④

Garlic Green Beans with Gorgonzola

I updated this green bean holiday side dish by adding a touch of white wine, fresh thyme and green onions. It's delicious and easy to make; my family loves it!

—**NANCY HEISHMAN** LAS VEGAS, NV

PREP: 20 MIN. • **COOK:** 3 HOURS
MAKES: 10 SERVINGS

- 2 pounds fresh green beans, trimmed and halved
- 1 can (8 ounces) sliced water chestnuts, drained
- 4 green onions, chopped
- 5 bacon strips, cooked and crumbled, divided
- ⅓ cup white wine or chicken broth
- 2 tablespoons minced fresh thyme or 2 teaspoons dried thyme
- 4 garlic cloves, minced
- 1½ teaspoons seasoned salt
- 1 cup (8 ounces) sour cream
- ¾ cup crumbled Gorgonzola cheese

1. Place green beans, water chestnuts, green onions and ¼ cup cooked bacon in a 4-qt. slow cooker. In a small bowl, mix wine, thyme, garlic and seasoned salt; pour over top. Cook, covered, on low 3-4 hours or until green beans are crisp-tender. Drain liquid from beans.

2. Just before serving, stir in sour cream; sprinkle with cheese and remaining bacon.

Butternut Squash with Whole Grain Pilaf

Fresh thyme really shines in this hearty slow-cooked side dish featuring tender butternut squash, nutritious whole grain pilaf and vitamin-packed baby spinach.

—*TASTE OF HOME* TEST KITCHEN

PREP: 15 MIN. • **COOK:** 4 HOURS
MAKES: 12 SERVINGS (¾ CUP EACH)

- 1 cup whole grain brown and red rice blend
- 1 can (14½ ounces) vegetable broth
- 1 medium onion, chopped
- ½ cup water
- 3 garlic cloves, minced
- 2 teaspoons minced fresh thyme or ½ teaspoon dried thyme
- ½ teaspoon salt
- ¼ teaspoon pepper
- 1 medium butternut squash (about 3 pounds), cut into ½-inch cubes
- 1 package (6 ounces) fresh baby spinach

In a 4-qt. slow cooker, combine the first nine ingredients. Cover and cook on low for 4-5 hours or until grains are tender. Just before serving, stir in spinach.

NOTE *This recipe was tested with RiceSelect Royal Blend Whole Grain Texmati Brown & Red Rice with Barley and Rye. Look for it in the rice aisle.*

BUTTERNUT SQUASH WITH WHOLE GRAIN PILAF

EXPRESS PREP READY IN ④

Slow-Cooked Broccoli

This crumb-topped side dish is quick to assemble and full of flavor. Since it simmers in a slow cooker, it frees up my oven for other things. This a great help when I'm preparing several items for a big meal at home.

—**CONNIE SLOCUM** ANTIOCH, TN

PREP: 10 MIN. • **COOK:** 2½ HOURS
MAKES: 8-10 SERVINGS

- 6 cups frozen chopped broccoli, partially thawed
- 1 can (10¾ ounces) condensed cream of celery soup, undiluted
- 1½ cups (6 ounces) shredded sharp cheddar cheese, divided
- ¼ cup chopped onion
- ½ teaspoon Worcestershire sauce
- ¼ teaspoon pepper
- 1 cup crushed butter-flavored crackers (about 25)
- 2 tablespoons butter

1. In a large bowl, combine the broccoli, soup, 1 cup cheese, onion, Worcestershire sauce and pepper. Pour into a greased 3-qt. slow cooker. Sprinkle crackers on top; dot with butter.

2. Cover and cook on high for 2½-3 hours. Sprinkle with remaining cheese. Cook 10 minutes longer or until the cheese is melted.

**SWEET & HOT
BAKED BEANS**

**HONEY-BUTTER
PEAS AND CARROTS**

**GREEN CHILI
CREAMED CORN**

Sweet & Hot Baked Beans

Baked beans belong at a barbecue. They're sweet with heat when you add pineapple and jalapenos.
—**ROBIN HAAS** CRANSTON, RI

PREP: 20 MIN. • **COOK:** 5 HOURS
MAKES: 12 SERVINGS (½ CUP EACH)

- 4 cans (15 ounces each) white kidney or cannellini beans, rinsed and drained
- 2 cans (8 ounces each) crushed pineapple, undrained
- 2 large onions, finely chopped
- 1 cup packed brown sugar
- 1 cup ketchup
- 10 bacon strips, cooked and crumbled
- ½ cup molasses
- ¼ cup canned diced jalapeno peppers
- 2 tablespoons white vinegar
- 4 garlic cloves, minced
- 4 teaspoons ground mustard
- ¼ teaspoon ground cloves

In a 3- or 4-qt. slow cooker, combine all ingredients. Cook, covered, on low 5-6 hours.

Honey-Butter Peas and Carrots

This classic combination of peas and carrots is enriched with a handful of flavor enhancers. Slow cooking allows the ingredients to meld for maximum richness.
—**THERESA KREYCHE** TUSTIN, CA

PREP: 15 MIN. • **COOK:** 5¼ HOURS
MAKES: 12 SERVINGS (½ CUP EACH)

- 1 pound carrots, sliced
- 1 large onion, chopped
- ¼ cup water
- ¼ cup butter, cubed
- ¼ cup honey
- 4 garlic cloves, minced

- 1 teaspoon salt
- 1 teaspoon dried marjoram
- ⅛ teaspoon white pepper
- 1 package (16 ounces) frozen peas

In a 3-qt. slow cooker, combine the first nine ingredients. Cook, covered, on low 5 hours. Stir in peas. Cook, covered, on high 15-25 minutes longer or until vegetables are tender.

EXPRESS PREP | READY IN 4
Green Chili Creamed Corn

When hosting big meals, I sometimes run out of burners. Then I realized my slow cooker could help by simmering corn and green chilies with pickled jalapenos.
—**PAT DAZIS** CHARLOTTE, NC

PREP: 10 MIN. • **COOK:** 3 HOURS
MAKES: 8 SERVINGS

- 6 cups fresh or frozen corn (about 30 ounces), thawed
- 1 package (8 ounces) cream cheese, cubed
- 1 jar (4 ounces) diced pimientos, drained
- 1 can (4 ounces) chopped green chilies
- ½ cup vegetable broth
- ¼ cup butter, cubed
- ¼ cup pickled jalapeno slices, coarsely chopped
- 1 tablespoon sugar
- ⅛ teaspoon crushed red pepper flakes

In a 3- or 4-qt. slow cooker, combine all ingredients. Cook, covered, on low 2½-3 hours or until heated through. Stir just before serving.

READY IN 4
Spiced Acorn Squash

Working full-time, I found I didn't always have the chance to cook the meals my family loved. So I re-created many of our favorites in the slow cooker! This treatment for squash is one of them. With only a handful of ingredients, a few moments of prep work and my slow cooker, I can easily set a comforting meal on the table.
—**CAROL GRECO** CENTEREACH, NY

PREP: 15 MIN. • **COOK:** 3½ HOURS
MAKES: 4 SERVINGS

- ¾ cup packed brown sugar
- 1 teaspoon ground cinnamon
- 1 teaspoon ground nutmeg
- 2 small acorn squash, halved and seeded
- ¾ cup raisins
- 4 tablespoons butter
- ½ cup water

1. In a small bowl, mix brown sugar, cinnamon and nutmeg; spoon into squash halves. Sprinkle with raisins. Top each with 1 tablespoon butter.
2. Wrap each half individually in heavy-duty foil, sealing tightly.
3. Pour water into a 5-qt. slow cooker. Place squash in slow cooker, cut side up (packets may be stacked). Cook, covered, on high 3½-4 hours or until squash is tender.
4. Remove squash from slow cooker. Carefully open foil to allow steam to escape.

SAVORY SAUSAGE
STUFFING

3. Stir in sausage. Add bread cubes and sage; toss to combine. Add chicken stock and wine. Stir in cranberries and, if desired, sunflower kernels. Transfer to a greased 6-qt. slow cooker.
4. Cook, covered, on low 2-3 hours or until heated through, stirring once.

Spiced Carrots & Butternut Squash

When I've got a lot going on, my slow cooker is my go-to tool for roasting veggies. The sweetness of the squash and carrots really complement the spicy seasonings.
—**COURTNEY STULTZ** COLUMBUS, KS

PREP: 15 MIN. • **COOK:** 4 HOURS
MAKES: 6 SERVINGS

- 5 **large carrots, cut into ½-inch pieces (about 3 cups)**
- 2 **cups cubed peeled butternut squash (1-inch)**
- 1 **tablespoon balsamic vinegar**
- 1 **tablespoon olive oil**
- 1 **tablespoon honey**
- 1 **teaspoon ground cinnamon**
- ½ **teaspoon salt**
- ½ **teaspoon ground cumin**
- ¼ **teaspoon chili powder**

Place carrots and squash in a 3-qt. slow cooker. In a small bowl, mix remaining ingredients; drizzle over vegetables and toss to coat. Cook, covered, on low 4-5 hours or until vegetables are tender. Gently stir before serving.

READY IN ④

Savory Sausage Stuffing

I always made the same old stuffing every year for the holidays. One Thanksgiving about 10 years ago, I decided to jazz up the recipe with pork sausage. Now I am "ordered" to make this same recipe every year for Thanksgiving and Christmas. Leftovers are even better the following day!
—**URSULA HERNANDEZ** WALTHAM, MN

PREP: 30 MIN. • **COOK:** 2 HOURS
MAKES: 16 SERVINGS (¾ CUP EACH)

- 1 **pound sage pork sausage**
- ½ **cup butter, cubed**
- ½ **pound fresh mushrooms, finely chopped**
- 6 **celery ribs, finely chopped**
- 2 **small onions, finely chopped**
- 2 **garlic cloves, minced**

- 1 **loaf (13 ounces) French bread, cut into ½-inch cubes (about 17 cups)**
- 4 **cups cubed multigrain bread (½-inch)**
- 1 **tablespoon rubbed sage**
- 1 **cup chicken stock**
- ½ **cup white wine or chicken stock**
- 1 **cup dried cranberries**
- ½ **cup sunflower kernels, optional**

1. In a large skillet, cook sausage over medium heat 4-6 minutes or until no longer pink, breaking into crumbles; drain.
2. In a stockpot, melt butter over medium heat. Add mushrooms, celery and onions; cook and stir 3-4 minutes or until tender. Add garlic; cook 1 minute longer. Remove from heat.

Onion-Garlic Hash Browns

Quick to assemble, this is a simple recipe I've served many times. Stir in hot sauce if you like a bit of heat. I love to top my finished dish with a sprinkling of shredded cheddar cheese. Try is as a breakfast side dish or alongside your dinner entree.

—**CINDI BOGER** ARDMORE, AL

PREP: 20 MIN. • **COOK:** 3 HOURS
MAKES: 12 SERVINGS (½ CUP EACH)

- 1 **large red onion, chopped**
- 1 **small sweet red pepper, chopped**
- 1 **small green pepper, chopped**
- ¼ **cup butter, cubed**
- 1 **tablespoon olive oil**
- 4 **garlic cloves, minced**
- 1 **package (30 ounces) frozen shredded hash brown potatoes**
- ½ **teaspoon salt**
- ½ **teaspoon pepper**
- 3 **drops hot pepper sauce, optional**
- 2 **teaspoons minced fresh parsley**

1. In a large skillet, saute onion and peppers in butter and oil until crisp-tender. Add garlic; cook 1 minute longer. Stir in the hash browns, salt, pepper and pepper sauce if desired.

2. Transfer to a 5-qt. slow cooker coated with cooking spray. Cover and cook on low for 3-4 hours or until heated through. Sprinkle with parsley before serving.

SPICED CARROTS &
BUTTERNUT SQUASH

ONION-GARLIC
HASH BROWNS

Sweet Onion & Red Bell Pepper Topping

As soon as the spring Vidalia onions hit the market, I make this relish. I use it on hot dogs, bruschetta, cream cheese and crackers. It's versatile.

—PAT HOCKETT OCALA, FL

PREP: 15 MIN. • **COOK:** 4 HOURS
MAKES: 4 CUPS

- 4 large sweet onions, thinly sliced (about 8 cups)
- 4 large sweet red peppers, thinly sliced (about 6 cups)
- ½ cup cider vinegar
- ¼ cup packed brown sugar
- 2 tablespoons canola oil
- 2 tablespoons honey
- 2 teaspoons celery seed
- ¾ teaspoon crushed red pepper flakes
- ½ teaspoon salt

In a 5- or 6-qt. slow cooker, combine all ingredients. Cook, covered, on low 4-5 hours or until vegetables are tender. Serve with a slotted spoon.

TOP TIP

I've found that a melon baller works great to scoop out the seeds and membranes from red bell peppers.
—CHARLINE S. SAN DIEGO, CA.

Easy Beans & Potatoes with Bacon

I love the combination of green beans with bacon, so I created this recipe. It's great for when you have company because you can start the side dish in the slow cooker and continue preparing the rest of your dinner.
—BARBARA BRITTAIN SANTEE, CA

PREP: 15 MIN. • **COOK:** 6 HOURS
MAKES: 10 SERVINGS

- 8 bacon strips, chopped
- 1½ pounds fresh green beans, trimmed and cut into 2-inch pieces (about 4 cups)
- 4 medium potatoes, peeled and cut into ½-inch cubes
- 1 small onion, halved and sliced
- ¼ cup reduced-sodium chicken broth
- ½ teaspoon salt
- ¼ teaspoon pepper

1. In a large skillet, cook bacon over medium heat until crisp, stirring occasionally. Remove to paper towels with a slotted spoon; drain, reserving 1 tablespoon drippings. Cover and refrigerate bacon until serving.

2. In a 5-qt. slow cooker, combine the remaining ingredients; stir in reserved drippings. Cover and cook on low for 6-8 hours or until potatoes are tender. Stir in bacon; heat through.

**EASY BEANS &
POTATOES WITH BACON**

Nebraska Creamed Corn

I brought this super-easy dish to a school potluck once and it was gone in no time. I've been asked to bring it to every function since.
—JESSICA MAXWELL ENGLEWOOD, NJ

PREP: 10 MIN. • **COOK:** 3 HOURS
MAKES: 9 SERVINGS

- 2 packages (one 16 ounces, one 12 ounces) frozen corn, thawed
- 1 package (8 ounces) cream cheese, cubed
- ¾ cup shredded cheddar cheese
- ¼ cup butter, melted
- ¼ cup heavy whipping cream
- ½ teaspoon salt
- ¼ teaspoon pepper

In a 3- or 4-qt. slow cooker, combine all ingredients. Cook, covered, on low 3 to 3½ hours or until cheese is melted and corn is tender. Stir just before serving.

PECAN-COCONUT SWEET POTATOES

Pecan-Coconut Sweet Potatoes

It's great to be able to make a tempting sweet potato dish ahead of time by putting it in the slow cooker. This tasty recipe includes sweet coconut and crunchy pecans.
—**REBECCA CLARK** WARRIOR, AL

PREP: 20 MIN. • **COOK:** 5 HOURS
MAKES: 6 SERVINGS

- ¼ cup packed brown sugar
- 2 tablespoons flaked coconut
- 2 tablespoons chopped pecans, toasted
- 1 teaspoon vanilla extract
- ½ teaspoon salt
- ¼ teaspoon ground cinnamon
- 2 pounds sweet potatoes, peeled and cut into ¾-inch cubes
- 1 tablespoon butter, melted
- ½ cup miniature marshmallows

1. In a small bowl, mix the first six ingredients. Place sweet potatoes in a 3-qt. slow cooker coated with cooking spray; sprinkle with brown sugar mixture. Drizzle with butter.

2. Cook, covered, on low 5-6 hours or until sweet potatoes are tender. Turn off slow cooker. Sprinkle marshmallows over potatoes; let stand, covered, 5 minutes before serving.

Slow-Cooked Mac 'n' Cheese

The name of this recipe alone is enough to make mouths water. This is comfort food at its finest: rich, hearty and extra-cheesy. It serves nine as a side dish, though you might want to make it your main course!
—**SHELBY MOLINA** WHITEWATER, WI

PREP: 25 MIN. • **COOK:** 2 HOURS
MAKES: 9 SERVINGS

- 2 cups uncooked elbow macaroni
- 1 can (12 ounces) reduced-fat evaporated milk
- 1½ cups fat-free milk
- ⅓ cup egg substitute
- 1 tablespoon butter, melted
- 8 ounces reduced-fat process cheese (Velveeta), cubed
- 2 cups (8 ounces) shredded sharp cheddar cheese, divided

1. Cook macaroni according to package directions; drain and rinse in cold water. Meanwhile, in a large bowl, combine the evaporated milk, milk, egg substitute and butter. Stir in the process cheese, 1½ cups sharp cheddar cheese and the macaroni.

2. Transfer to a 3-qt. slow cooker coated with cooking spray. Cover and cook on low for 2-3 hours or until center is set, stirring once. Sprinkle with remaining sharp cheddar cheese.

Nutty Apple Butter

As a New England native, I love apple-picking season. Grab some apples and peanut butter to make this creamy PB&J spread. Use it to coat sliced fruit or spread it on a sandwich or graham crackers.
—**BRANDIE CRANSHAW** RAPID CITY, SD

PREP: 20 MIN. • **COOK:** 8 HOURS
MAKES: 5 CUPS

- 4 **pounds apples (about 8 large), peeled and chopped**
- ¾ **to 1 cup sugar**
- ¼ **cup water**
- 3 **teaspoons ground cinnamon**
- ¼ **teaspoon ground nutmeg**
- ¼ **teaspoon ground cloves**
- ¼ **teaspoon ground allspice**
- ¼ **cup creamy peanut butter**

1. In a greased 5-qt. slow cooker, combine the first seven ingredients. Cook, covered, on low 8-10 hours or until the apples are tender.
2. Whisk in peanut butter until apple mixture is smooth. Cool to room temperature. Store in an airtight container in the refrigerator.

NUTTY APPLE BUTTER

EXPRESS PREP
Mushroom Wild Rice

This is one of my favorite recipes from my mother. With only seven ingredients, it's quick to assemble in the morning before I leave for work. By the time I get home, all sorts of mouthwatering aromas have filled the house.

—**BOB MALCHOW** MONON, IN

PREP: 5 MIN. • **COOK:** 7 HOURS
MAKES: 12-16 SERVINGS

- 2¼ **cups water**
- 1 **can (10½ ounces) condensed beef consomme, undiluted**
- 1 **can (10½ ounces) condensed French onion soup, undiluted**
- 3 **cans (4 ounces each) mushroom stems and pieces, drained**
- ½ **cup butter, melted**
- 1 **cup uncooked brown rice**
- 1 **cup uncooked wild rice**

In a 3-qt. slow cooker, combine all ingredients. Cover and cook on low for 7-8 hours or until rice is tender.

TOP TIP

We feed a lot of people at Thanksgiving and Christmas dinner, so my sisters and I always set up a big buffet on the kitchen counter. We put each side dish in a slow cooker (mashed potatoes, scalloped corn, squash, gravy and so forth) to keep everything warm. Guests bring the breads, rolls, salads and pies. If someone arrives late, they still can have a hot delicious meal.

—**MARLA C.** SMYRNA, NY

EXPRESS PREP READY IN ④
Cheesy Creamed Corn

Even those who usually don't like corn will ask for a second helping of this creamy, cheesy side dish. It's a favorite of mine because it is easy to make, calling for ingredients that I usually have on hand.

—**MARY ANN TRUITT** WICHITA, KS

PREP: 5 MIN. • **COOK:** 3 HOURS
MAKES: 12 SERVINGS

- 3 **packages (16 ounces each) frozen corn**
- 2 **packages (one 8 ounces, one 3 ounces) cream cheese, cubed**
- ¼ **cup butter, cubed**
- 3 **tablespoons water**
- 3 **tablespoons milk**
- 2 **tablespoons sugar**
- 6 **slices process American cheese, cut into small pieces**

In a 4- or 5-qt. slow cooker, combine all ingredients. Cook, covered, on low 3-4 hours or until heated through and cheese is melted, stirring once.

Sweet Potato Stuffing

Mom likes to make sure there will be enough stuffing to satisfy our large family. For our holiday gatherings, she slow-cooks this tasty sweet potato dressing in addition to the traditional stuffing that's cooked inside the turkey.

—**KELLY POLLOCK** LONDON, ON

PREP: 15 MIN. • **COOK:** 4 HOURS
MAKES: 10 SERVINGS

- ¼ **cup butter, cubed**
- ½ **cup chopped celery**
- ½ **cup chopped onion**
- ½ **cup chicken broth**
- ½ **teaspoon salt, optional**
- ½ **teaspoon rubbed sage**
- ½ **teaspoon poultry seasoning**
- ½ **teaspoon pepper**
- 6 **cups dry bread cubes**
- 1 **large sweet potato, cooked, peeled and finely chopped**
- ¼ **cup chopped pecans**

1. In a Dutch oven, heat butter over medium-high heat. Add celery and onion; cook and stir until tender. Stir in broth and seasonings. Add remaining ingredients; toss to combine.
2. Transfer to a greased 3-qt. slow cooker. Cook, covered, on low 4 hours or until heated through.

CHEESY CREAMED CORN

SWEET POTATO STUFFING

SLOW-COOKED
GREEN BEANS

PARSLEY SMASHED
POTATOES

⑤ INGREDIENTS *EXPRESS* PREP
READY IN ④

Slow-Cooked Green Beans

I was asked to do a cooking demo for a group of women from my church. After spending hours researching side dishes, I combined a few to make these green beans my own.
—**ALICE WHITE** WILLOW SPRING, NC

PREP: 10 MIN. • **COOK:** 2 HOURS
MAKES: 12 SERVINGS

- 3 **packages (16 ounces each) frozen French-style green beans, thawed**
- ½ **cup packed brown sugar**
- ½ **cup butter, melted**
- 1½ **teaspoons garlic salt**
- ¾ **teaspoon reduced-sodium soy sauce**

Place green beans in a 5-qt. slow cooker. In a small bowl, mix remaining ingredients; pour over beans and toss to coat. Cook, covered, on low 2-3 hours or until heated through. Serve with a slotted spoon.

Parsley Smashed Potatoes

I love potatoes but not the work involved in making mashed potatoes from scratch. I came up with this easy homemade version using my slow cooker. The best part is I can use the leftover broth for soup the next day!
—**KATIE HAGY** BLACKSBURG, SC

PREP: 20 MIN. • **COOK:** 6 HOURS
MAKES: 8 SERVINGS

- 16 **small red potatoes (about 2 pounds)**
- 1 **celery rib, sliced**
- 1 **medium carrot, sliced**
- ¼ **cup finely chopped onion**
- 2 **cups chicken broth**
- 1 **tablespoon minced fresh parsley**
- 1½ **teaspoons salt, divided**
- 1 **teaspoon pepper, divided**
- 1 **garlic clove, minced**
- 2 **tablespoons butter, melted**
  Additional minced fresh parsley

1. Place potatoes, celery, carrot and onion in a 4-qt. slow cooker. In a small bowl, mix broth, parsley, 1 teaspoon salt, ½ teaspoon pepper and garlic; pour over vegetables. Cook, covered, on low 6-8 hours or until potatoes are tender.

2. Transfer potatoes from slow cooker to a 15x10x1-in. pan; discard cooking liquid and vegetables. Using the bottom of a measuring cup, flatten potatoes slightly.

3. Transfer to a large bowl; drizzle with butter. Sprinkle with remaining salt and pepper; toss to coat. Sprinkle with additional minced parsley.

DID YOU KNOW?

Red potatoes are ideal for slow-cooker recipes. The small spuds hold their shape well no matter how they're cooked, making them a great addition to slow-cooked side dishes as well as potato salads and soups.

Scalloped Taters

This creamy and comforting side dish tastes great with almost any entree, and it is truly a snap to assemble with convenient frozen hash browns. It's the best way to prepare potatoes when the oven is full of other dishes.
—**LUCINDA WOLKER** SOMERSET, PA

PREP: 10 MIN. • **COOK:** 3 HOURS
MAKES: 12 SERVINGS

- 1 package (2 pounds) frozen cubed hash brown potatoes
- 1 can (10¾ ounces) condensed cream of chicken soup, undiluted
- 1½ cups whole milk
- 1 cup (4 ounces) shredded cheddar cheese
- ½ cup plus 1 tablespoon butter, melted, divided
- ¼ cup dried minced onion
- ½ teaspoon salt
- ⅛ teaspoon pepper
- ¾ cup crushed cornflakes

1. In a large bowl, combine the hash browns, soup, milk, cheese, ½ cup butter, onion, salt and pepper. Pour into a greased 5-qt. slow cooker. Cover and cook on low for 3-4 hours or until the potatoes are tender.

2. Just before serving, combine the cornflake crumbs and remaining butter in a pie plate. Bake at 350° for 4-6 minutes or until golden brown. Stir the potatoes; sprinkle with crumb topping.

Cheesy Spinach

My daughter often serves this comforting favorite at church suppers. There is never any left!
—**FRANCES MOORE** DECATUR, IL

PREP: 10 MIN. • **COOK:** 5 HOURS
MAKES: 6-8 SERVINGS

- 2 packages (10 ounces each) frozen chopped spinach, thawed and well drained
- 2 cups (16 ounces) 4% cottage cheese
- 1½ cups cubed process cheese (Velveeta)
- 3 large eggs, lightly beaten
- ¼ cup butter, cubed
- ¼ cup all-purpose flour
- 1 teaspoon salt

In a large bowl, combine all ingredients. Pour into a greased 3-qt. slow cooker. Cover and cook on high for 1 hour. Reduce heat to low; cook 4-5 hours longer or until a knife inserted near the center comes out clean.

SCALLOPED TATERS

Shoepeg Corn Side Dish

READY IN 4

If shoepeg corn isn't available in your region, then you can use regular canned corn; it works just as well.

—**GLORIA SCHUTZ** TRENTON, IL

PREP: 20 MIN. • **COOK:** 3 HOURS
MAKES: 8 SERVINGS

- 1 can (14½ ounces) French-style green beans, drained
- 2 cans (7 ounces each) white or shoepeg corn
- 1 can (10¾ ounces) condensed cream of mushroom soup, undiluted
- 1 jar (4½ ounces) sliced mushrooms, drained
- ½ cup slivered almonds
- ½ cup shredded cheddar cheese
- ½ cup sour cream
- ¾ cup French-fried onions

In a 3-qt. slow cooker, combine the first seven ingredients. Cover and cook on low for 3-4 hours or until vegetables are tender, stirring occasionally. Sprinkle with onions during the last 15 minutes of cooking.

Old-Fashioned Peach Butter

Cinnamon and ground cloves add down-home flavor to this spread for toast or biscuits. Using the slow cooker eliminates much of the stirring required when simmering fruit butter on the stovetop.

—**MARILOU ROBINSON** PORTLAND, OR

PREP: 25 MIN.
COOK: 9 HOURS + COOLING
MAKES: 9 CUPS

- 14 cups coarsely chopped peeled fresh or frozen peaches (about 5½ pounds)
- 2½ cups sugar
- 4½ teaspoons lemon juice
- 1½ teaspoons ground cinnamon
- ¾ teaspoon ground cloves
- ½ cup quick-cooking tapioca

1. In a large bowl, combine the peaches, sugar, lemon juice, cinnamon and cloves. Transfer to a 5-qt. slow cooker. Cover and cook on low for 8-10 hours or until peaches are very soft, stirring occasionally.
2. Stir in tapioca. Cook, uncovered, on high for 1 hour or until thickened. Pour into jars or freezer containers; cool to room temperature, about 1 hour. Cover and refrigerate up to 3 weeks or freeze up to 1 year.
FREEZE OPTION *Thaw peach butter in the refrigerator for 1-2 days; use within 3 weeks.*

Marmalade-Glazed Carrots

EXPRESS PREP

This side dish is ideal when you'd like to serve your vegetables in a different way for a special dinner. Cinnamon and nutmeg season baby carrots that are simmered with orange marmalade and brown sugar.

—**BARB RUDYK** VERMILION, AB

PREP: 10 MIN. • **COOK:** 5½ HOURS
MAKES: 6 SERVINGS

- 2 pounds fresh carrots halved lenthwise and cut into 2-inch pieces
- ½ cup orange marmalade
- 3 tablespoons cold water, divided
- 2 tablespoons brown sugar
- 1 tablespoon butter, melted
- ½ teaspoon ground cinnamon
- ¼ teaspoon salt
- ¼ teaspoon ground nutmeg
- ⅛ teaspoon pepper
- 1 tablespoon cornstarch

1. In a 3-qt. slow cooker, combine the carrots, marmalade, 1 tablespoon water, brown sugar, butter and seasonings. Cover and cook on low for 5-6 hours or until carrots are tender.
2. Combine cornstarch and remaining water until smooth; stir into carrot mixture. Cover and cook on high for 30 minutes or until thickened. Serve with a slotted spoon.

SHOEPEG CORN SIDE DISH

OLD-FASHIONED PEACH BUTTER

MARMALADE-GLAZED CARROTS

PORK AND BEEF BARBECUE, 154

179

81

120

Easy Entrees

Turn here for all your dinnertime solutions! Whether you're looking for a beef, poultry or pork main course, these slow-cooked entrees hit the spot! You'll even find seafood and pasta recipes that make meals as simple as can be.

SLOW COOKER MAC N CHEESE, 160

CHILE COLORADO BURRITOS

Chile Colorado Burritos

When I was growing up in Southern California, this was one of my favorite Mexican dishes. It's hard to find now that I live in the Midwest—except in my kitchen!

—**KELLY MCCULLEY** DES MOINES, IA

PREP: 20 MIN. • **COOK:** 6¼ HOURS
MAKES: 8 SERVINGS

- 2 **pounds boneless beef chuck roast, cut into 1½-inch pieces**
- 2 **cans (10 ounces each) enchilada sauce**
- 1 **teaspoon beef bouillon granules**
- 1 **can (16 ounces) refried beans, optional**
- 8 **flour tortillas (8 inches)**
- 1 **cup (4 ounces) shredded Colby-Monterey Jack cheese Chopped green onions, optional**

1. In a 4-qt. slow cooker, combine beef, enchilada sauce and bouillon granules. Cook, covered, on low 6-8 hours or until meat is tender.
2. Preheat oven to 425°. Using a slotted spoon, remove meat from sauce. Skim fat from sauce. If desired, spoon about ¼ cup beans across center of each tortilla; top with ⅓ cup meat. Fold the bottom and sides of tortilla over filling and roll up.
3. Place in a greased 11x7-in. baking dish. Pour 1 cup sauce over top; sprinkle with cheese. Bake, uncovered, 10-15 minutes or until cheese is melted. If desired, sprinkle with green onions.

Garlic-Sesame Beef

My mom received this marinade recipe from a neighbor while she lived in Seoul, South Korea, which is where I was adopted from. Mom created heritage night for my brother and me. As a busy mother of four, I keep her tradition alive but let the slow cooker do the work!

—JACKIE BROWN FAIRVIEW, NC

PREP: 15 MIN. + MARINATING
COOK: 5 HOURS
MAKES: 6 SERVINGS

- 6 green onions, sliced
- ½ cup sugar
- ½ cup water
- ½ cup reduced-sodium soy sauce
- ¼ cup sesame oil
- 3 tablespoons sesame seeds, toasted
- 2 tablespoons all-purpose flour
- 4 garlic cloves, minced
- 1 beef sirloin tip roast (3 pounds), thinly sliced
  Additional sliced green onions and toasted sesame seeds
  Hot cooked rice

1. In a large resealable plastic bag, mix the first eight ingredients. Add beef; seal bag and turn to coat. Refrigerate 8 hours or overnight.
2. Pour beef and marinade into a 3-qt. slow cooker. Cook, covered, on low 5-7 hours or until the meat is tender.
3. Using a slotted spoon, remove beef to a serving platter; sprinkle with additional green onions and sesame seeds. Serve with rice.

GARLIC-SESAME BEEF

Potato Pizza Casserole

Here's a fun, full-flavored meal-in-one the whole family will go for. It's great on weeknights when everyone comes through the door hungry at the same time.

—TYLER SHERMAN WILLIAMSBURG, VA

PREP: 25 MIN. • **COOK:** 4 HOURS
MAKES: 8 SERVINGS

- 1 pound ground beef
- ½ pound sliced fresh mushrooms
- 1 medium green pepper, chopped
- 1 small onion, chopped
- 2 jars (14 ounces each) pizza sauce
- 1 can (10¾ ounces) condensed cheddar cheese soup, undiluted
- ½ cup 2% milk
- 1 teaspoon Italian seasoning
- ½ teaspoon garlic salt
- ¼ teaspoon crushed red pepper flakes
- 1 package (32 ounces) frozen cubed hash brown potatoes, thawed
- 15 slices pepperoni, chopped
- 2 cups (8 ounces) shredded Italian cheese blend

1. In a large skillet, cook the beef, mushrooms, green pepper and onion until the meat is no longer pink; drain.
2. Meanwhile, in a large bowl, combine the pizza sauce, soup, milk, Italian seasoning, garlic salt and pepper flakes. Stir in the potatoes, pepperoni and beef mixture.
3. Transfer half of the meat mixture to a 5-qt slow cooker. Sprinkle with half of the cheese; repeat layers. Cover and cook on low for 4-5 hours or until potatoes are tender.

Italian Beef

I make this beef in the slow cooker when I'm having a party so I don't have to spend so much time in the kitchen. The meat smells so delicious, I can hardly keep my husband from helping himself ahead of time! For a very robust sandwich, serve the shredded beef on a roll spread with horseradish sauce.

—**LORI HAYES** VENICE, FL

PREP: 5 MIN. • **COOK:** 10 HOURS
MAKES: 14 SERVINGS

- 1 beef top round roast (4 pounds)
- 2 cups water
- 2 tablespoons Italian seasoning
- 1 teaspoon each salt, dried oregano, dried basil, garlic powder, dried parsley flakes and pepper
- 1 bay leaf
- 14 French rolls (5 inches long)

1. Cut roast in half; place in a 5-qt. slow cooker. Combine the water and seasonings; pour over roast. Cover and cook on low for 10-12 hours or until meat is very tender. Discard bay leaf.
2. Remove meat and shred with a fork. Skim fat from cooking juices; return meat to slow cooker. Serve on rolls.

Mexican Beef-Stuffed Peppers

I grew up eating stuffed peppers and thought my husband would love them as well. He didn't at first, but then I created this slow-cooked recipe. He loves fajitas and tacos, so I created stuffed peppers with all of his favorite flavors tucked inside. What a hit!

—**NICOLE SULLIVAN** ARVADA, CO

PREP: 15 MIN. • **COOK:** 5 HOURS
MAKES: 4 SERVINGS

- 4 medium green or sweet red peppers
- 1 pound ground beef
- 1 package (8.8 ounces) ready-to-serve Spanish rice
- 2 cups (8 ounces) shredded Colby-Monterey Jack cheese, divided
- 1½ cups salsa
- 1 tablespoon hot pepper sauce
- 1 cup water
- 2 tablespoons minced fresh cilantro

1. Cut tops off peppers and remove seeds; set aside. In a large skillet, cook beef over medium heat until no longer pink; drain.
2. Stir in the rice, 1½ cups cheese, salsa and pepper sauce. Spoon into peppers. Transfer to a 5-qt. slow cooker. Pour water around peppers.
3. Cover and cook on low for 5-6 hours or until peppers are tender and filling is heated through. Top with remaining cheese; sprinkle with cilantro.

Java Roast Beef

Coffee adds richness to the gravy in this filling entree.

—**CHARLA SACKMANN** ORANGE CITY, IA

PREP: 10 MIN. • **COOK:** 8 HOURS
MAKES: 12 SERVINGS

- 5 garlic cloves, minced
- 1½ teaspoons salt
- ¾ teaspoon pepper
- 1 boneless beef chuck roast (3 to 3½ pounds)
- 1½ cups strong brewed coffee
- 2 tablespoons cornstarch
- ¼ cup cold water

1. Mix garlic, salt and pepper; rub over beef. Transfer to a 4-qt. slow cooker. Pour coffee around meat. Cook, covered, on low 8-10 hours or until meat is tender.
2. Remove roast to a serving plate; keep warm. Transfer cooking juices to a small saucepan; skim off fat. Bring to a boil. In a small bowl, mix cornstarch and water until smooth; gradually stir into cooking juices. Bring to a boil; cook and stir 1-2 minutes or until thickened. Serve with roast.

HOW TO

CARVE A CHUCK ROAST

❶ To carve a chuck roast, first separate the individual muscles by cutting around each muscle and bone.
❷ Carve across the grain of the meat to desired thickness.

Slow-Cooker Sloppy Joes

On hot summer days, this simmers without heating up the kitchen while I work on the rest of the meal. It's easy to double or triple for crowds, and if there are any leftovers, you can freeze them to enjoy later.

—CAROL LOSIER BALDWINSVILLE, NY

PREP: 20 MIN. • **COOK:** 3 HOURS
MAKES: 8 SERVINGS

- 1½ **pounds ground beef**
- 2 **celery ribs, chopped**
- 1 **small onion, chopped**
- 1 **bottle (12 ounces) chili sauce**
- 2 **tablespoons brown sugar**
- 2 **tablespoons sweet pickle relish**
- 1 **tablespoon Worcestershire sauce**
- 1 **teaspoon salt**
- ⅛ **teaspoon pepper**
- 8 **hamburger buns, split**

1. In a large skillet, cook beef, celery and onion over medium-high heat 8-10 minutes or until beef is no longer pink, breaking up beef into crumbles; drain. Transfer to a 3-qt. slow cooker.

2. Stir in chili sauce, brown sugar, pickle relish, Worcestershire sauce, salt and pepper. Cook, covered, on low 3-4 hours or until heated through and flavors are blended. Spoon meat mixture onto bun bottoms. Replace tops.

JAVA ROAST BEEF

SLOW-COOKER SLOPPY JOES

**MEAT-LOVER'S
PIZZA HOT DISH**

**SPRING HERB
ROAST**

HOME-STYLE STEW

Meat-Lover's Pizza Hot Dish

I make this hearty casserole for the men who help us out during harvest. Every year they say it's the best, hands down. You can add any pizza toppings your family likes.

—BROOK BOTHUN CANBY, MN

PREP: 25 MIN. • **COOK:** 3¼ HOURS
MAKES: 10 SERVINGS

- 1 **pound ground beef**
- 1 **pound bulk Italian sausage**
- 1 **medium onion, chopped**
- 1 **cup sliced fresh mushrooms**
- 4 **cans (8 ounces each) no-salt-added tomato sauce**
- 2 **cans (15 ounces each) pizza sauce**
- 1 **package (16 ounces) penne pasta**
- 1 **cup water**
- 1 **can (6 ounces) tomato paste**
- 1 **package (3½ ounces) sliced pepperoni**
- 1 **teaspoon Italian seasoning**
- 2 **cups (8 ounces) shredded part-skim mozzarella cheese, divided**
- 2 **cups (8 ounces) shredded cheddar cheese, divided**

1. In a large skillet, cook beef, sausage, onion and mushrooms over medium heat 10-12 minutes or until meat is no longer pink and vegetables are tender, breaking up meat into crumbles; drain.

2. Transfer meat mixture to a greased 6-qt. slow cooker. Stir in tomato sauce, pizza sauce, pasta, water, tomato paste, pepperoni and Italian seasoning. Cook, covered, on low 3-4 hours or until pasta is tender.

3. Stir thoroughly; mix in 1 cup mozzarella cheese and 1 cup cheddar cheese. Sprinkle remaining cheese over top. Cook, covered, 15-20 minutes longer or until cheese is melted.

Spring Herb Roast

You might forget about this roast while it's cooking, but the marvelous aroma won't let you forget for long! We serve it with mashed potatoes or brown rice.

—DONNA ROBERTS MANHATTAN, KS

PREP: 20 MIN.
COOK: 4 HOURS + STANDING
MAKES: 8 SERVINGS

- 2 **large onions, halved and sliced (about 3 cups)**
- ½ **pound sliced fresh mushrooms**
- 1 **beef rump roast or bottom round roast (3 to 4 pounds)**
- 2 **teaspoons salt**
- ½ **teaspoon pepper**
- 1 **tablespoon canola oil**
- 1½ **cups water**
- 2 **tablespoons tomato paste**
- 3 **garlic cloves, minced**
- ½ **teaspoon each dried basil, marjoram and thyme**
  Minced fresh parsley

1. Place onions and mushrooms in a 5- or 6-qt. slow cooker. Sprinkle roast with salt and pepper. In a large skillet, heat oil over medium-high heat, brown roast on all sides. Transfer to slow cooker.

2. In a bowl, mix water, tomato paste, garlic, basil, marjoram and thyme; pour over roast. Cook, covered, on low 4-5 hours or until meat is tender (a thermometer should read at least 145°).

3. Remove roast from slow cooker; tent with foil. Let stand 15 minutes before slicing. Serve with onion mixture; sprinkle with parsley.

Home-Style Stew

My husband and I both work full time, so quick meals are important. Because this stew always tastes great, it's a regular menu item for us.

—MARIE SHANKS TERRE HAUTE, IN

PREP: 20 MIN. • **COOK:** 6 HOURS
MAKES: 5 SERVINGS

- 2 **packages (16 ounces each) frozen vegetables for stew**
- 1½ **pounds beef stew meat, cut into 1-inch cubes**
- 1 **can (10¾ ounces) condensed cream of mushroom soup, undiluted**
- 1 **can (10¾ ounces) condensed tomato soup, undiluted**
- 1 **envelope reduced-sodium onion soup mix**

1. Place vegetables in a 5-qt. slow cooker. In a large nonstick skillet coated with cooking spray, brown beef on all sides.

2. Transfer to slow cooker. Combine the remaining ingredients; pour over the top.

3. Cover and cook on low for 6-8 hours or until meat is tender.

DID YOU KNOW?

Browning beef in a small amount of fat before slow cooking helps to seal in the juices. It also creates savory pan drippings, which can be used to flavor a gravy, and gives the meat a deep rich color that can't be achieved with slow cooking alone.

Autumn Beef Stew

Let the aroma of this savory supper instantly set you in a good mood. Chock-full of tender beef, hearty potatoes and colorful carrots, this down-home dinner is a longtime staple in my kitchen.

—MARGARET SHAUER GREAT BEND, KS

PREP: 15 MIN. • **COOK:** 8 HOURS
MAKES: 8 SERVINGS

- 12 small red potatoes, halved
- 1 pound carrots, cut into 1-inch pieces
- 1 large onion, cut into wedges
- 2 pounds beef stew meat, cut into 1-inch cubes
- ⅓ cup butter
- 1 tablespoon all-purpose flour
- 1 cup water
- 1 teaspoon salt
- 1 teaspoon dried parsley flakes
- ½ teaspoon celery seed
- ½ teaspoon dried thyme
- ⅛ teaspoon pepper

1. Place potatoes, carrots and onion in a 5-qt. slow cooker. In a large skillet, brown beef in butter. Transfer beef to slow cooker with a slotted spoon.
2. Stir flour into the pan drippings until blended; cook and stir until browned. Gradually add water. Bring to a boil; cook and stir for 2 minutes or until thickened. Add salt, parsley, celery seed, thyme and pepper; pour over beef.
3. Cover and cook on low for 8-9 hours or until meat and vegetables are tender.

Chipotle Carne Guisada

It's nice to have a meal that is both easy to prepare and sure-to-please. This is my go-to dinner when I have guests but no time.

—ADRIENNE SPENRATH AUSTIN, TX

PREP: 30 MIN. • **COOK:** 6 HOURS
MAKES: 8 SERVINGS

- 2 tablespoons canola oil
- 2½ pounds beef stew meat
- 1 can (8 ounces) tomato sauce
- ¾ cup water
- 2 chopped chipotle peppers in adobo sauce plus 2 tablespoons sauce
- 12 garlic cloves, minced
- 1 tablespoon chili powder
- 1½ teaspoons ground cumin
- 1 teaspoon beef bouillon granules
- ½ teaspoon pepper
- ¼ teaspoon salt
  Hot cooked rice or warmed flour tortillas, optional

1. In a large skillet, heat oil over medium-high heat. Brown beef in batches. Transfer meat to a 3-qt. slow cooker. Stir in tomato sauce, water, chipotle peppers, adobo sauce, garlic, chili powder, cumin, bouillon, pepper and salt.
2. Cook, covered, on low 6-8 hours or until meat is tender. If desired, serve with rice.

Slow Cooker French Dip Sandwiches

These sandwiches are a standout addition to any buffet. The sauce is dipping perfection!

—HOLLY NEUHARTH MESA, AZ

PREP: 15 MIN. • **COOK:** 8 HOURS
MAKES: 12 SERVINGS

- 1 beef rump or bottom round roast (3 pounds)
- 1½ teaspoons onion powder
- 1½ teaspoons garlic powder
- ½ teaspoon Creole seasoning
- 1 carton (26 ounces) beef stock
- 12 whole wheat hoagie buns, split
- 6 ounces Havarti cheese, cut into 12 slices

1. Cut roast in half. Mix onion powder, garlic powder and Creole seasoning; rub onto beef. Place in a 5-qt. slow cooker; add stock. Cook, covered, on low 8-10 hours or until meat is tender.
2. Remove beef; cool slightly. Skim fat from cooking juices. When cool enough to handle, shred the beef with two forks and return to the slow cooker.
3. Place buns on ungreased baking sheets, cut side up. Using tongs, place beef on bun bottoms. Place cheese on bun tops. Broil 3-4 in. from heat 1-2 minutes or until cheese is melted. Close the sandwiches; serve with cooking juices.
NOTE *The following spices may be substituted for 1 teaspoon Creole seasoning: ¼ teaspoon each salt, garlic powder and paprika; and a pinch each of dried thyme, ground cumin and cayenne pepper.*

CHIPOTLE CARNE GUISADA

SLOW COOKER FRENCH DIP
SANDWICHES

SLOW-COOKED
COFFEE POT ROAST

NO-FUSS BEEF ROAST

EXPRESS PREP

Slow-Cooked Coffee Pot Roast

My family raves about my gravy when I prepare this recipe. Whenever I'm fishing for compliments, this pot roast is a sure hit!

—JANET DOMINICK BAGLEY, MN

PREP: 5 MIN. • **COOK:** 9½ HOURS
MAKES: 10-12 SERVINGS

- 2 **medium onions, thinly sliced**
- 2 **garlic cloves, minced**
- 1 **boneless beef chuck roast (3½-4 pounds), quartered**
- 1 **cup brewed coffee**
- ¼ **cup soy sauce**
- ¼ **cup cornstarch**
- 6 **tablespoons cold water**

1. Place half of the onions in a 5-qt. slow cooker. Top with garlic and half of the beef. Top with remaining onion and beef. Combine coffee and soy sauce; pour over beef. Cover and cook on low for 9-10 hours or until meat is tender.

2. Combine cornstarch and water until smooth; stir into cooking juices. Cover and cook on high for 30 minutes or until gravy is thickened.

⑤INGREDIENTS EXPRESS PREP

No-Fuss Beef Roast

You just need a few ingredients to create this tangy roast that feeds a bunch. The gravy is tasty on mashed potatoes, too.

—JEANIE BEASLEY TUPELO, MS

PREP: 10 MIN. • **COOK:** 6 HOURS
MAKES: 8 SERVINGS

- 1 **boneless beef chuck roast (3 to 4 pounds)**
- 1 **can (14½ ounces) stewed tomatoes, cut up**
- 1 **can (10¾ ounces) condensed cream of mushroom soup, undiluted**
- 1 **envelope Lipton beefy onion soup mix**
- ¼ **cup cornstarch**
- ½ **cup cold water**

1. Cut roast in half. Transfer to a 5-qt. slow cooker. In a small bowl, combine the tomatoes, soup and soup mix; pour over meat. Cover and cook on low for 6-8 hours or until meat is tender.

2. Remove meat to a serving platter; keep warm. Skim fat from cooking juices; transfer to a large saucepan. Bring liquid to a boil. Combine cornstarch and water until smooth; stir into the pan. Bring to a boil; cook and stir for 2 minutes or until thickened. Serve with roast.

DID YOU KNOW?

Opening the lid of a slow cooker to sneak a peek can greatly extend the cooking time. If you want to check cooking progress, slowly spin the lid in place so the condensation drips off and you can easily see inside.

Family-Favorite Italian Beef Sandwiches

With only a few ingredients, this roast beef is a snap to throw together. And after simmering all day, the meat is so tender and juicy! The sandwiches became a family favorite at our house right away.

—**LAUREN ADAMSON** LAYTON, UT

PREP: 10 MIN.
COOK: 8 HOURS
MAKES: 12 SERVINGS

- 1 jar (16 ounces) sliced pepperoncini, undrained
- 1 can (14½ ounces) diced tomatoes, undrained
- 1 medium onion, chopped
- ½ cup water
- 2 packages Italian salad dressing mix
- 1 teaspoon dried oregano
- ½ teaspoon garlic powder
- 1 beef rump roast or bottom round roast (3 to 4 pounds)
- 12 Italian rolls, split

1. Combine the first seven ingredients in a 5- or 6-qt. slow cooker. Cook, covered, on low 8-10 hours or until meat is tender.
2. Remove roast; cool slightly. Skim fat from cooking juices. Shred meat with two forks.
3. Return meat and cooking juices to slow cooker; heat through. Serve on rolls.

FAMILY-FAVORITE ITALIAN BEEF SANDWICHES

Tender Beef over Noodles

I dress up thrifty stew meat with noodles and a sweet red sauce for this satisfying main dish. It's great with a salad and garlic bread.

—**OLIVIA GUST** SALEM, OR

PREP: 15 MIN. • **COOK:** 5½ HOURS
MAKES: 2 SERVINGS

- ½ to ¾ pound beef stew meat
- ⅓ cup chopped onion
- 1 teaspoon canola oil
- 1 cup water, divided
- ⅓ cup ketchup
- 1 tablespoon brown sugar
- 1 tablespoon Worcestershire sauce
- ½ teaspoon paprika
- ¼ teaspoon ground mustard
- 3 tablespoons all-purpose flour
- 1 cup uncooked egg noodles
  Minced fresh parsley, optional

1. In a small skillet, brown beef and onion in oil; drain. Transfer to a 1½-qt. slow cooker.
2. In a small bowl, combine ½ cup water, ketchup, brown sugar, Worcestershire sauce, paprika and mustard; pour over meat. Cover and cook on low for 5 hours or until meat is tender.
3. Combine flour and remaining water until smooth; stir into meat mixture. Cover and cook 30 minutes longer or until thickened.
4. Meanwhile, cook noodles according to package directions; drain. Stir in parsley if desired. Serve with beef.

MEXICAN SHREDDED BEEF WRAPS

Mexican Shredded Beef Wraps

I first served this go-to beef slow cooker recipe for my son's baptism. I made a double batch and fed a crowd of 20 easily!
—**AMY LENTS** GRAND FORKS, ND

PREP: 20 MIN. • **COOK:** 6 HOURS
MAKES: 6 SERVINGS

- 1 small onion, finely chopped
- 1 jalapeno pepper, seeded and minced
- 3 garlic cloves, minced
- 1 boneless beef chuck roast (2 to 3 pounds)
- ½ teaspoon salt
- ½ teaspoon pepper
- 1 can (8 ounces) tomato sauce
- ¼ cup lime juice
- 1 tablespoon chili powder
- 1 teaspoon ground cumin
- ¼ teaspoon cayenne pepper
- 6 flour or whole wheat tortillas (8 inches)
  Optional toppings: torn romaine, chopped tomatoes and sliced avocado

1. Place onion, jalapeno and garlic in a 4-qt. slow cooker. Sprinkle roast with salt and pepper; place over vegetables. In a small bowl, mix tomato sauce, lime juice, chili powder, cumin and cayenne; pour over roast.
2. Cook, covered, on low 6-8 hours or until meat is tender. Remove roast; cool slightly. Shred meat with two forks; return to slow cooker. Serve beef on tortillas with toppings of your choice.
NOTE *Wear disposable gloves when cutting hot peppers; the oils can burn skin. Avoid touching your face.*

Slow Cooker Pot Roast

I work full time but love to make home-cooked meals for my husband and son. It's a comfort to walk in and smell this simmering roast that I know will be fall-apart tender and delicious.

—**GINA JACKSON** OGDENSBURG, NY

PREP: 15 MIN. • **COOK:** 6 HOURS
MAKES: 6 SERVINGS

- 1 **cup warm water**
- 1 **tablespoon beef base**
- ½ **pound sliced fresh mushrooms**
- 1 **large onion, coarsely chopped**
- 3 **garlic cloves, minced**
- 1 **boneless beef chuck roast (3 pounds)**
- ½ **teaspoon pepper**
- 1 **tablespoon Worcestershire sauce**
- ¼ **cup butter, cubed**
- ⅓ **cup all-purpose flour**
- ¼ **teaspoon salt**

1. In a 5- or 6-qt. slow cooker, whisk water and beef base; add mushrooms, onion and garlic. Sprinkle roast with pepper; transfer to slow cooker. Drizzle with Worcestershire sauce. Cook, covered, on low 6-8 hours or until meat is tender.

2. Remove roast to a serving platter; tent with foil. Strain cooking juices, reserving vegetables. Skim fat from cooking juices. In a large saucepan, melt butter over medium heat. Stir in flour and salt until smooth; gradually whisk in cooking juices. Bring to a boil, stirring constantly; cook and stir 1-2 minutes or until thickened. Stir in cooked vegetables. Serve with roast.

NOTE *Look for beef base near the broth and bouillon.*

Slow-Cooked Beef Brisket

When my husband and I were both working full-time, we loved this recipe's 10-hour cook time. The beef is delicious after it simmers all day in the slow cooker, and the chili sauce adds a unique touch to the gravy.

—**ANNA STODOLAK** VOLANT, PA

PREP: 10 MIN. • **COOK:** 8½ HOURS
MAKES: 8 SERVINGS

- 1 **large onion, sliced**
- 1 **fresh beef brisket (3 to 4 pounds), cut in half**
- ¼ **teaspoon pepper**
- 1 **jar (4½ ounces) sliced mushrooms, drained**
- ¾ **cup beef broth**
- ½ **cup chili sauce**
- ¼ **cup packed brown sugar**
- 2 **garlic cloves, minced**
- ¼ **cup all-purpose flour**
- ¼ **cup cold water**

1. Place onion in a 5-qt. slow cooker. Rub brisket with pepper; place over onion. Top with mushrooms. In a small bowl, combine the broth, chili sauce, brown sugar and garlic; pour over brisket. Cover and cook on low for 8-10 hours or until meat is tender.

2. Remove brisket and keep warm. In a small bowl, combine flour and water until smooth; stir into cooking juices. Cover and cook on high for 30 minutes or until thickened. Slice brisket; serve with gravy.

NOTE *This is a fresh beef brisket, not corned beef.*

SLOW COOKER POT ROAST

SLOW-COOKED TEX-MEX FLANK STEAK

BRISKET WITH CRANBERRY GRAVY

Slow-Cooked Tex-Mex Flank Steak

This flavorful, tender beef dish has been a go-to recipe for many years; it's a meal lifesaver on days when I'm going to be late getting home.
—**ANNE MERRILL** CROGHAN, NY

PREP: 20 MIN. • **COOK:** 6 HOURS
MAKES: 4 SERVINGS

- 1 tablespoon canola oil
- 1 beef flank steak (1½ pounds)
- 1 large onion, sliced
- ⅓ cup water
- 1 can (4 ounces) chopped green chilies
- 2 tablespoons cider vinegar
- 2 to 3 teaspoons chili powder
- 1 teaspoon garlic powder
- 1 teaspoon sugar
- ½ teaspoon salt
- ⅛ teaspoon pepper

1. In a large skillet, heat oil over medium-high heat; brown steak on both sides. Transfer to a 3-qt. slow cooker.
2. Add onion to same skillet; cook and stir 1-2 minutes or until crisp-tender. Add water to pan; cook 30 seconds, stirring to loosen browned bits from pan. Stir in remaining ingredients; return to a boil. Pour over steak.
3. Cook, covered, on low 6-8 hours or until meat is tender. Slice steak across the grain; serve with onion mixture.

⑤INGREDIENTS

Brisket with Cranberry Gravy

Cranberry sauce adds a pleasant sweetness to this dish. You can also use jellied sauce instead of whole berry sauce if you prefer.
—**NINA HALL** SPOKANE, WA

PREP: 25 MIN. • **COOK:** 8 HOURS
MAKES: 6-8 SERVINGS

- 1 fresh beef brisket (2½ pounds)
- ½ teaspoon salt
- ¼ teaspoon pepper
- 1 can (14 ounces) whole-berry cranberry sauce
- 1 can (8 ounces) tomato sauce
- ½ cup chopped onion
- 1 tablespoon prepared mustard

1. Rub brisket with salt and pepper; place in a 5-qt. slow cooker. Combine the cranberry sauce, tomato sauce, onion and mustard; pour over brisket.
2. Cover and cook on low for 8-10 hours or until meat is tender. Remove brisket; thinly slice across the grain. Skim fat from cooking juices; serve with brisket.
NOTE *This is a fresh beef brisket, not corned beef.*

TOP TIP

To carve a boneless roast, cut the meat vertically across the grain into ¼ in. to ½ in. slices. If the roast is tied, remove the string as you carve to help hold the roast together.

Sassy Pot Roast

We lost this recipe for several years, so it's even more special to us now that we found it again. It is such a satisfying and heartwarming way to end a busy day.

—**SUSAN BURKETT** MONROEVILLE, PA

PREP: 15 MIN. • **COOK:** 8 HOURS
MAKES: 8 SERVINGS

- 1 boneless beef chuck roast (2 pounds)
- ½ teaspoon salt
- ½ teaspoon pepper
- 2 teaspoons olive oil
- 1 large onion, chopped
- 1 can (8 ounces) tomato sauce
- ¼ cup water
- ¼ cup lemon juice
- ¼ cup cider vinegar
- ¼ cup ketchup
- 2 tablespoons brown sugar
- 1 tablespoon Worcestershire sauce
- ½ teaspoon ground mustard
- ½ teaspoon paprika

1. Sprinkle beef with salt and pepper. In a large skillet, brown beef in oil on all sides; drain.

2. Transfer to a 4-qt. slow cooker. Sprinkle with onion. Combine the remaining ingredients; pour over the meat.

3. Cover and cook on low for 8-10 hours or until meat is tender. Skim fat. If desired, thicken cooking liquid.

Slow-Cooked Chunky Chili

Pork sausage, ground beef and plenty of beans make this chili a marvelous meal. I keep serving-size containers of it in my freezer at all times so I can quickly warm up bowls on busy days.

—**MARGIE SHAW** GREENBRIER, AR

PREP: 15 MIN. • **COOK:** 4 HOURS
MAKES: 3 QUARTS

- 1 pound ground beef
- 1 pound bulk pork sausage
- 4 cans (16 ounces each) kidney beans, rinsed and drained
- 2 cans (14½ ounces each) diced tomatoes, undrained
- 2 cans (10 ounces each) diced tomatoes and green chilies, undrained
- 1 large onion, chopped
- 1 medium green pepper, chopped
- 1 envelope taco seasoning
- ½ teaspoon salt
- ¼ teaspoon pepper

1. In a large skillet, cook beef and sausage over medium heat until meat is no longer pink; drain. Transfer to a 5-qt. slow cooker. Stir in the remaining ingredients.

2. Cover and cook on high for 4-5 hours or until vegetables are tender. Serve desired amount. Cool the remaining chili; transfer to freezer bags or containers. Freeze for up to 3 months.

TO USE FROZEN CHILI *Thaw in the refrigerator; place in saucepan and heat through. Add water if desired.*

SASSY POT ROAST

SWEET & TANGY
BEEF ROAST

SWEET AND SOUR
BRISKET

BURGUNDY BEEF

Sweet & Tangy Beef Roast

Here's a tasty change to classic beef roast. I love to serve this for family dinners because I know it will always be well-appreciated.

—**RACHEL VAN ORDEN** ANNVILLE, PA

PREP: 10 MIN.
COOK: 7 HOURS + STANDING
MAKES: 8 SERVINGS

- 1 tablespoon canola oil
- 1 boneless beef chuck roast (4 pounds)
- 2 medium onions, sliced into ½-inch rings
- 1 cup plus 2 tablespoons water, divided
- ¾ cup honey barbecue sauce
- ½ cup red pepper jelly
- 3 tablespoons hoisin sauce
- 2 tablespoons cornstarch

1. In a large skillet, heat oil over medium heat. Brown roast on all sides. Transfer to a 5-qt. slow cooker; add onions and 1 cup water.
2. In a small bowl, mix barbecue sauce, jelly and hoisin sauce; pour over meat. Cook, covered, on low 7-9 hours or until meat is tender.
3. Remove roast from slow cooker; tent with foil. Let stand 10 minutes before slicing.
4. Meanwhile, skim fat from cooking juices; transfer juices to a small saucepan. Bring to a boil. Mix cornstarch and remaining water until smooth. Stir into pan. Return to a boil; cook and stir 1-2 minutes or until thickened. Serve with roast and onions.

Sweet and Sour Brisket

Here's one dish that never gets old in our house. This brisket is tender and juicy with a great sweet and sour twist. We'd eat it every night if we could!

—**JOLIE ALBERTAZZIE**
MORENO VALLEY, CA

PREP: 15 MIN. • **COOK:** 8 HOURS
MAKES: 10 SERVINGS

- 1 can (28 ounces) crushed tomatoes
- 1 medium onion, halved and thinly sliced
- ½ cup raisins
- ¼ cup packed brown sugar
- 2 tablespoons lemon juice
- 3 garlic cloves, minced
- 1 fresh beef brisket (3 pounds)
- ½ teaspoon salt
- ¼ teaspoon pepper

1. In a small bowl, combine the tomatoes, onion, raisins, brown sugar, lemon juice and garlic. Pour half into a 4- or 5-qt. slow cooker coated with cooking spray. Sprinkle meat with salt and pepper. Transfer to slow cooker. Top with remaining tomato mixture. Cover and cook on low for 8-10 hours or until meat is tender.
2. Remove brisket to a serving platter and keep warm. Skim fat from cooking juices. Thinly slice meat across the grain. Serve with tomato mixture.
NOTE *This is a fresh beef brisket, not corned beef.*

Burgundy Beef

When my adult children are coming over for dinner, this is their request. All three of them and their significant others love this dish.

—**URILLA CHEVERIE** ANDOVER, MA

PREP: 10 MIN. • **COOK:** 8¼ HOURS
MAKES: 10 SERVINGS

- 4 pounds beef top sirloin steak, cut into 1-inch cubes
- 3 large onions, sliced
- 1 cup water
- 1 cup burgundy wine or beef broth
- 1 cup ketchup
- ¼ cup quick-cooking tapioca
- ¼ cup packed brown sugar
- ¼ cup Worcestershire sauce
- 4 teaspoons paprika
- 1½ teaspoons salt
- 1 teaspoon minced garlic
- 1 teaspoon ground mustard
- 2 tablespoons cornstarch
- 3 tablespoons cold water
  Hot cooked noodles

1. In a 5-qt. slow cooker, combine the first 12 ingredients. Cover and cook on low for 8-9 hours or until meat is tender.
2. Combine cornstarch and water until smooth; stir into pan juices. Cover and cook on high for 15 minutes or until the gravy is thickened. Serve with noodles.

Slow-Cooked Meat Loaf

My husband and I both work late, so it's great to come home to a classic homemade meat loaf with mashed potatoes and veggies on the side. It only serves two so there aren't any leftovers. Best of all, it reminds me of a comforting supper that my mom would make.

—**GINGER CORTESE** HOLLSOPPLE, PA

PREP: 15 MIN. • **COOK:** 5 HOURS
MAKES: 2 SERVINGS

- 1 can (10¾ ounces) condensed cream of celery soup, undiluted
- 1¼ cups water
- 1 large egg
- ¼ cup dry bread crumbs
- 2 tablespoons grated Parmesan cheese
- 1½ teaspoons dried parsley flakes
- ½ teaspoon garlic powder
- ¼ teaspoon onion powder
- ⅛ teaspoon salt, optional
- ⅛ teaspoon pepper
- ½ pound lean ground beef (90% lean)
  Hot mashed potatoes, optional

1. In a small bowl, combine soup and water until blended. Pour half into a 1½-qt. slow cooker. Cover and refrigerate remaining soup mixture.

2. In a small bowl, combine the egg, bread crumbs, cheese, parsley, garlic powder, onion powder, salt if desired and pepper. Crumble beef over mixture and mix well.

3. Shape into a loaf; place in slow cooker. Cover and cook on low for 5-6 hours or until meat is no longer pink and a thermometer reads 160°.

4. For gravy, place reserved soup mixture in a small saucepan; cook over low heat until heated through. Serve the meat loaf and gravy with mashed potatoes if desired.

Best Ever Roast Beef

This is the best roast beef I've ever had, and it's great for family dinners! Leftovers are wonderful simply stirred into fried rice.

—**CAROLINE FLYNN** TROY, NY

PREP: 15 MIN. • **COOK:** 7 HOURS
MAKES: 6 SERVINGS

- 1 boneless beef chuck roast (4 pounds), trimmed
- 1 large sweet onion, chopped
- 1⅓ cups plus 3 tablespoons water, divided
- 1 can (10½ ounces) condensed French onion soup
- 1 cup packed brown sugar
- ⅓ cup reduced-sodium soy sauce
- ¼ cup cider vinegar
- 6 garlic cloves, minced
- 1 teaspoon ground ginger
- ¼ teaspoon pepper
- 3 tablespoons cornstarch

1. Cut roast in half. Transfer to a 5-qt. slow cooker; add onion and 1⅓ cups water. In a small bowl, combine the soup, brown sugar, soy sauce, vinegar, garlic, ginger and pepper; pour over top. Cover and cook on low for 7-8 hours or until meat is tender.

2. Remove meat to a serving platter and keep warm.

3. Skim fat from cooking juices; transfer to a small saucepan. Bring liquid to a boil. Combine cornstarch and remaining water until smooth; gradually stir into the pan. Bring to a boil; cook and stir for 2 minutes or until thickened. Serve with the roast.

Mushroom-Beef Spaghetti Sauce

I made this meal for the first time years ago, and I've been going back to it ever since. The savory sauce is well worth the wait, and extras freeze well for busy nights.

—**MEG FISHER** MARIETTA, GA

PREP: 20 MIN. • **COOK:** 6-8 HOURS
MAKES: 12 SERVINGS (1½ QUARTS)

- 1 pound lean ground beef (90% lean)
- ½ pound sliced fresh mushrooms
- 1 small onion, chopped
- 2 cans (14½ ounces each) diced tomatoes, undrained
- 1 can (12 ounces) tomato paste
- 1 can (8 ounces) tomato sauce
- 1 cup reduced-sodium beef broth
- 2 tablespoons dried parsley flakes
- 1 tablespoon brown sugar
- 1 teaspoon dried basil
- 1 teaspoon dried oregano
- 1 teaspoon salt
- ¼ teaspoon pepper

1. In a large nonstick skillet, cook the beef, mushrooms and onion over medium heat until meat is no longer pink; drain. Transfer to a 3-qt. slow cooker.

2. Stir in the tomatoes, tomato paste, tomato sauce, broth, parsley, brown sugar, basil, oregano, salt and pepper. Cover and cook on low for 6-8 hours.

SLOW COOKER GOLOMBKI

Slow Cooker Golombki

I modified my mom's classic Polish dish to fit my hectic life. Instead of boiling the cabbage and then filling it with beef, I just toss the ingredients in the slow cooker. It's much easier and tastes just as good.

—**MARY WALKER** CLERMONT, FL

PREP: 25 MIN. • **COOK:** 6 HOURS
MAKES: 8 SERVINGS

- 1 **pound ground beef**
- 1 **small onion, chopped**
- 1 **cup uncooked converted rice**
- ¾ **teaspoon salt**
- ¼ **teaspoon pepper**
- 1 **jar (24 ounces) meatless spaghetti sauce**
- 2 **cans (10¾ ounces each) condensed tomato soup, undiluted**
- 1 **cup water**
- ½ **teaspoon sugar**
- 1 **medium head cabbage, chopped**

1. In a large skillet, cook beef and onion over medium heat until meat is no longer pink; drain. Stir in the rice, salt and pepper. In a large bowl, combine the spaghetti sauce, soup, water and sugar.

2. In a 5-qt. slow cooker, layer one third of the sauce, half of the beef mixture and one third of the cabbage. Repeat layers; top with remaining sauce and cabbage.

3. Cover and cook on low for 6-8 hours or until cabbage and rice are tender.

HEARTY BUSY-DAY STEW

EXPRESS *PREP*
Hearty Busy-Day Stew

When I was still living in Missouri, a friend gave me all of her family cookbooks. I got the idea for this easy stew from one of these books. Believe it or not, the taco seasoning adds just the right touch.
—**KRISTEN HILLS** LAYTON, UT

PREP: 10 MIN. • **COOK:** 7½ HOURS
MAKES: 6 SERVINGS

- 1½ **pounds beef stew meat**
- 1½ **pounds potatoes (about 3 medium), peeled and cut into 1-inch cubes**
- 1 **can (14½ ounces) diced tomatoes, undrained**
- 1 **can (14½ ounces) beef broth**
- 2½ **cups fresh baby carrots (about 12 ounces)**
- 1 **large tomato, chopped**
- 1 **medium onion, chopped**
- 2 **tablespoons taco seasoning**
- 2 **garlic cloves, minced**
- ½ **teaspoon salt**
- 2 **tablespoons cornstarch**
- 2 **tablespoons cold water**

1. In a 5- or 6-qt. slow cooker, combine the first ten ingredients. Cook, covered, on low 7-9 hours or until the beef and vegetables are tender.

2. In a small bowl, mix cornstarch and water until smooth; gradually stir into stew. Cook, covered, on high 30-45 minutes longer or until stew is slightly thickened.

Beef 'N' Bean Torta

This zesty dish is a favorite of mine because it has a wonderful Southwestern taste and is easy to prepare. I serve it on nights when we have only a few minutes to eat before running off to various meetings or sporting events.
—JOAN HALLFORD
NORTH RICHLAND HILLS, TX

PREP: 30 MIN. • **COOK:** 4 HOURS
MAKES: 4 SERVINGS

- 1 **pound ground beef**
- 1 **small onion, chopped**
- 1 **can (15 ounces) pinto or black beans, rinsed and drained**
- 1 **can (10 ounces) diced tomatoes and green chilies, undrained**
- 1 **can (2¼ ounces) sliced ripe olives, drained**
- 1½ **teaspoons chili powder**
- ½ **teaspoon salt**
- ⅛ **teaspoon pepper**
- 3 **drops hot pepper sauce**
- 4 **flour tortillas (8 inches)**
- 1 **cup (4 ounces) shredded cheddar cheese**
  Minced fresh cilantro, optional
  Salsa, sour cream, shredded lettuce and chopped tomatoes, optional

1. Cut four 20x3-in. strips of heavy-duty foil; crisscross so they resemble spokes of a wheel. Place strips on the bottom and up the sides of a 5-qt. slow cooker. Coat strips with cooking spray.
2. In a large skillet, cook beef and onion over medium heat until meat is no longer pink; drain. Stir in the beans, tomatoes, olives, chili powder, salt, pepper and hot pepper sauce. Spoon about 1⅔ cups into prepared slow cooker; top with one tortilla and ¼ cup cheese. Repeat layers three times.
3. Cover and cook on low for 4-5 hours or until heated through. Using foil strips as handles, remove the tortilla stack to a platter. Sprinkle with cilantro. Serve with salsa, sour cream, lettuce and tomatoes if desired.

Braised Beef Short Ribs

My slow cooker is like a reliable friend when I work very long shifts. It is great to come home to these saucy, well-seasoned ribs in the evening. My mother used to make them for her family, and now I do, too.
—CHERYL MARTINETTO
GRAND RAPIDS, MN

PREP: 15 MIN. • **COOK:** 6 HOURS
MAKES: 4 SERVINGS

- 4 **pounds bone-in beef short ribs**
- 2 **tablespoons canola oil**
- 2½ **cups sliced onions**
- 1½ **cups beef broth**
- 1½ **cups chili sauce**
- ⅔ **cup cider vinegar**
- 1 **tablespoon brown sugar**
- 2 **teaspoons paprika**
- 1½ **teaspoons curry powder**
- 1 **teaspoon minced garlic**
- 1 **teaspoon salt**
- ½ **teaspoon ground mustard**
- ½ **teaspoon pepper**

In a large skillet, brown ribs in oil in batches. Transfer to a 5-qt. slow cooker; add onions. Combine the remaining ingredients; pour over ribs. Cover and cook on low for 6-8 hours or until meat is tender.

BEEF 'N' BEAN TORTA

Steak San Marino

As a busy pastor's wife and mother of three, this delicious, inexpensive dish helps my day run smoother. The steak is tender and flavorful.
—**LAEL GRIESS** HULL, IA

PREP: 15 MIN. • **COOK:** 7 HOURS
MAKES: 6 SERVINGS

- ¼ cup all-purpose flour
- ½ teaspoon salt
- ½ teaspoon pepper
- 1 beef top round steak (1½ pounds), cut into six pieces
- 2 large carrots, sliced
- 1 celery rib, sliced
- 1 can (8 ounces) tomato sauce
- 2 garlic cloves, minced
- 1 bay leaf
- 1 teaspoon Italian seasoning
- ½ teaspoon Worcestershire sauce
- 3 cups hot cooked brown rice

1. In a large resealable plastic bag, combine the flour, salt and pepper. Add beef, a few pieces at a time, and shake to coat. Transfer to a 4-qt. slow cooker.
2. In a small bowl, combine the carrots, celery, tomato sauce, garlic, bay leaf, Italian seasoning and Worcestershire sauce. Pour over beef. Cover and cook on low for 7-9 hours or until beef is tender. Discard bay leaf. Serve with rice.
FREEZE OPTION *Place cooked steak and vegetables in freezer containers; top with sauce. Cool and freeze. To use, partially thaw in refrigerator overnight. Heat through in a covered saucepan, gently stirring and adding a little water if necessary.*

EXPRESS PREP
Shredded Beef au Jus

My mom found this recipe in a farm journal soon after she and my dad got married. The tender beef has been a family favorite for years, and Dad still requests it often.
—**DANIELLE BRANDT** RUTHTON, MN

PREP: 10 MIN. • **COOK:** 6 HOURS
MAKES: 8 SERVINGS

- 1 boneless beef chuck roast (3 pounds)
- 2 cups water
- 2 teaspoons beef bouillon granules
- 1½ teaspoons dried oregano
- 1 teaspoon garlic salt
- 1 teaspoon seasoned salt
- ¼ teaspoon dried rosemary, crushed
- 8 hamburger buns, split

1. Cut roast in half; place in a 4- or 5-qt. slow cooker. In a small bowl, mix water, bouillon granules and seasonings; pour over meat.
2. Cook, covered, on low 6-8 hours or until tender. Remove beef; cool slightly. Meanwhile, skim fat from the cooking liquid.
3. Shred meat with two forks; return to slow cooker. Using a slotted spoon, place meat on bun bottoms. Replace tops. Serve with the additional cooking liquid on the side.

Melt-in-Your-Mouth Meat Loaf

When my husband and I were first married, he refused to eat meat loaf because he said it was bland and dry. Then I prepared this version, and it became his favorite meal.
—**SUZANNE CODNER** STARBUCK, MN

PREP: 15 MIN.
COOK: 5¼ HOURS + STANDING
MAKES: 6 SERVINGS

- 2 large eggs
- ¾ cup milk
- ⅔ cup seasoned bread crumbs
- 2 teaspoons dried minced onion
- 1 teaspoon salt
- ½ teaspoon rubbed sage
- 1½ pounds ground beef
- ¼ cup ketchup
- 2 tablespoons brown sugar
- 1 teaspoon ground mustard
- ½ teaspoon Worcestershire sauce

1. In a large bowl, combine the first six ingredients. Crumble beef over mixture and mix well (mixture will be moist). Shape into a round loaf; place in a 5-qt. slow cooker. Cover and cook on low for 5-6 hours or until no pink remains and a thermometer reads 160°.
2. In a small bowl, whisk the ketchup, brown sugar, mustard and Worcestershire sauce. Spoon over the meat loaf. Cook 15 minutes longer or until heated through. Let stand for 10-15 minutes before slicing.

STEAK SAN MARINO

SHREDDED BEEF
AU JUS

MELT-IN-YOUR-MOUTH
MEAT LOAF

SIMPLY DELICIOUS ROAST
BEEF SANDWICHES

CHIPOTLE BEEF CHILI

Simply Delicious Roast Beef Sandwiches

Mushrooms add a tasty change-of-pace touch to these comforting roast beef sandwiches. I like to pile the shredded beef high on Kaiser rolls.
—SCOTT POWELL PHILLIPSBURG, NJ

PREP: 15 MIN. • **COOK:** 8 HOURS
MAKES: 15 SERVINGS

- 1 beef rump roast or bottom round roast (3 to 4 pounds)
- 1 can (10¾ ounces) condensed cream of mushroom soup, undiluted
- 1 envelope onion soup mix
- 2 celery ribs, finely chopped
- 1 jar (6 ounces) sliced mushrooms, drained
- 15 kaiser rolls, split

1. Cut roast in half; transfer to a 5-qt. slow cooker. Combine soup and soup mix; stir in celery. Pour over meat. Cover and cook on low for 8-10 hours or until meat is tender, adding mushrooms during the last hour of cooking.
2. Remove meat from slow cooker. Skim fat from cooking juices. When cool enough to handle, shred meat with two forks and return to slow cooker; heat through. Spoon ½ cup onto each roll.

Chipotle Beef Chili

This is one of my favorite recipes! I make this chili for parties and late night meals. It always gets rave reviews, and it freezes well.
—STEVEN SCHEND GRAND RAPIDS, MI

PREP: 15 MIN. • **COOK:** 6 HOURS
MAKES: 8 SERVINGS (ABOUT 2½ QUARTS)

- 2 pounds beef flank steak, cut into 1-inch pieces
- 2 to 4 chipotle peppers in adobo sauce, chopped
- ¼ cup chopped onion
- 1 tablespoon chili powder
- 2 garlic cloves, minced
- 1 teaspoon salt
- ½ teaspoon ground cumin
- 3 cans (15 ounces each) tomato puree
- 1 can (14½ ounces) beef broth
- ¼ cup minced fresh cilantro

In a 4- or 5-qt. slow cooker, combine the first nine ingredients. Cook, covered, on low 6-8 hours or until meat is tender. Stir in cilantro.
FREEZE OPTION *Freeze cooled chili in freezer containers. To use, partially thaw in refrigerator overnight. Heat through in a saucepan, stirring occasionally and adding a little broth or water if necessary.*

EXPRESS PREP
Smoked Beef Brisket

This slow-cooked beef brisket has a sensational smoky taste. It's one of my family's favorites any time of the year. Try it tonight!
—DANA CEBOLSKI BESSEMER, MI

PREP: 10 MIN. • **COOK:** 8 HOURS
MAKES: 6 SERVINGS

- 1 fresh beef brisket (2½ pounds)
- 1 tablespoon Liquid Smoke, optional
- 1 teaspoon salt
- ½ teaspoon pepper
- ½ cup chopped onion
- ½ cup ketchup
- 2 teaspoons Dijon mustard
- ½ teaspoon celery seed

1. Place beef in a 3-qt. slow cooker; rub with Liquid Smoke if desired. Sprinkle with salt and pepper. Top with onion. Combine the ketchup, mustard and celery seed; spread over meat.
2. Cover and cook on low for 8-10 hours or until meat is tender. Remove and keep warm.
3. Transfer cooking juices to a blender; cover and process until smooth. Serve with brisket, thinly sliced across the grain.
NOTE *This is a fresh beef brisket, not corned beef.*

TOP TIP

To ensure even cooking when using the slow cooker, cut roasts over 3 pounds in half. Trim fat from meat before placing in the slow cooker to avoid greasy gravy. Add more flavor to gravy by first browning the meat in a skillet. Then scrape all of the browned bits from the bottom of the skillet and add to the slow cooker along with the meat.

(5) INGREDIENTS

Dilly Beef Sandwiches

My younger sister, Jean, shared this recipe with me. It puts a twist on the traditional barbecue sandwich, and it has been proven to be a crowd-pleaser at my house. Plus, it is incredibly convenient to make in the slow cooker.

—DONNA BLANKENHEIM MADISON, WI

PREP: 15 MIN.
COOK: 8 HOURS + COOLING
MAKES: 10-12 SERVINGS

- 1 boneless beef chuck roast (3 to 4 pounds)
- 1 jar (16 ounces) whole dill pickles, undrained
- ½ cup chili sauce
- 2 garlic cloves, minced
- 10 to 12 hamburger buns, split

1. Cut roast in half and place in a 3-qt. slow cooker. Add pickles with juice, chili sauce and garlic. Cover and cook on low for 8-9 hours or until beef is tender.
2. Discard pickles. Remove roast. When cool enough to handle, shred the meat. Return to the slow cooker and heat through.
3. Using a slotted spoon, fill each bun with about ½ cup of the meat mixture.

Flavorful Beef in Gravy

Served over noodles, this fantastic supper showcases tender chunks of savory beef stew meat. I use canned soups and onion soup mix to make the mouthwatering gravy.

—CHERYL SINDERGARD PLOVER, IA

PREP: 15 MIN. • **COOK:** 7 HOURS
MAKES: 10-12 SERVINGS

- ⅓ cup all-purpose flour
- 3 pounds beef stew meat, cut into 1-inch cubes
- 3 tablespoons canola oil
- 2 cans (10¾ ounces each) condensed cream of mushroom soup, undiluted
- 1 can (10¾ ounces) condensed golden mushroom soup, undiluted
- 1 can (10¾ ounces) condensed cream of celery soup, undiluted
- 1⅓ cups milk
- 1 envelope onion soup mix
  Hot cooked noodles or mashed potatoes

1. Place flour in a large resealable plastic bag; add beef and toss to coat. In a skillet, brown beef in oil.
2. Transfer beef to a 5-qt. slow cooker. Stir in the soups, milk and soup mix. Cover and cook on low for 7-8 hours or until the meat is tender. Serve with noodles or potatoes.

Barbecue Beef Brisket

Brisket is such a simple dish, and it is satisfying when it is slow cooked to perfection. Try serving the entree alongside heaping mounds of mashed potatoes.

—TASTE OF HOME TEST KITCHEN

PREP: 20 MIN. • **COOK:** 6 HOURS
MAKES: 6 SERVINGS

- 1 fresh beef brisket (3 pounds)
- 1 cup barbecue sauce
- ½ cup finely chopped onion
- 2 tablespoons Worcestershire sauce
- 1 tablespoon prepared horseradish
- 1 teaspoon salt
- ½ teaspoon pepper
- 3 tablespoons cornstarch
- ¼ cup cold water

1. Cut brisket in half; place in a 5-qt. slow cooker. Combine the barbecue sauce, onion, Worcestershire sauce, horseradish, salt and pepper; pour over beef. Cover and cook on low for 6-7 hours or until meat is tender.
2. Remove beef and keep warm. Transfer cooking juices to a large saucepan; bring to a boil. Combine cornstarch and water until smooth. Gradually stir into pan. Bring to a boil; cook and stir for 2 minutes or until thickened. Slice meat across the grain; serve with the gravy.
NOTE *This is a fresh beef brisket, not corned beef.*

Zesty Orange Beef

I put this recipe together in the morning before I leave for work. In the evening, all I have to do is quickly cook some rice, and dinner is served.
—**DEBORAH PUETTE** LILBURN, GA

PREP: 15 MIN. • **COOK:** 5 HOURS
MAKES: 5 SERVINGS

- 1 beef top sirloin steak (1½ pounds), cut into ¼-inch strips
- 2½ cups sliced fresh shiitake mushrooms
- 1 medium onion, cut into wedges
- 3 dried hot chilies
- ¼ cup packed brown sugar
- ¼ cup orange juice
- ¼ cup reduced-sodium soy sauce
- 3 tablespoons cider vinegar
- 1 tablespoon cornstarch
- 1 tablespoon minced fresh gingerroot
- 1 tablespoon sesame oil
- 2 garlic cloves, minced
- 1¾ cups fresh snow peas
- 1 tablespoon grated orange peel
  Hot cooked rice

1. Place beef in a 4-qt. slow cooker. Add the mushrooms, onion, and chilies. In a small bowl, combine the brown sugar, orange juice, soy sauce, vinegar, cornstarch, ginger, oil and garlic. Pour over meat.

2. Cover and cook on high for 5-6 hours or until meat is tender, adding snow peas during the last 30 minutes of cooking. Stir in orange peel. Serve with rice.

BARBECUE BEEF BRISKET

ZESTY ORANGE BEEF

CURRY CHICKEN STEW

Curry Chicken Stew

My Grandma Inky grew up in India and passed down this recipe to my mother, who passed it down to me. The recipe brings back fond memories of the family gathered around the table. I tweaked it a bit to fit my toddler's taste buds, but it's just as scrumptious as the original.
—TERESA FLOWERS SACRAMENTO, CA

PREP: 15 MIN. • **COOK:** 4 HOURS
MAKES: 6 SERVINGS

- 2 cans (14½ ounces each) chicken broth
- 1 can (10¾ ounces) condensed cream of chicken soup, undiluted
- 1 tub Knorr concentrated chicken stock
- 4 garlic cloves, minced
- 1 tablespoon curry powder
- ¼ teaspoon salt
- ¼ teaspoon cayenne pepper
- ¼ teaspoon pepper
- 6 boneless skinless chicken breasts (6 ounces each)
- 1 medium green pepper, cut into thin strips
- 1 medium onion, thinly sliced
  Hot cooked rice
  Chopped fresh cilantro and chutney, optional

1. In a large bowl, combine the first eight ingredients. Place chicken, green pepper and onion in a 5- or 6-qt. slow cooker; pour broth mixture over top. Cook, covered, on low 4-5 hours or until chicken and vegetables are tender.
2. Remove chicken and cool slightly. Cut or shred meat into bite-size pieces and return to slow cooker; heat through. Serve with rice. If desired, top with cilantro and chutney.

Saucy BBQ Chicken Thighs

Barbecued chicken gets a makeover in this recipe. The combination of ingredients makes for a mellow, not-too-sweet flavor that's a bit more sophisticated than you'd expect. Try it over rice or pasta.

—**SHARON FRITZ** MORRISTOWN, TN

PREP: 15 MIN. • **COOK:** 5 HOURS
MAKES: 6 SERVINGS

- 6 **boneless skinless chicken thighs (about 1½ pounds)**
- ½ **teaspoon poultry seasoning**
- 1 **medium onion, chopped**
- 1 **can (14½ ounces) diced tomatoes, undrained**
- 1 **can (8 ounces) tomato sauce**
- ½ **cup barbecue sauce**
- ¼ **cup orange juice**
- 1 **teaspoon garlic powder**
- ¾ **teaspoon dried oregano**
- ½ **teaspoon hot pepper sauce**
- ¼ **teaspoon pepper**
  Hot cooked brown rice, optional

1. Place chicken in a 3-qt. slow cooker; sprinkle with poultry seasoning. Top with onion and tomatoes. In a small bowl, mix tomato sauce, barbecue sauce, orange juice and seasonings; pour over top.

2. Cook, covered, on low 5-6 hours or until chicken is tender. If desired, serve with rice.

FREEZE OPTION *Place cooked chicken mixture in freezer containers. Cool and freeze. To use, partially thaw in refrigerator overnight. Microwave, covered, on high in a microwave-safe dish until heated through, gently stirring and adding a little water if necessary.*

Easy Turkey Sloppy Joes

Letting all the flavors combine in the slow cooker is the key to these mildly sweet sloppy joes. This recipe is sure to be a keeper, and since it calls for ground turkey, you can feel good about serving it to your family.

—**LISA ANN PANZINO DINUNZIO** VINELAND, NJ

PREP: 20 MIN. • **COOK:** 4 HOURS
MAKES: 10 SERVINGS

- 2 **pounds lean ground turkey**
- 1 **medium onion, finely chopped**
- 1 **small green pepper, chopped**
- 2 **cans (8 ounces each) no-salt-added tomato sauce**
- 1 **cup water**
- 2 **envelopes sloppy joe mix**
- 1 **tablespoon brown sugar**
- 10 **hamburger buns, split**

1. In a large nonstick skillet coated with cooking spray, cook the turkey, onion and pepper over medium heat until meat is no longer pink; drain. Transfer to a 3-qt. slow cooker.

2. Stir in the tomato sauce, water, sloppy joe mix and brown sugar. Cover and cook on low for 4-5 hours or until flavors are blended. Spoon ½ cup onto each bun.

SAUCY BBQ CHICKEN THIGHS

Rosemary Cashew Chicken

Here's a flavorful entree with a hint of citrus and the delightful crunch of cashews. It's great for weekend parties or weeknight family dinners.

—RUTH ANDREWSON
LEAVENWORTH, WA

PREP: 15 MIN. • **COOK:** 4 HOURS
MAKES: 4-6 SERVINGS

- 1 broiler/fryer chicken (3 to 4 pounds), cut up and skin removed
- 1 medium onion, thinly sliced
- ⅓ cup thawed orange juice concentrate
- 1 teaspoon dried rosemary, crushed
- 1 teaspoon salt
- ¼ teaspoon cayenne pepper
- 2 tablespoons all-purpose flour
- 3 tablespoons water
- ¼ to ½ cup chopped cashews
  Hot cooked pasta

1. Place chicken in a 3-qt. slow cooker. Combine the onion, orange juice concentrate, rosemary, salt and cayenne; pour over chicken. Cover and cook on low for 4-5 hours or until chicken juices run clear. Remove the chicken and keep warm.
2. In a saucepan, combine flour and water until smooth. Stir in cooking juices. Bring to a boil; cook and stir for 2 minutes or until thickened. Stir in cashews. Pour over chicken. Serve with pasta.

READY IN 4

Creamy Garlic-Lemon Chicken

I needed an easy way to prepare my family's favorite meal, lemon chicken, and found it in this recipe. I serve the chicken over a bed of rice or couscous and spoon some of the creamy sauce over the top.

—NANETTE SLAUGHTER
SAMMAMISH, WA

PREP: 15 MIN. • **COOK:** 3 HOURS
MAKES: 6 SERVINGS

- 1 cup vegetable broth
- 1½ teaspoons grated lemon peel
- 3 tablespoons lemon juice
- 2 tablespoons capers, drained
- 3 garlic cloves, minced
- ½ teaspoon pepper
- 6 boneless skinless chicken breast halves (6 ounces each)
- 2 tablespoons butter
- 2 tablespoons all-purpose flour
- ½ cup heavy whipping cream
  Hot cooked rice

1. In a small bowl, combine the first six ingredients. Place chicken in a 5-qt. slow cooker; pour broth mixture over chicken. Cook, covered, on low 3-4 hours or until chicken is tender.
2. Remove chicken from slow cooker; keep warm. In a large saucepan, melt butter over medium heat. Stir in flour until smooth; gradually whisk in cooking juices. Bring to a boil, stirring constantly; cook and stir 1-2 minutes or until thickened. Remove from heat and stir in cream. Serve chicken and rice with the sauce.

Slow Cooker Chicken Cacciatore

My husband and I milk 125 cows, so there are days when there's just no time left for cooking. It's really nice to come into the house at night and smell this wonderful entree simmering on its own.

—AGGIE ARNOLD-NORMAN LIBERTY, PA

PREP: 15 MIN. • **COOK:** 6 HOURS
MAKES: 6 SERVINGS

- 2 medium onions, thinly sliced
- 1 broiler/fryer chicken (3 to 4 pounds), cut up and skin removed
- 2 garlic cloves, minced
- 1 to 2 teaspoons dried oregano
- 1 teaspoon salt
- ½ teaspoon dried basil
- ¼ teaspoon pepper
- 1 bay leaf
- 1 can (14½ ounces) diced tomatoes, undrained
- 1 can (8 ounces) tomato sauce
- 1 can (4 ounces) mushroom stems and pieces, drained or 1 cup sliced fresh mushrooms
- ¼ cup white wine or water
  Hot cooked pasta

1. Place onions in a 5-qt. slow cooker. Add the chicken, seasonings, tomatoes, tomato sauce, mushrooms and wine.
2. Cover and cook on low for 6-8 hours or until chicken is tender. Discard bay leaf. Serve chicken with sauce over pasta.

CREAMY GARLIC-LEMON CHICKEN

SLOW COOKER CHICKEN CACCIATORE

SLOW-ROASTED CHICKEN WITH VEGETABLES

CRANBERRY CHICKEN

CAROLINA-STYLE VINEGAR BBQ CHICKEN

Slow-Roasted Chicken with Vegetables

The aroma of rosemary and garlic is mouthwatering, and this recipe could not be easier. Just a few minutes of prep and you'll come home to a delicious dinner. Even if you're not an experienced cook, this will make you look like a pro.

—**ANITA BELL** HERMITAGE, TN

PREP: 15 MIN.
COOK: 6 HOURS + STANDING
MAKES: 6 SERVINGS

- 2 medium carrots, halved lengthwise and cut into 3-inch pieces
- 2 celery ribs, halved lengthwise and cut into 3-inch pieces
- 8 small red potatoes, quartered
- ¾ teaspoon salt, divided
- ⅛ teaspoon pepper
- 1 medium lemon, halved
- 2 garlic cloves, crushed
- 1 broiler/fryer chicken (3 to 4 pounds)
- 1 tablespoon dried rosemary, crushed
- 1 tablespoon lemon juice
- 1 tablespoon olive oil
- 2½ teaspoons paprika

1. Place carrots, celery and potatoes in a 6-qt. slow cooker; toss with ¼ teaspoon salt and pepper. Place lemon halves and garlic in chicken cavity. Tuck wings under chicken; tie drumsticks together. Place chicken over vegetables in slow cooker, breast side up. Mix rosemary, lemon juice, oil, paprika and remaining salt; rub over chicken.

2. Cook, covered, on low 6-8 hours or until a thermometer inserted in thickest part of thigh reads 170°-175°; and vegetables are tender.

3. Remove chicken to a serving platter; tent with foil. Let stand 15 minutes before carving. Serve with vegetables.

EXPRESS PREP
Cranberry Chicken

This dish is delicious, easy and oh-so good, particularly when it's served with rice and a side vegetable. Everyone in the family just loves it! It's lovely for the holidays, but tasty any time of year.

—**EDITH HOLLIDAY** FLUSHING, MI

PREP: 10 MIN. • **COOK:** 5 HOURS
MAKES: 6 SERVINGS

- 1 broiler/fryer chicken (3 to 4 pounds), cut up
- 1 can (14 ounces) whole-berry cranberry sauce
- 1 cup barbecue sauce
- 1 small onion, finely chopped
- 1 celery rib, finely chopped
- ½ teaspoon salt
- ¼ teaspoon pepper
  Hot cooked rice

Place chicken in a 3-qt. slow cooker. In a small bowl, combine the cranberry sauce, barbecue sauce, onion, celery, salt and pepper; pour over chicken. Cover and cook on low for 5-6 hours or until the chicken is tender. Serve with rice.

FREEZE OPTION *Cover and freeze cooled chicken and sauce in freezer containers. To use, partially thaw in refrigerator overnight. Reheat in a foil-lined 13x9-in. baking dish in a preheated 325° oven until heated through, covering if necessary to prevent excess browning.*

⑤ INGREDIENTS EXPRESS PREP
Carolina-Style Vinegar BBQ Chicken

I live in Georgia but I appreciate the tangy, sweet and slightly spicy taste of Carolina vinegar chicken. I make my version in the slow cooker and when you walk in the door after being gone all day, the heavenly aroma will knock you off your feet!

—**RAMONA PARRIS** MARIETTA, GA

PREP: 10 MIN. • **COOK:** 4 HOURS
MAKES: 6 SERVINGS

- 2 cups water
- 1 cup white vinegar
- ¼ cup sugar
- 1 tablespoon reduced-sodium chicken base
- 1 teaspoon crushed red pepper flakes
- ¾ teaspoon salt
- 1½ pounds boneless skinless chicken breasts
- 6 whole wheat hamburger buns, split, optional

1. In a small bowl, mix the first six ingredients. Place chicken in a 3-qt. slow cooker; add vinegar mixture. Cook, covered, on low 4-5 hours or until chicken is tender.

2. Remove chicken; cool slightly. Reserve 1 cup cooking juices; discard remaining juices. Shred chicken with two forks. Return meat and reserved cooking juices to slow cooker; heat through. If desired, serve chicken mixture on buns.

NOTE *Look for chicken base near the broth and bouillon.*

READY IN 4

Creamy Chicken Fettuccine

Convenient canned soup and processed American cheese hurry along the assembly of this creamy sauce that is loaded with delicious chunks of chicken.

—MELISSA COWSER GREENVILLE, TX

PREP: 15 MIN. • **COOK:** 3 HOURS
MAKES: 6 SERVINGS

- 1½ **pounds boneless skinless chicken breasts, cut into cubes**
- ½ **teaspoon garlic powder**
- ½ **teaspoon onion powder**
- ⅛ **teaspoon pepper**
- 1 **can (10¾ ounces) condensed cream of chicken soup, undiluted**
- 1 **can (10¾ ounces) condensed cream of celery soup, undiluted**
- 4 **ounces process cheese (Velveeta), cubed**
- 1 **can (2¼ ounces) sliced ripe olives, drained**
- 1 **jar (2 ounces) diced pimientos, drained, optional**
- 1 **package (16 ounces) fettuccine or spaghetti**

1. Place the chicken in a 3-qt. slow cooker; sprinkle with garlic powder, onion powder and pepper. Top with soups. Cover and cook on high for 3-4 hours or until chicken is no longer pink.
2. Stir in the cheese, olives and pimientos if desired. Cover and cook until cheese is melted. Meanwhile, cook fettuccine according to package directions; drain. Serve with chicken.

Red Pepper Chicken

Chicken breasts are treated to black beans, red peppers and juicy tomatoes in this southwestern supper. We love it served with rice that's been cooked in chicken broth.

—PIPER SPIWAK VIENNA, VA

PREP: 15 MIN. • **COOK:** 6 HOURS
MAKES: 4 SERVINGS

- 4 **boneless skinless chicken breast halves (4 ounces each)**
- 1 **can (15 ounces) black beans, rinsed and drained**
- 1 **can (14½ ounces) Mexican stewed tomatoes, undrained**
- 1 **jar (12 ounces) roasted sweet red peppers, drained and cut into strips**
- 1 **large onion, chopped**
- ½ **teaspoon salt**
   Pepper to taste
   Hot cooked rice

Place the chicken in a 3-qt. slow cooker. In a bowl, combine the beans, tomatoes, red peppers, onion, salt and pepper. Pour over the chicken. Cover and cook on low for 6 hours or until chicken is tender. Serve with rice.

TOP TIP

To cut down on side dish prep time, I always cook extra rice or noodles and portion out the leftovers to freeze in resealable storage bags. Later, it's easy to take them out of the bag, pop them in the microwave and have a hot side in a snap!
—JEAN B. OCONOMOWOC, WI

EXPRESS PREP

Herbed Chicken and Tomatoes

I put a tangy spin on poultry with just a few ingredients. Recipes such as this are really a plus when you work a full-time job but still want to put a healthy, satisfying meal on the table.

—REBECCA POPKE LARGO, FL

PREP: 10 MIN. • **COOK:** 5 HOURS
MAKES: 4 SERVINGS

- 1 **pound boneless skinless chicken breasts, cut into 1½-inch pieces**
- 2 **cans (14½ ounces each) Italian diced tomatoes, undrained**
- 1 **envelope Lipton savory herb with garlic soup mix**
- ¼ **teaspoon sugar**
   Hot cooked pasta
   Shredded Parmesan cheese

In a 3-qt. slow cooker, combine the chicken, tomatoes, soup mix and sugar. Cover and cook on low for 5-6 hours or until chicken is no longer pink. Serve with pasta; sprinkle with cheese.

**SLOW COOKER CHICKEN &
BLACK BEAN SOFT TACOS**

Slow Cooker Chicken & Black Bean Soft Tacos

My husband and I love Mexican food, and these tacos have become one of our favorite meals. Try setting out the toppings in different bowls on the table so everyone can create their own tacos.

—**LAURA RODRIGUEZ** WILLOUGHBY, OH

PREP: 20 MIN. • **COOK:** 4¼ HOURS
MAKES: 6 SERVINGS

- 1 **can (8 ounces) crushed pineapple**
- ½ **cup salsa**
- 2 **green onions, sliced**
- 1 **teaspoon grated lime peel**
- ¼ **cup lime juice**
- ½ **teaspoon chili powder**
- ¼ **teaspoon garlic powder**
- ¼ **teaspoon ground cumin**
- ⅛ **teaspoon each salt, cayenne pepper and pepper**
- 1 **pound boneless skinless chicken thighs**
- 1 **can (15 ounces) black beans, rinsed and drained**
- 12 **flour tortillas (6 inches), warmed**
   Toppings: shredded Mexican cheese blend, shredded lettuce and chopped avocado

1. In a small bowl, combine the first five ingredients; stir in seasonings. Place chicken in a 3-qt. slow cooker; add pineapple mixture. Cook, covered, on low 4-5 hours or until chicken is tender.
2. Remove chicken; cool slightly. Shred meat with two forks; return to slow cooker. Stir in beans. Cook, covered, on low 15-20 minutes longer or until heated through. Using a slotted spoon, serve chicken mixture in tortillas with toppings.

SLOW-COOKED
COCONUT CHICKEN

LEMONY
TURKEY BREAST

EXPRESS *PREP*

Slow-Cooked Coconut Chicken

One of my favorite things about this recipe is how incredible it makes my home smell. Everyone who comes by asks, "What are you cooking?" And anyone who tastes it goes home with the recipe.

—**ANN SMART** NORTH LOGAN, UT

PREP: 10 MIN. • **COOK:** 4 HOURS
MAKES: 6 SERVINGS

- ½ cup light coconut milk
- 2 tablespoons brown sugar
- 2 tablespoons reduced-sodium soy sauce
- 2 garlic cloves, minced
- ⅛ teaspoon ground cloves
- 6 boneless skinless chicken thighs (about 1½ pounds)
- 6 tablespoons flaked coconut, toasted
  Minced fresh cilantro

In a large bowl, combine the first five ingredients. Place chicken in a 3-qt. slow cooker. Pour coconut milk mixture over top. Cook, covered, on low 4-5 hours or until chicken is tender. Serve with coconut and cilantro.

NOTE *To toast coconut, bake in a shallow pan in a 350° oven for 5-10 minutes or cook in a skillet over low heat until golden brown, stirring occasionally.*

EXPRESS *PREP*

Lemony Turkey Breast

Lemon and a hint of garlic add a lovely touch to tender slices of slow-cooked turkey breast. I usually serve the gravy over a combination of white and brown rice, along with broccoli for a healthy meal.

—**LYNN LAUX** BALLWIN, MO

PREP: 10 MIN. • **COOK:** 5 HOURS
MAKES: 14 SERVINGS

- 1 bone-in turkey breast (5 to 6 pounds)
- 1 medium lemon, halved
- 1 teaspoon salt-free lemon-pepper seasoning
- 1 teaspoon garlic salt
- 4 teaspoons cornstarch
- ½ cup reduced-sodium chicken broth

1. Remove skin from turkey. Pat turkey dry with paper towels; spray turkey with cooking spray. Place breast side up in a 5-qt. slow cooker. Squeeze half of the lemon over turkey; sprinkle with lemon-pepper and garlic salt. Place lemon halves under turkey.

2. Cover and cook on low for 5-7 hours or until meat is tender. Remove turkey and keep warm. Discard lemon.

3. For gravy, pour cooking liquid into a measuring cup; skim fat. In a saucepan, combine cornstarch and broth until smooth. Gradually stir in cooking liquid. Bring to a boil; cook and stir for 2 minutes or until thickened. Serve with turkey.

Sweet-and-Sour Chicken

No one will believe this dish is made in the slow cooker. Adding the onions, pineapple and snow peas later in the process keeps them from becoming over-cooked and sustains their color.
—**DOROTHY HESS** HARTWELL, GA

PREP: 15 MIN. • **COOK:** 3 HOURS 20 MIN.
MAKES: 5 SERVINGS

- 1¼ pounds boneless skinless chicken breasts, cut into 1-inch strips
- 1 tablespoon canola oil
  Salt and pepper to taste
- 1 can (8 ounces) pineapple chunks
- 1 can (8 ounces) sliced water chestnuts, drained
- 2 medium carrots, sliced
- 2 tablespoons soy sauce
- 4 teaspoons cornstarch
- 1 cup sweet-and-sour sauce
- ¼ cup water
- 1½ teaspoons ground ginger
- 3 green onions, cut into 1-inch pieces
- 1½ cups fresh or frozen snow peas
  Hot cooked rice

1. In a large skillet, saute chicken in oil for 4-5 minutes; drain. Sprinkle with salt and pepper. Drain pineapple, reserving juice; set pineapple aside. In a 5-qt. slow cooker, combine the chicken, water chestnuts, carrots, soy sauce and pineapple juice. Cover and cook on low for 3 hours or until chicken juices run clear.

2. In a small bowl, combine the cornstarch, sweet-and-sour sauce, water and ginger until smooth. Stir into the slow cooker. Add onions and reserved pineapple; cover and cook on high for 15 minutes or until thickened. Add peas; cook 5 minutes longer. Serve with rice.

EXPRESS PREP

Chicken Veggie Alfredo

My family loves this dinner! It's easy to make and a great way to save time after a busy day. If you like, add other veggies to suit your family's tastes.
—**JENNIFER JORDAN** HUBBARD, OH

PREP: 10 MIN. • **COOK:** 6 HOURS
MAKES: 4 SERVINGS

- 4 boneless skinless chicken breast halves (4 ounces each)
- 1 tablespoon canola oil
- 1 jar (16 ounces) Alfredo sauce
- 1 can (15¼ ounces) whole kernel corn, drained
- 1 cup frozen peas, thawed
- 1 jar (4½ ounces) sliced mushrooms, drained
- ½ cup chopped onion
- ½ cup water
- ½ teaspoon garlic salt
- ¼ teaspoon pepper
  Hot cooked linguine

1. In a large skillet, brown chicken in oil. Transfer to a 3-qt. slow cooker. In a large bowl, combine the Alfredo sauce, corn, peas, mushrooms, onion, water, garlic salt and pepper.

2. Pour over chicken. Cover and cook on low for 6-8 hours or until a thermometer reads 170°. Serve with linguine.

SWEET-AND-SOUR CHICKEN

Creamy Italian Chicken

Italian salad dressing mix is like a secret weapon for adding flavor to this comforting specialty. The dinner is rich, delicious and certainly special enough for guests.

—**MAURA MCGEE** TALLAHASSEE, FL

PREP: 15 MIN. • **COOK:** 4 HOURS
MAKES: 4 SERVINGS

- 4 boneless skinless chicken breast halves (4 ounces each)
- 1 envelope Italian salad dressing mix
- ¼ cup water
- 1 package (8 ounces) cream cheese, softened
- 1 can (10¾ ounces) condensed cream of chicken soup, undiluted
- 1 can (4 ounces) mushroom stems and pieces, drained
    Hot cooked pasta or rice
    Fresh oregano leaves, optional

1. Place the chicken in a 3-qt. slow cooker. Combine salad dressing mix and water; pour over chicken. Cover and cook on low for 3 hours.
2. In a small bowl, beat cream cheese and soup until blended. Stir in mushrooms. Pour over chicken. Cook 1 hour longer or until chicken is tender. Serve with pasta or rice. Garnish with oregano if desired.

Mushroom Chicken Cacciatore

I pump up chicken's flavor by slow-cooking it in a zesty tomato sauce. It's great for company. Toss a salad and you're ready to eat.

—**JANE BONE** CAPE CORAL, FL

PREP: 20 MIN. • **COOK:** 4 HOURS
MAKES: 4 SERVINGS

- 4 boneless skinless chicken breast halves (about 1½ pounds)
- 2 tablespoons canola oil
- 1 can (15 ounces) tomato sauce
- 2 cans (4 ounces each) sliced mushrooms, drained
- 1 medium onion, chopped
- ¼ cup red wine or chicken broth
- 2 garlic cloves, minced
- 1¼ teaspoons dried oregano
- ½ teaspoon dried thyme
- ⅛ to ¼ teaspoon salt
- ⅛ teaspoon pepper
    Hot cooked spaghetti

1. In a large skillet, brown chicken in oil on both sides. Transfer to a 3-qt. slow cooker. In a bowl, combine the tomato sauce, mushrooms, onion, wine, garlic, oregano, thyme, salt and pepper; pour over chicken.
2. Cover and cook on low for 4-5 hours or until meat is tender. Serve with spaghetti.

DID YOU KNOW?

Cacciatore is a general term used to refer to a tomato-based Italian-inspired sauce. It usually contains mushrooms and onions, though some versions might also include bell peppers and wine. This vibrant sauce is served over meats, such as chicken, beef and pork.

Busy-Day Chicken Fajitas

When I don't have much time to cook supper, chicken fajitas from the slow cooker are a delicious way to keep my family satisfied. If you aren't cooking for youngsters, try spicing things up with medium or hot picante sauce.

—**MICHELE FURRY** PLAINS, MT

PREP: 20 MIN. • **COOK:** 4 HOURS
MAKES: 6 SERVINGS

- 1 pound boneless skinless chicken breasts
- 1 can (15 ounces) black beans, rinsed and drained
- 1 medium green pepper, cut into strips
- 1 large onion, sliced
- 1½ cups picante sauce
- ½ teaspoon garlic powder
- ½ teaspoon ground cumin
- 12 flour tortillas (6 inches), warmed
- 2 cups (8 ounces) shredded cheddar cheese
    Optional toppings: thinly sliced green onions, chopped tomatoes and sour cream, optional

1. Place chicken in a 4-qt. slow cooker; add black beans, pepper and onion. In a small bowl, mix picante sauce, garlic powder and cumin; pour over top. Cook, covered, on low 4-5 hours or until chicken is tender.
2. Remove chicken and cool slightly. Shred meat with two forks and return to slow cooker; heat through. Serve with tortillas, cheese and toppings of your choice.

Slow Cooker Roast Chicken

Roast chicken is easy to make in a slow cooker. We save shredded chicken for busy weeknights.
—**COURTNEY STULTZ** COLUMBUS, KS

PREP: 20 MIN.
COOK: 4 HOURS + STANDING
MAKES: 6 SERVINGS

- 2 medium carrots, cut into 1-inch pieces
- 1 medium onion, cut into 1-inch pieces
- 2 garlic cloves, minced
- 2 teaspoons olive oil
- 1 teaspoon dried parsley flakes
- 1 teaspoon pepper
- ¾ teaspoon salt
- ½ teaspoon dried oregano
- ½ teaspoon rubbed sage
- ½ teaspoon chili powder
- 1 broiler/fryer chicken (4 to 5 pounds)

1. Place carrots and onion in a 6-qt. slow cooker. In a small bowl, mix garlic and oil. In another bowl, mix dry seasonings.

2. Tuck wings under chicken; tie drumsticks together. With fingers, carefully loosen skin from chicken breast; rub garlic mixture under the skin. Secure skin to underside of breast with toothpicks.

3. Place chicken in slow cooker over vegetables, breast side up; sprinkle with seasoning mixture. Cook, covered, on low 4-5 hours (a thermometer inserted in thigh should read at least 170°).

4. Remove chicken from slow cooker; tent with foil. Let chicken stand 15 minutes before carving.

BUSY-DAY CHICKEN FAJITAS

SLOW COOKER ROAST CHICKEN

CREAMY CHICKEN THIGHS & NOODLES

SHREDDED TURKEY SANDWICHES

EXPRESS PREP

Creamy Chicken Thighs & Noodles

This meal is a both tasty and hearty. I make it when I want a very easy dinner that's also comforting.
—**CHRISTINA PETRI** ALEXANDRIA, MN

PREP: 10 MIN. • **COOK:** 7 HOURS
MAKES: 8 SERVINGS

- 8 **boneless skinless chicken thighs (about 2 pounds)**
- 2 **cans (10¾ ounces each) condensed cream of mushroom soup, undiluted**
- 1 **can (10¾ ounces) condensed cream of chicken soup, undiluted**
- 1 **cup (8 ounces) sour cream**
- 2 **tablespoons paprika**
- ½ **teaspoon onion powder**
- ¼ **teaspoon salt**
- ¼ **teaspoon cayenne pepper**
  Hot cooked wide egg noodles

Place chicken in a greased 4-qt. slow cooker. In a large bowl, combine soups, sour cream and seasonings; pour over chicken. Cook, covered, on low 7-9 hours or until chicken is tender. Serve with egg noodles.

⑤ INGREDIENTS

Shredded Turkey Sandwiches

This simple slow-cooked sandwich gets its zesty twist from onion soup mix and beer. In total, it only takes five ingredients to make the recipe!
—**JACKI KNUTH** OWATONNA, MN

PREP: 15 MIN. • **COOK:** 7 HOURS
MAKES: 24 SERVINGS

- 2 **boneless skinless turkey breast halves (2 to 3 pounds each)**
- 1 **bottle (12 ounces) beer or nonalcoholic beer**
- ½ **cup butter, cubed**
- 1 **envelope onion soup mix**
- 24 **French rolls, split**

1. Place turkey in a 5-qt. slow cooker. Combine the beer, butter and soup mix; pour over meat. Cover and cook on low for 7-9 hours or until meat is tender.
2. Shred meat and return to slow cooker; heat through. Serve on rolls.

DID YOU KNOW?

One advantage of the slow cooker is that it uses very little energy. Because of its low wattage, a slow cooker running for 10 hours will cost about 25 cents, depending on utility prices in your region. Using the slow cooker at least once a week over an entire year could mean significant savings.

Slow-Cooked Jambalaya

A combo of chicken, sausage and shrimp makes my jambalaya extra hearty. Featuring canned items and other kitchen staples, it's perfect for casual get-togethers.

—SHERRY HUNTWORK GRETNA, NE

PREP: 20 MIN. • **COOK:** 6¼ HOURS
MAKES: 12 SERVINGS

- 1 pound smoked kielbasa or Polish sausage, sliced
- ½ pound boneless skinless chicken breasts, cut into 1-inch cubes
- 1 can (14½ ounces) beef broth
- 1 can (14½ ounces) diced tomatoes, undrained
- 2 celery ribs, chopped
- ⅓ cup tomato paste
- 4 garlic cloves, minced
- 1 tablespoon dried parsley flakes
- 1½ teaspoons dried basil
- 1 teaspoon cayenne pepper
- ½ teaspoon salt
- ½ teaspoon dried oregano
- 1 pound cooked medium shrimp, peeled and deveined
- 2 cups cooked rice

1. In a 4-qt. slow cooker, combine the first 12 ingredients. Cover and cook on low for 6-7 hours or until chicken is no longer pink.
2. Stir in shrimp and rice. Cover and cook 15 minutes longer or until heated through.

SLOW-COOKED JAMBALAYA

Snappy Southwest Chicken

My delicious low-fat dish gets even better with a garnish of reduced-fat sour cream and fresh cilantro. With just 15 minutes of prep, you'll be out of the kitchen in no time.

—BRANDI CASTILLO SANTA MARIA, CA

PREP: 15 MIN. • **COOK:** 6 HOURS
MAKES: 6 SERVINGS

- 2 cans (15 ounces each) black beans, rinsed and drained
- 1 can (14½ ounces) reduced-sodium chicken broth
- 1 can (14½ ounces) diced tomatoes with mild green chilies, undrained
- ½ pound boneless skinless chicken breast
- 1 jar (8 ounces) chunky salsa
- 1 cup frozen corn
- 1 tablespoon dried parsley flakes
- 1 teaspoon ground cumin
- ¼ teaspoon pepper
- 3 cups hot cooked rice

1. In a 2- or 3-qt. slow cooker, combine the beans, broth, tomatoes, chicken, salsa, corn and seasonings. Cover and cook on low for 6-8 hours or until a thermometer reads 170°.
2. Shred chicken with two forks and return to the slow cooker; heat through. Serve with rice.
FREEZE OPTION *After shredding chicken, freeze cooled mixture in freezer containers. To use, partially thaw in refrigerator overnight. Heat through in a saucepan, stirring occasionally and adding a little broth or water if necessary.*

SUNDAY CHICKEN SUPPER

Sunday Chicken Supper

Here's a hearty, homespun dinner that satisfies even the biggest appetites. I love the convenience of cooking my chicken and veggies in the same wonderful dish.
—**RUTHANN MARTIN** LOUISVILLE, OH

PREP: 15 MIN. • **COOK:** 6 HOURS
MAKES: 4 SERVINGS

- 4 **medium carrots, cut into 2-inch pieces**
- 1 **medium onion, chopped**
- 1 **celery rib, cut into 2-inch pieces**
- 2 **cups cut fresh green beans (2-inch pieces)**
- 5 **small red potatoes, quartered**
- 1 **broiler/fryer chicken (3 to 3½ pounds), cut up**
- 4 **bacon strips, cooked and crumbled**
- 1½ **cups hot water**
- 2 **teaspoons chicken bouillon granules**
- 1 **teaspoon salt**
- ½ **teaspoon dried thyme**
- ½ **teaspoon dried basil**
   Pinch pepper

1. In a 5-qt. slow cooker, layer the first seven ingredients in order listed. In a small bowl, combine the water, bouillon, salt, thyme, basil and pepper; pour over the top. Do not stir.

2. Cover and cook on low for 6-8 hours or until vegetables are tender and chicken juices run clear. Remove chicken and vegetables. Thicken cooking juices for gravy if desired.

Chicken Stew

When you'd rather not be in the kitchen, it's great to rely on a slow-cooker stew. Chicken, vegetables and seasonings give this specialty a great flavor, and it's even lower in fat than most stews.

—**LINDA EMERY** BEARDEN, AR

PREP: 10 MIN. • **COOK:** 4½ HOURS
MAKES: 10 SERVINGS

- 2 **pounds boneless skinless chicken breasts, cut into 1-inch cubes**
- 2 **cans (14½ ounces each) reduced-sodium chicken broth**
- 3 **cups cubed peeled potatoes**
- 1 **cup chopped onion**
- 1 **cup sliced celery**
- 1 **cup thinly sliced carrots**
- 1 **teaspoon paprika**
- ½ **teaspoon pepper**
- ½ **teaspoon rubbed sage**
- ½ **teaspoon dried thyme**
- 1 **can (6 ounces) no-salt-added tomato paste**
- ¼ **cup cold water**
- 3 **tablespoons cornstarch**
  Shredded Parmesan cheese, optional

1. In a 5-qt. slow cooker, combine the first 11 ingredients; cover and cook on high for 4 hours.
2. Mix water and cornstarch until smooth; stir into stew. Cook, covered, 30 minutes more or until the vegetables are tender. If desired, sprinkle with Parmesan cheese.

Greek Dinner

The amount of garlic might seem high, but you get every bit of the flavor without it overpowering the other ingredients.

—**TERRI CHRISTENSEN** MONTAGUE, MI

PREP: 20 MIN. • **COOK:** 5 HOURS
MAKES: 6 SERVINGS

- 6 **medium Yukon Gold potatoes, quartered**
- 1 **broiler/fryer chicken (3½ pounds), cut up and skin removed**
- 2 **large onions, quartered**
- 1 **whole garlic bulb, separated and peeled**
- 3 **teaspoons dried oregano**
- 1 **teaspoon salt**
- ¾ **teaspoon pepper**
- ½ **cup plus 1 tablespoon water, divided**
- 1 **tablespoon olive oil**
- 4 **teaspoons cornstarch**

1. Place potatoes in a 5-qt. slow cooker. Add the chicken, onions and garlic.
2. Combine the oregano, salt, pepper and ½ cup water; pour over chicken and vegetables. Drizzle with oil. Cover and cook on low for 5-6 hours or until chicken juices run clear and vegetables are tender.
3. Remove chicken and vegetables to a serving platter; keep warm. Strain cooking juices and skim fat; transfer to a small saucepan. Bring the liquid to a boil. Combine the cornstarch and remaining water until smooth. Gradually stir into the pan. Bring to a boil; cook and stir for 2 minutes or until thickened. Serve with chicken and vegetables.

CHICKEN STEW

READY IN ④
Shredded Chicken Gyros

Our family has no links to Greece of any kind, but we always have a great time at Salt Lake City's annual Greek Festival. One of my favorite things is the food. My kids are big fans of this Greek-inspired meal.

—**CAMILLE BECKSTRAND** LAYTON, UT

PREP: 20 MIN. • **COOK:** 3 HOURS
MAKES: 8 SERVINGS

- 2 **medium onions, chopped**
- 6 **garlic cloves, minced**
- 1 **teaspoon lemon-pepper seasoning**
- 1 **teaspoon dried oregano**
- ½ **teaspoon ground allspice**
- ½ **cup water**
- ½ **cup lemon juice**
- ¼ **cup red wine vinegar**
- 2 **tablespoons olive oil**
- 2 **pounds boneless skinless chicken breasts**
- 8 **whole pita breads**
  Toppings: tzatziki sauce, torn romaine and sliced tomato, cucumber and onion

1. In a 3-qt. slow cooker, combine the first nine ingredients; add the chicken. Cook, covered, on low 3-4 hours or until chicken is tender (a thermometer should read at least 165°).
2. Remove chicken from slow cooker. Shred with two forks; return to slow cooker. Using tongs, place chicken mixture on pita breads. Serve with toppings.

READY IN ④
Chipotle Pulled Chicken

I love chicken that has a spicy kick to it, so this is a go-to meal when I'm looking for something extra tasty.

—**TAMRA PARKER** MANLIUS, NY

PREP: 15 MIN. • **COOK:** 3 HOURS
MAKES: 12 SERVINGS

- 2 **cups ketchup**
- 1 **small onion, finely chopped**
- ¼ **cup Worcestershire sauce**
- 3 **tablespoons reduced-sodium soy sauce**
- 2 **tablespoons brown sugar**
- 2 **tablespoons cider vinegar**
- 3 **garlic cloves, minced**
- 1 **tablespoon molasses**
- 2 **teaspoons dried oregano**
- 2 **teaspoons minced chipotle pepper in adobo sauce plus 1 teaspoon sauce**
- 1 **teaspoon ground cumin**
- 1 **teaspoon smoked paprika**
- ¼ **teaspoon salt**
- ¼ **teaspoon crushed red pepper flakes**
- 2½ **pounds boneless skinless chicken breasts**
- 12 **sesame seed hamburger buns, split and toasted**

1. In a 3-qt. slow cooker, combine the first 14 ingredients; add chicken. Cook, covered, on low 3-4 hours or until chicken is tender (a thermometer should read at least 165°).
2. Remove chicken from slow cooker. Shred with two forks; return to slow cooker. Using tongs, place chicken mixture on bun bottoms. Replace tops.
FREEZE OPTION *Freeze cooled meat mixture and sauce in freezer containers. To use, partially thaw in refrigerator overnight. Heat through in a saucepan, stirring occasionally.*

EXPRESS PREP
Chicken a la King

When I know I'll be having a busy day with little time to prepare a meal, I use my slow cooker to make this longtime favorite.

—**ELEANOR MIELKE** SNOHOMISH, WA

PREP: 10 MIN. • **COOK:** 7½ HOURS
MAKES: 6 SERVINGS

- 1 **can (10¾ ounces) reduced-fat reduced-sodium condensed cream of chicken soup, undiluted**
- 3 **tablespoons all-purpose flour**
- ¼ **teaspoon pepper**
  Dash cayenne pepper
- 1 **pound boneless skinless chicken breasts, cubed**
- 1 **celery rib, chopped**
- ½ **cup chopped green pepper**
- ¼ **cup chopped onion**
- 1 **package (10 ounces) frozen peas, thawed**
- 2 **tablespoons diced pimientos, drained**
  Hot cooked rice

In a 3-qt. slow cooker, combine soup, flour, pepper and cayenne until smooth. Stir in chicken, celery, green pepper and onion. Cover and cook on low for 7-8 hours or until meat juices run clear. Stir in peas and pimientos. Cook 30 minutes longer or until heated through. Serve with rice.

SHREDDED CHICKEN GYROS

CHIPOTLE
PULLED CHICKEN

CHICKEN A LA KING

SLOW COOKER MUSHROOM
CHICKEN & PEAS

CHUNKY CHICKEN
CACCIATORE

EXPRESS PREP | READY IN (4)

Slow Cooker Mushroom Chicken & Peas

Some amazingly fresh mushrooms I found at our local farmers market inspired this recipe. When you start with the best ingredients, you can't go wrong.
—**JENNIFER TIDWELL** FAIR OAKS, CA

PREP: 10 MIN. • **COOK:** 3 HOURS 10 MIN.
MAKES: 4 SERVINGS

- **4 boneless skinless chicken breast halves (6 ounces each)**
- **1 envelope onion mushroom soup mix**
- **1 cup water**
- **½ pound sliced baby portobello mushrooms**
- **1 medium onion, chopped**
- **4 garlic cloves, minced**
- **2 cups frozen peas**

1. Place chicken in a 3-qt. slow cooker. Sprinkle with soup mix, pressing to help seasonings adhere. Add water, mushrooms, onion and garlic.

2. Cook, covered, on low 3-4 hours or until chicken is tender (a thermometer inserted in chicken should read at least 165°). Stir in peas; cook, covered, 10 minutes longer or until heated through.

EXPRESS PREP

Chunky Chicken Cacciatore

Look in your fridge for anything else you want to add, such as red pepper, mushrooms, extra zucchini, you name it. And if you're a vegetarian, go ahead and leave out the chicken.
—**STEPHANIE LOAIZA** LAYTON, UT

PREP: 10 MIN.
COOK: 4 HOURS
MAKES: 6 SERVINGS

- **6 boneless skinless chicken thighs (about 1½ pounds)**
- **1 jar (24 ounces) garden-style spaghetti sauce**
- **2 medium zucchini, cut into 1-inch slices**
- **1 medium green pepper, cut into 1-inch pieces**
- **1 large sweet onion, coarsely chopped**
- **½ teaspoon dried oregano**
   Hot cooked spaghetti
   Sliced ripe olives and shredded Parmesan cheese, optional

1. Place the first six ingredients in a 3-qt. slow cooker. Cook, covered, on low 4-5 hours or until the chicken is tender.

2. Coarsely shred chicken with two forks. Serve chicken and vegetables with spaghetti. Sprinkle with olives and cheese if desired.

Ham 'n' Swiss Chicken

This saucy casserole allows you to enjoy all the rich flavor of traditional chicken Cordon Bleu with less effort. It's a snap to layer the ingredients and let them cook all afternoon.

—**DOROTHY WITMER** EPHRATA, PA

PREP: 10 MIN. • **COOK:** 4 HOURS
MAKES: 6 SERVINGS

- 2 **large eggs**
- 2 **cups milk, divided**
- ½ **cup butter, melted**
- ½ **cup chopped celery**
- 1 **teaspoon finely chopped onion**
- 8 **slices bread, cubed**
- 12 **slices deli ham, chopped**
- 2 **cups (8 ounces) shredded Swiss cheese**
- 2½ **cups cubed cooked chicken**
- 1 **can (10¾ ounces) condensed cream of chicken soup, undiluted**

1. In a large bowl, whisk eggs and 1½ cups milk. Add butter, celery and onion; stir in bread crumbs.
2. Place half of the mixture in a greased 3-qt. slow cooker; top with half of the ham, cheese and chicken. Combine soup and remaining milk; pour half over chicken. Repeat layers.
3. Cook, covered on low 4-5 hours or until a thermometer inserted into bread mixture reads 160°.

Sweet Pepper Chicken

Sweet red and green pepper strips add attractive color to this delicious chicken. Put it in the slow cooker before getting ready for church on Sunday morning. It'll be ready to eat by the time you get home.

—**ANN JOHNSON** DUNN, NC

PREP: 10 MIN. • **COOK:** 4 HOURS
MAKES: 6 SERVINGS

- 6 **bone-in chicken breast halves (8 ounces each), skin removed**
- 1 **tablespoon canola oil**
- 2 **cups sliced fresh mushrooms**
- 1 **medium onion, halved and sliced**
- 1 **medium green pepper, julienned**
- 1 **medium sweet red pepper, julienned**
- 1 **can (10¾ ounces) condensed cream of chicken soup, undiluted**
- 1 **can (10¾ ounces) condensed cream of mushroom soup, undiluted**
  Hot cooked rice

1. In a large skillet, brown chicken in oil on both sides. Transfer to a 5-qt. slow cooker. Top with mushrooms, onion and peppers. Combine the soups; pour over vegetables.
2. Cover and cook on low for 4-5 hours or until a thermometer reads 170°. Serve with rice.

HAM 'N' SWISS CHICKEN

Busy Mom's Chicken Fajitas

Staying at home with a young child makes preparing dinner a challenge, but a slow cooker is an easy way to make a healthy, low-fat meal. The meat in these fajitas is tender, and the veggies and beans provide fiber.

—**SARAH NEWMAN** MAHTOMEDI, MN

PREP: 15 MIN. • **COOK:** 5 HOURS
MAKES: 6 SERVINGS

- 1 pound boneless skinless chicken breast halves
- 1 can (16 ounces) kidney beans, rinsed and drained
- 1 can (14½ ounces) diced tomatoes with mild green chilies, drained
- 1 each medium green, sweet red and yellow peppers, julienned
- 1 medium onion, halved and sliced
- 2 teaspoons ground cumin
- 2 teaspoons chili powder
- 1 garlic clove, minced
- ¼ teaspoon salt
- 6 flour tortillas (8 inches), warmed
  Shredded lettuce and chopped tomatoes, optional

1. In a 3-qt. slow cooker, combine the chicken, beans, tomatoes, peppers, onion and seasonings. Cover and cook on low for 5-6 hours or until chicken is tender.
2. Remove chicken; cool slightly. Shred chicken and return to the slow cooker; heat through.
3. Spoon about ¾ cup chicken mixture down the center of each tortilla. Top with lettuce and tomatoes if desired.

EXPRESS PREP
Slow Cooker Chicken Dinner

This meal-in-one, which includes juicy chicken and veggies in a creamy sauce, is always a welcome treat.

—**JENET CATTAR** NEPTUNE BEACH, FL

PREP: 10 MIN. • **COOK:** 8 HOURS
MAKES: 4 SERVINGS

- 6 medium red potatoes, cut into chunks
- 4 medium carrots, cut into ½-inch pieces
- 4 boneless skinless chicken breast halves
- 1 can (10¾ ounces) condensed cream of chicken soup, undiluted
- 1 can (10¾ ounces) condensed cream of mushroom soup, undiluted
- ⅛ teaspoon garlic salt
- 2 to 4 tablespoons mashed potato flakes, optional

1. Place potatoes and carrots in a 5-qt. slow cooker. Top with chicken. Combine soups and garlic salt; pour over chicken.
2. Cover and cook on low for 8 hours or until meat and vegetables are tender. To thicken, stir potato flakes into the gravy and cook 30 minutes longer, if desired.

READY IN ④
Party-Time Wings

Here are some irresistible, fall-off-the-bone chicken wings. Chili sauce and powder give them just a bit of heat, while molasses lends a hint of sweetness. These make a great dinner without much fuss.

—**SHARON MORCILIO** JOSHUA TREE, CA

PREP: 15 MIN. • **COOK:** 3 HOURS
MAKES: ABOUT 4 DOZEN

- 5 pounds chicken wings (about 25 wings)
- 1 bottle (12 ounces) chili sauce
- ¼ cup lemon juice
- ¼ cup molasses
- 2 tablespoons Worcestershire sauce
- 6 garlic cloves, minced
- 1 tablespoon chili powder
- 1 tablespoon salsa
- 1 teaspoon garlic salt
- 3 drops hot pepper sauce

1. Cut chicken wings into three sections; discard wing tips. Place wings in a 5-qt. slow cooker.
2. In a small bowl, combine the remaining ingredients; pour over chicken. Stir to coat. Cook, covered, on low 3-4 hours or until chicken is tender.
NOTE *Uncooked chicken wing sections (wingettes) may be substituted for whole chicken wings.*

SLOW COOKER
CHICKEN DINNER

PARTY-TIME WINGS

GREEK GARLIC CHICKEN

SPRING-THYME CHICKEN STEW

CORNISH HENS WITH POTATOES

Greek Garlic Chicken

Lively flavors of the Greek Isles come through in this robust chicken entree. I created it so we could have a homemade dinner after a busy day out and about.

—**MARGEE BERRY** WHITE SALMON, WA

PREP: 20 MIN. • **COOK:** 3½ HOURS
MAKES: 6 SERVINGS

- ½ cup chopped onion
- 1 tablespoon plus 1 teaspoon olive oil, divided
- 3 tablespoons minced garlic
- 2½ cups chicken broth, divided
- ¼ cup pitted Greek olives, chopped
- 3 tablespoons chopped sun-dried tomatoes (not packed in oil)
- 1 tablespoon quick-cooking tapioca
- 2 teaspoons grated lemon peel
- 1 teaspoon dried oregano
- 6 boneless skinless chicken breast halves (6 ounces each)
- 1¾ cups uncooked couscous
- ½ cup crumbled feta cheese

1. In a small skillet, saute onion in 1 tablespoon oil until crisp-tender. Add garlic; cook 1 minute longer.
2. Transfer to a 5-qt. slow cooker. Stir in ¾ cup broth, olives, tomatoes, tapioca, lemon peel and oregano. Add chicken. Cover and cook on low for 3½-4 hours or until chicken is tender.
3. In a large saucepan, bring remaining oil and broth to a boil. Stir in couscous. Cover and remove from the heat; let stand for 5 minutes or until broth is absorbed. Serve with chicken; sprinkle with feta cheese.

Spring-Thyme Chicken Stew

During a long winter, my husband and I were in need of something warm, comforting and bright. This stew was the perfect thing. It always reminds me of the days my mom would make chicken soup.

—**AMY CHASE** VANDERHOOF, BC

PREP: 15 MIN. • **COOK:** 7 HOURS
MAKES: 4 SERVINGS

- 1 pound small red potatoes, halved
- 1 large onion, finely chopped
- ¾ cup shredded carrots
- 3 tablespoons all-purpose flour
- 6 garlic cloves, minced
- 2 teaspoons grated lemon peel
- 2 teaspoons dried thyme
- ½ teaspoon salt
- ¼ teaspoon pepper
- 1½ pounds boneless skinless chicken thighs, halved
- 2 cups reduced-sodium chicken broth
- 2 bay leaves
- 2 tablespoons minced fresh parsley

1. Place potatoes, onion and carrots in a 3-qt. slow cooker. Sprinkle with flour, garlic, lemon peel, thyme, salt and pepper; toss to coat. Place chicken over top. Add broth and bay leaves.
2. Cook, covered, on low 7-9 hours or until chicken and vegetables are tender. Remove bay leaves. Sprinkle servings with parsley.

Cornish Hens with Potatoes

This is a wonderful meal with only a fraction of the work you'd expect. This special slow-cooked dinner is delicious served with green beans and French bread.

—**DEBORAH RANDALL** ABBEVILLE, LA

PREP: 20 MIN.
COOK: 6-8 HOURS
MAKES: 4 SERVINGS

- 4 Cornish game hens (20 to 24 ounces each)
- 2 tablespoons canola oil
- 4 large red potatoes, cut into ⅛-inch slices
- 4 bacon strips, cut into 1-inch pieces
  Lemon-pepper seasoning and garlic powder to taste
  Minced fresh parsley

1. In a large skillet, brown hens in oil. Place the potatoes in a 5-qt. slow cooker. Top with the hens and bacon. Sprinkle with lemon-pepper and garlic powder.
2. Cover and cook on low for 6-8 hours or until a thermometer reads 180° and potatoes are tender. Thicken the cooking juices if desired. Sprinkle the hens with parsley.

Fruited Chicken

I've worked full time for more than 30 years, and this convenient recipe has been a lifesaver. Try it when you need a simple dinner that offers a delightful change-of-pace flavor.

—**MIRIEN CHURCH** AURORA, CO

PREP: 10 MIN. • **COOK:** 4 HOURS
MAKES: 6 SERVINGS

- 1 large onion, sliced
- 6 boneless skinless chicken breast halves (6 ounces each)
- ⅓ cup orange juice
- 2 tablespoons soy sauce
- 2 tablespoons Worcestershire sauce
- 2 tablespoons Dijon mustard
- 1 tablespoon grated orange peel
- 2 garlic cloves, minced
- ½ cup chopped dried apricots
- ½ cup dried cranberries
  Hot cooked rice

1. Place onion and chicken in a 5-qt. slow cooker. Combine the orange juice, soy sauce, Worcestershire sauce, mustard, orange peel and garlic; pour over chicken. Sprinkle with apricots and cranberries.
2. Cover and cook on low for 4-5 hours or until a thermometer reads 170°. Serve with rice.
FREEZE OPTION *Freeze cooled chicken mixture in freezer containers. To use, partially thaw in refrigerator overnight. Heat through in a covered saucepan, gently stirring and adding a little broth or water if necessary.*

Sweet and Tangy Chicken

If you need an easy dish for a casual dinner party, this is just the thing. Spicy barbecue sauce blends with sweet pineapple for a crowd-pleasing entree that preps in minutes.

—**MARY ZAWLOCKI** GIG HARBOR, WA

PREP: 10 MIN. • **COOK:** 8 HOURS
MAKES: 8 SERVINGS

- 8 boneless skinless chicken breast halves (4 ounces each)
- 1 bottle (18 ounces) barbecue sauce
- 1 can (20 ounces) pineapple chunks, undrained
- 1 medium green pepper, chopped
- 1 medium onion, chopped
- 2 garlic cloves, minced
  Hot cooked rice

1. Place four chicken breasts in a 5-qt. slow cooker. Combine the barbecue sauce, pineapple, green pepper, onion and garlic; pour half over the chicken. Top with remaining chicken and sauce.
2. Cover and cook on low for 8-9 hours or until chicken is tender. Thicken sauce if desired. Serve the chicken and sauce with rice.

Butter & Herb Turkey

My kids love turkey for dinner, and this easy recipe lets me make it whenever I want. No special occasion required! The meat is so tender it falls right off the bone.

—**ROCHELLE POPOVIC** SOUTH BEND, IN

PREP: 10 MIN. • **COOK:** 5 HOURS
MAKES: 12 SERVINGS (3 CUPS GRAVY)

- 1 bone-in turkey breast (6 to 7 pounds)
- 2 tablespoons butter, softened
- ½ teaspoon dried rosemary, crushed
- ½ teaspoon dried thyme
- ¼ teaspoon garlic powder
- ¼ teaspoon pepper
- 1 can (14½ ounces) chicken broth
- 3 tablespoons cornstarch
- 2 tablespoons cold water

1. Rub turkey with butter. Combine the rosemary, thyme, garlic powder and pepper; sprinkle over turkey.
2. Place in a 6-qt. slow cooker. Pour broth over top. Cover and cook on low for 5-6 hours or until tender.
3. Remove turkey to a serving platter; keep warm. Skim fat from cooking juices; transfer to a small saucepan. Bring to a boil. Combine cornstarch and water until smooth. Gradually stir into the pan. Bring to a boil; cook and stir for 2 minutes or until thickened. Serve with turkey.

Wine-Braised Chicken with Pearl Onions

My family favorite was handed down from my grandmother in London. She made it for every family gathering. It was always the first food at the table and the first to disappear.

—**WAYNE E BARNES** MONTGOMERY, AL

PREP: 10 MIN. • **COOK:** 7 HOURS
MAKES: 4 SERVINGS

- 8 **boneless skinless chicken thighs (about 2 pounds)**
- 1 **package (14.4 ounces) pearl onions, thawed**
- 1 **can (10¾ ounces) condensed cream of chicken soup, undiluted**
- ¼ **cup white wine or chicken broth**
- 2 **teaspoons minced fresh parsley**
- 1 **teaspoon dried tarragon**
- ½ **teaspoon salt**
- ¼ **teaspoon dried rosemary, crushed**
  Hot cooked rice or pasta
  Minced fresh parsley, optional

1. Place chicken and onions in a 4-qt. slow cooker. In a small bowl, combine soup, wine and seasonings; pour over chicken and onions. Cook, covered, on low 7-8 hours or until chicken is tender.
2. Remove chicken; skim fat from cooking juices. Serve cooking juices with chicken and rice. If desired, sprinkle with parsley.

WINE-BRAISED CHICKEN WITH PEARL ONIONS

APPLE BALSAMIC CHICKEN

CHILI-LIME CHICKEN TOSTADAS

Apple Balsamic Chicken

I just love the sweet and tart flavor that balsamic vinegar gives to this dish. It's easy to prepare and after simmering for a few hours, the chicken thighs are very tender and flavorful.
—**JULI SNAER** ENID, OK

PREP: 15 MIN. • **COOK:** 4 HOURS
MAKES: 4 SERVINGS

- 4 **bone-in chicken thighs (about 1½ pounds), skin removed**
- ½ **cup chicken broth**
- ¼ **cup apple cider or juice**
- ¼ **cup balsamic vinegar**
- 2 **tablespoons lemon juice**
- ½ **teaspoon salt**
- ½ **teaspoon garlic powder**
- ½ **teaspoon dried thyme**
- ½ **teaspoon paprika**
- ½ **teaspoon pepper**
- 2 **tablespoons butter**
- 2 **tablespoons all-purpose flour**

1. Place chicken in a 1½-qt. slow cooker. In a small bowl, combine the broth, cider, vinegar, lemon juice and seasonings; pour over meat. Cover and cook on low for 4-5 hours or until chicken is tender.

2. Remove chicken; keep warm. Skim fat from cooking liquid. In a small saucepan, melt butter; stir in flour until smooth. Gradually add cooking liquid. Bring to a boil; cook and stir for 2-3 minutes or until thickened. Serve with chicken.

EXPRESS PREP

Chili-Lime Chicken Tostadas

The flavor of this tender chicken is delicious with a hint of lime. It has just the right amount of heat to spice it up but keep it family-friendly.
—**LAURA POWELL** SOUTH JORDAN, UT

PREP: 10 MIN. • **COOK:** 5 HOURS
MAKES: 5 SERVINGS

- 4 **pounds bone-in chicken breast halves, skin removed**
- 1 **medium onion, chopped**
- 1 **can (4 ounces) chopped green chilies**
- 3 **tablespoons lime juice**
- 4½ **teaspoons chili powder**
- 4 **garlic cloves, minced**
- 10 **tostada shells**
- 1 **can (16 ounces) fat-free refried beans**
  Optional ingredients: Shredded cabbage, shredded cheddar cheese, salsa, sour cream, sliced ripe olives and guacamole

1. In a 4-qt. slow cooker, combine chicken and onion. In a small bowl, combine the green chilies, lime juice, chili powder and garlic; pour over chicken. Cover and cook on low for 5-6 hours or until the meat is tender.

2. Remove chicken; cool slightly. Set aside ⅔ cup cooking juices. Discard remaining juices. Shred chicken with two forks and return to slow cooker. Stir in reserved cooking juices.

3. Spread tostadas with refried beans; top with chicken. Layer with cabbage, cheese, salsa, sour cream, olives and guacamole if desired.

Mandarin Turkey Tenderloin

My husband grew up in an area with lots of turkey farms, so he learned early to love dishes that use turkey. This makes a tasty dinner that requires no last minute fussing, so I like to serve it when I have company.
—**LORIE MINER** KAMAS, UT

PREP: 15 MIN. • **COOK:** 4½ HOURS
MAKES: 8 SERVINGS

- 8 **turkey breast tenderloins (4 ounces each)**
- ½ **teaspoon ground ginger**
- ½ **teaspoon crushed red pepper flakes**
- 1 **can (11 ounces) mandarin oranges, drained**
- 1 **cup sesame ginger marinade**
- ½ **cup chicken broth**
- 1 **package (16 ounces) frozen stir-fry vegetable blend, thawed**
- 1 **tablespoon sesame seeds, toasted**
- 1 **green onion, sliced**
   Hot cooked rice, optional

1. Place turkey in a 3-qt. slow cooker. Sprinkle with ginger and pepper flakes. Top with oranges. In a small bowl, combine marinade and broth; pour over turkey. Cover and cook on low for 4-5 hours or until a thermometer reads 170°.
2. Stir vegetables into the slow cooker. Cover and cook 30 minutes longer or until vegetables are heated through.
3. Sprinkle with sesame seeds and green onion. Serve with rice if desired.

FREEZE OPTION *Cool turkey mixture. Freeze in freezer containers. To use, partially thaw in refrigerator overnight. Heat through slowly in a covered skillet until a thermometer inserted in turkey reads 165°, stirring occasionally and adding a little broth or water if necessary. Garnish as directed.*

MANDARIN TURKEY TENDERLOIN

Pineapple Chicken

This quick-to-prep recipe tastes a little like sweet-and-sour chicken. It's delicious and perfect over rice.
—**FRANCISCA MESIANO**
NEWPORT NEWS, VA

PREP: 15 MIN. • **COOK:** 4 HOURS
MAKES: 4 SERVINGS

- 4 **bone-in chicken breast halves (12 to 14 ounces each), skin removed**
- 1 **tablespoon canola oil**
- 1 **can (20 ounces) sliced pineapple**
- ⅓ **cup packed brown sugar**
- ¼ **cup cornstarch**
- 2 **tablespoons lemon juice**
- ¾ **teaspoon salt**
- ¼ **teaspoon ground ginger**
   Hot cooked rice

1. In a large skillet, brown chicken in oil. Transfer to a greased 4-qt. slow cooker. Drain pineapple, reserving juice; place pineapple over chicken. Whisk the brown sugar, cornstarch, lemon juice, salt, ginger and reserved juice until smooth; pour over top.
2. Cover and cook on low for 4-5 hours or until chicken is tender. Serve with rice.

EXPRESS PREP

Wild Rice Turkey Dinner

We live in the northwoods of Wisconsin, and the wild rice, squash and cranberries I use for this dish are all locally grown. I combine these ingredients with turkey tenderloins for a complete and satisfying supper.

—TABITHA DODGE CONOVER, WI

PREP: 10 MIN. • **COOK:** 6 HOURS
MAKES: 4 SERVINGS

- ¾ cup uncooked wild rice
- 1 medium butternut squash, peeled, seeded and cut into 1-inch pieces
- 1 medium onion, cut into 1-inch pieces
- 2 turkey breast tenderloins (8 ounces each)
- 3 cups chicken broth
- ½ teaspoon salt
- ½ teaspoon pepper
- ½ teaspoon dried thyme
- ½ cup dried cranberries

1. In a 4 qt. slow cooker, layer the rice, squash, onion and turkey. Add broth; sprinkle with salt, pepper and thyme. Cover and cook on low for 6-8 hours or until the meat is tender.

2. Remove turkey; cut into slices. Stir cranberries into rice mixture. Using a slotted spoon, serve squash mixture with turkey.

EXPRESS PREP

Chicken Chili

Assemble this midday and your delicious meal will be ready at dinnertime. What could be better?

—TASTE OF HOME TEST KITCHEN

PREP: 10 MIN. • **COOK:** 5 HOURS
MAKES: 6 SERVINGS

- 1½ pounds boneless skinless chicken breasts, cut into ½-inch cubes
- 1 cup chopped onion
- 3 tablespoons canola oil
- 1 can (15 ounces) white kidney or cannellini beans, rinsed and drained
- 1 can (14½ ounces) diced tomatoes, undrained
- 1 can (14½ ounces) diced tomatoes with mild green chilies, undrained
- 1 cup frozen corn
- 1 teaspoon salt
- 1 teaspoon ground cumin
- 1 teaspoon minced garlic
- ½ teaspoon celery salt
- ½ teaspoon ground coriander
- ½ teaspoon pepper
  Sour cream and shredded cheddar cheese, optional

1. In a large skillet, saute chicken and onion in oil for 5 minutes or until chicken is browned.

2. Transfer to a 5-qt. slow cooker. Stir in the beans, tomatoes, corn and seasonings. Cover and cook on low for 5 hours or until chicken is no longer pink. Garnish with sour cream and cheese if desired.

Slow-Cooked Turkey Stroganoff

I have been making this tasty dish for more than 30 years. Our family loves turkey, and I make a variety of turkey dinners, but this is our favorite. The tarragon comes through nicely, and cream of celery soup lends a mild but welcome flavor.

—CINDY ADAMS TRACY, CA

PREP: 20 MIN. • **COOK:** 6 HOURS
MAKES: 6 SERVINGS

- 4 turkey thighs (about 4 pounds)
- 1 large onion, halved and thinly sliced
- 1 can (10¾ ounces) condensed cream of celery soup, undiluted
- ⅓ cup water
- 3 garlic cloves, minced
- 2 teaspoons dried tarragon
- ½ teaspoon salt
- ½ teaspoon pepper
- ½ cup sour cream
  Hot cooked egg noodles

1. Place turkey and onion in a 5-qt. slow cooker. In a large bowl, whisk soup, water, garlic, tarragon, salt and pepper until blended; pour over top. Cook, covered, on low 6-8 hours or until meat is tender.

2. Remove turkey from slow cooker. When cool enough to handle, remove meat from bones; discard bones. Shred meat with two forks.

3. Whisk sour cream into cooking juices; return meat to slow cooker. Serve with noodles.

Polynesian Pull Chicken

This dish has a unique taste that really spices up weeknights.

—BECKY WALCH MANTECA, CA

PREP: 15 MIN. • **COOK:** 3¼ HOURS
MAKES: 6 SERVINGS

- 2 **pounds boneless skinless chicken breasts**
- 1 **cup barbecue sauce**
- 1 **cup crushed pineapple, undrained**
- 1 **medium onion, chopped**
- ¾ **cup frozen pepper strips, thawed**
- ¼ **cup flaked coconut**
- 1 **tablespoon minced garlic**
- 1 **tablespoon reduced-sodium soy sauce**
- 1 **teaspoon salt**
- 1 **tablespoon cornstarch**
- ¼ **cup water**
- 6 **hoagie buns, split**
  Minced fresh cilantro, optional

1. In a 3- or 4-qt. slow cooker, combine the first nine ingredients. Cook, covered, on low 3-4 hours or until a thermometer reads 165°. Remove chicken; cool slightly.

2. Meanwhile, in a small bowl, mix cornstarch and water until smooth; gradually stir into cooking juices. Cook, covered, on high 15-20 minutes or until sauce is thickened. Shred chicken with two forks. Return to slow cooker; heat through.

3. Serve with buns and, if desired, sprinkle with cilantro.

SLOW-COOKED TURKEY STROGANOFF

POLYNESIAN PULL CHICKEN

GARLIC-APPLE PORK ROAST

⑤INGREDIENTS *EXPRESS PREP*

Garlic-Apple Pork Roast

This is the meal I am known for among family and friends. The garlic and apple flavors complement the pork. It's delicious served with steamed fresh asparagus and roasted red potatoes.

—JENNIFER LOOS
WASHINGTON BORO, PA

PREP: 10 MIN.
COOK: 8 HOURS + STANDING
MAKES: 12 SERVINGS

- 1 boneless pork loin roast (3½-4 pounds)
- 1 jar (12 ounces) apple jelly
- ½ cup water
- 2½ teaspoons minced garlic
- 1 tablespoon dried parsley flakes
- 1 to 1½ teaspoons seasoned salt
- 1 to 1½ teaspoons pepper

1. Cut the roast in half; place in a 5-qt. slow cooker. In a small bowl, combine the jelly, water and garlic; pour over roast. Sprinkle with parsley, salt and pepper.
2. Cover and cook on low for 8-10 hours or until meat is tender. Let stand for 15 minutes before slicing. Serve with cooking juices if desired.

5 INGREDIENTS *EXPRESS PREP*

Easy Chili Verde

I love chili verde, and I always order it if it's on the menu at restaurants. A few years ago I figured out how to make an easy, tasty version at home. There are never leftovers when I make it for my family.

—JULIE ROWLAND SALT LAKE CITY, UT

PREP: 10 MIN. • **COOK:** 5 HOURS
MAKES: 12 SERVINGS (3 QUARTS)

- 1 boneless pork shoulder roast (4 to 5 pounds), cut into 1-inch pieces
- 3 cans (10 ounces each) green enchilada sauce
- 1 cup salsa verde
- 1 can (4 ounces) chopped green chilies
- ½ teaspoon salt
  Hot cooked rice
  Sour cream, optional

In a 5-qt. slow cooker, combine pork, enchilada sauce, salsa verde, green chilies and salt. Cook, covered, on low 5-6 hours or until pork is tender. Serve with rice. If desired, top with sour cream.

EASY CHILI VERDE

Italian Sausage Hoagies

In southeastern Wisconsin, our cuisine is greatly influenced by both the Germans and Italians who immigrated to this area. When preparing these sandwiches, we usually substitute German bratwurst for the Italian sausage, so we blend the two influences with absolutely delicious results.

—CRAIG WACHS RACINE, WI

PREP: 15 MIN. • **COOK:** 4 HOURS
MAKES: 10 SERVINGS

- 10 Italian sausage links
- 2 tablespoons olive oil
- 1 jar (24 ounces) meatless spaghetti sauce
- ½ medium green pepper, julienned
- ½ medium sweet red pepper, julienned
- ½ cup water
- ¼ cup grated Romano cheese
- 2 tablespoons dried oregano
- 2 tablespoons dried basil
- 2 loaves French bread (20 inches)

1. In a large skillet over medium-high heat, brown sausage in oil; drain. Transfer to a 5-qt. slow cooker. Add the spaghetti sauce, peppers, water, cheese, oregano and basil. Cover and cook on low for 4 hours or until sausage is no longer pink.

2. Slice each French bread lengthwise but not all of the way through; cut each loaf widthwise into five pieces. Fill each with sausage, peppers and sauce.

Potato Sausage Supper

I fix this comforting dish at least once a month. I've even taken the hearty layered casserole to family reunions, and I always return with an empty slow cooker.

—**PATRICIA GINN** DELPHI, IN

PREP: 15 MIN. • **COOK:** 6 HOURS
MAKES: 6-8 SERVINGS

- 4 medium potatoes, peeled and sliced
- 1 pound smoked kielbasa or Polish sausage, cut into ½-inch slices
- 2 medium onions, sliced and separated into rings
- 1 can (10¾ ounces) condensed cheddar cheese soup, undiluted
- 1 can (10¾ ounces) condensed cream of celery soup, undiluted
- 1 package (10 ounces) frozen peas, thawed

1. In a greased 5-qt. slow cooker; layer a third of each of the potatoes, sausage, onions and cheese soup. Repeat layers twice.
2. Pour celery soup over the top. Cover and cook on low for 5-6 hours or until the potatoes are tender.
3. Add peas and cook 30 minutes longer.

READY IN ④

Hash Brown Egg Breakfast

I love this slow cooker breakfast dish. It's great for potlucks because it's easy to carry and is always popular.

—**NANCY MARION** FROSTPROOF, FL

PREP: 15 MIN. • **COOK:** 3½ HOURS
MAKES: 12 SERVINGS (1⅓ CUPS EACH)

- 1 package (32 ounces) frozen cubed hash brown potatoes, thawed
- 2 cups cubed fully cooked ham
- 1½ cups (6 ounces) shredded cheddar cheese
- 1 large green pepper, chopped
- 1 medium onion, chopped
- 12 large eggs, lightly beaten
- 1 cup 2% milk
- 1 teaspoon salt
- 1 teaspoon pepper

1. Layer a third of the potatoes, ham, cheese, green pepper and onion in a greased 6-qt. slow cooker. Repeat layers twice.
2. In a large bowl, whisk the eggs, milk, salt and pepper; pour over top. Cover and cook on high for 30 minutes.
3. Reduce heat to low; cook for 2½-3½ hours or until a thermometer reads 160°.

EXPRESS *PREP*

Tender Spareribs

Even my three little ones love this easy-to-make meal. The succulent meat falls right off the bone!

—**JULIE CZMER** WEST BLOOMFIELD, MI

PREP: 10 MIN. • **COOK:** 5½ HOURS
MAKES: 8 SERVINGS

- 4 pounds pork spareribs, cut into serving-size pieces
- ¼ cup soy sauce
- ¼ cup prepared mustard
- ¼ cup molasses
- 3 tablespoons cider vinegar
- 2 tablespoons Worcestershire sauce
- 1 to 2 teaspoons hot pepper sauce

Place ribs in a 5-qt. slow cooker. Combine the remaining ingredients; pour over ribs. Cover and cook on low for 5-6 hours or until meat is tender.

DID YOU KNOW?

Spareribs are the curved ribs from the pork belly. While they are the least meaty of the rib varieties, they offer a strong, succulent pork flavor.

HASH BROWN
EGG BREAKFAST

TENDER SPARERIBS

SLOW COOKER KALUA PORK & CABBAGE

READY IN ④

Pork Chops with Sauerkraut

I pair tender pork chops with tangy sauerkraut in this filling entree. It's so quick and easy to put together, and it leaves everyone satisfied.

—STEPHANIE MILLER OMAHA, NE

PREP: 15 MIN. • **COOK:** 3 HOURS
MAKES: 4 SERVINGS

- 4 **bone-in center-cut pork loin chops (8 ounces each)**
- 2 **tablespoons canola oil**
- 1 **jar (32 ounces) sauerkraut, undrained**
- ¾ **cup packed brown sugar**
- 1 **medium green pepper, sliced**
- 1 **medium onion, sliced**

1. In a large skillet over medium heat, brown pork chops in oil for 3-4 minutes on each side; drain. In a 5-qt. slow cooker, combine the sauerkraut and brown sugar. Top with the pork chops, green pepper and onion.
2. Cover and cook on low for 3 to 4 hours or until meat is tender. Serve with a slotted spoon.

DID YOU KNOW?

It's important to pack brown sugar into the measuring cup. The moisture in brown sugar traps air between the crystals; packing it down insures an accurate measurement. *Taste of Home* recipes specify packed brown sugar in the ingredients.

⑤ INGREDIENTS
Slow Cooker Kalua Pork & Cabbage

This is a great way to have pork for dinner. It's always one of the most unique dishes at parties...and one of the most popular.

—RHOLINELLE DETORRES
SAN JOSE, CA

PREP: 20 MIN. • **COOK:** 9 HOURS
MAKES: 12 SERVINGS

- 7 **bacon strips, divided**
- 1 **boneless pork shoulder butt roast (3 to 4 pounds), well trimmed**
- 1 **tablespoon coarse sea salt**
- 1 **medium head cabbage (about 2 pounds), coarsely chopped**

1. Line bottom of a 6-qt. slow cooker with four bacon strips. Sprinkle all sides of roast with salt; place in slow cooker. Arrange remaining bacon over top of roast.
2. Cook, covered, on low 8-10 hours or until pork is tender. Add cabbage, spreading cabbage around roast. Cook, covered, 1 to 1¼ hours longer or until the cabbage is tender.
3. Remove pork to a serving bowl; shred pork with two forks. Using a slotted spoon, add cabbage to pork and toss to combine. If desired, skim fat from some of the cooking juices and stir into pork mixture or serve on the side.

HAM AND BEAN STEW

Ham and Bean Stew

You only need five ingredients to fix this thick and flavorful stew. I top bowls of it with shredded cheese. This stew is perfect with hot dogs and burgers in the summer, grilled cheese sandwiches in the fall or on it's own as a winter warmer-upper!

—TERESA D'AMATO EAST GRANBY, CT

PREP: 5 MIN. • **COOK:** 7 HOURS
MAKES: 6 SERVINGS

- 2 cans (16 ounces each) baked beans
- 2 medium potatoes, peeled and cubed
- 2 cups cubed fully cooked ham
- 1 celery rib, chopped
- ½ cup water

In a 3-qt. slow cooker, combine all ingredients; mix well. Cover and cook on low for 7 hours or until the potatoes are tender.

ROOT BEER PULLED PORK SANDWICHES

CRANBERRY-MUSTARD PORK LOIN

COUNTRY PORK CHOP SUPPER

Root Beer Pulled Pork Sandwiches

My husband is a huge fan of pulled pork sandwiches, so my sister shared this incredibly easy recipe with me. At potlucks and family dinners, nobody can get enough of this root beer-braised version. You should try it and see for yourself!

—**CAROLYN PALM** WALTON, NY

PREP: 20 MIN. • **COOK:** 8½ HOURS
MAKES: 12 SERVINGS

- 1 boneless pork shoulder butt roast (3 to 4 pounds)
- 1 can (12 ounces) root beer or cola
- 1 bottle (18 ounces) barbecue sauce
- 12 kaiser rolls, split

1. Place roast in a 4- or 5-qt. slow cooker. Add root beer; cook, covered, on low 8-10 hours or until meat is tender.
2. Remove roast; cool slightly. Discard cooking juices. Shred pork with two forks; return to slow cooker. Stir in barbecue sauce. Cook, covered, until heated through, about 30 minutes. Serve on rolls.
FREEZE OPTION *Freeze cooled meat mixture in freezer containers. To use, partially thaw in refrigerator overnight. Heat through in a saucepan, stirring occasionally and adding a little water if necessary.*

Cranberry-Mustard Pork Loin

My dressed-up pork loin is so easy that you only have to spend a few minutes preparing it. The roast is always a hit with guests because it's very tasty—and with me because it comes together fast.

—**LAURA COOK** WILDWOOD, MO

PREP: 15 MIN. • **COOK:** 4 HOURS
MAKES: 8 SERVINGS

- 1 boneless pork loin roast (2 pounds)
- 1 can (14 ounces) whole-berry cranberry sauce
- ¼ cup Dijon mustard
- 3 tablespoons brown sugar
- 3 tablespoons lemon juice
- 1 tablespoon cornstarch
- ¼ cup cold water

1. Place roast in a 3-qt. slow cooker. Combine the cranberry sauce, mustard, brown sugar and lemon juice; pour over roast. Cover and cook on low for 4-5 hours or until meat is tender. Remove roast and keep warm.
2. Strain cooking juices into a 2-cup measuring cup; add enough water to measure 2 cups. In a small saucepan, combine cornstarch and cold water until smooth; stir in cooking juices. Bring to a boil; cook and stir for 2 minutes or until thickened. Serve with pork.

Country Pork Chop Supper

Dinner doesn't get much easier than this quick and hearty all-in-one slow cooker meal. And if you ask me, it doesn't get much tastier, either!

—**SANDY MULLEN** GAGE, OK

PREP: 10 MIN. • **COOK:** 5 HOURS
MAKES: 6 SERVINGS

- 6 boneless pork loin chops (½ inch thick and 4 ounces each)
- 2 jars (12 ounces each) pork gravy
- 1 can (10¾ ounces) condensed cream of mushroom soup, undiluted
- 2 tablespoons ketchup
- 1 tablespoon minced chives
- 1 teaspoon pepper
- 1 teaspoon reduced-sodium soy sauce
- ½ teaspoon seasoned salt
- 3 medium potatoes, peeled and quartered
- 1 package (16 ounces) frozen mixed vegetables

1. Place pork chops in a greased 5-qt. slow cooker. In a large bowl, combine the gravy, soup, ketchup, chives, pepper, soy sauce and seasoned salt; pour over pork.
2. Stir in potatoes; cover and cook on low for 4-5 hours. Stir in the vegetables and cook 1 hour longer or until the meat and potatoes are tender.

Tender Pork Roast

(5) INGREDIENTS **EXPRESS** PREP

A fall-apart-tender pork roast is always a wonderful entree for company. It never fails to please.

—**LAVERNE PETERSON**
MINNEAPOLIS, MN

PREP: 5 MIN. • **COOK:** 8 HOURS
MAKES: 8 SERVINGS

- 1 boneless pork loin roast (3 pounds)
- 1 can (8 ounces) tomato sauce
- ¾ cup soy sauce
- ½ cup sugar
- 2 teaspoons ground mustard

1. Cut roast in half; place in a 5-qt. slow cooker. Combine remaining ingredients; pour over roast. Cover and cook on low for 8-9 hours or until meat is tender.

2. Remove roast to a serving platter and keep warm. If desired, skim fat from cooking juices and thicken for gravy.

DID YOU KNOW?

A pork loin chop has a T-bone-shaped bone, with meat on both sides of the bone. The rib chop has meat nestled between the rib and backbone. Center cut chops are boneless. A blade chop may have bones from the shoulder blade, rib and back.

Pork Chop Dinner

EXPRESS PREP

Canned soup creates a comforting gravy for tender pork and potatoes in this simple supper idea. Feel free to change the amount of onion soup mix to suit your tastes.

—**MIKE AVERY** BATTLE CREEK, MI

PREP: 10 MIN. • **COOK:** 6 HOURS
MAKES: 4 SERVINGS

- 6 to 8 medium carrots (1 pound), coarsely chopped
- 3 to 4 medium potatoes, cubed
- 4 boneless pork loin chops (¾ inch thick)
- 1 large onion, sliced
- 1 envelope onion soup mix
- 2 cans (10¾ ounces each) condensed cream of mushroom soup, undiluted

Place carrots and potatoes in a 3-qt. slow cooker. Top with pork chops, onion, soup mix and soup. Cover and cook on low for 6-8 hours or until meat and vegetables are tender.

Saucy Ranch Pork and Potatoes

(5) INGREDIENTS

My sister Elyse shared a tasty ranch pork roast recipe with me. I tweaked it so I could use what was already in my pantry, and this dish was the result.

—**KENDRA ADAMSON** LAYTON, UT

PREP: 20 MIN. • **COOK:** 4 HOURS
MAKES: 6 SERVINGS

- 2 pounds red potatoes (about 6 medium), cut into ¾-inch cubes
- ¼ cup water
- 6 boneless pork loin chops (6 ounces each)
- 2 cans (10¾ ounces each) condensed cream of chicken soup, undiluted
- 1 cup 2% milk
- 1 envelope ranch salad dressing mix
  Minced fresh parsley, optional

1. Place potatoes and water in a large microwave-safe dish. Microwave, covered, on high for 3-5 minutes or until potatoes are almost tender; drain.

2. Transfer potatoes and pork chops to a 4- or 5-qt. slow cooker. In a bowl, mix condensed soup, milk and salad dressing mix; pour over pork chops. Cook, covered, on low 4-5 hours or until pork and potatoes are tender (a thermometer inserted in pork should read at least 145°). If desired, sprinkle with parsley.

Pork Chops & Acorn Squash

My husband and I can never get enough of the fresh acorn squash from our garden. These chops cook up sweet and tender in the slow cooker, and the marvelous comfort-food flavor doesn't take my whole day to prepare. What a great way to enjoy garden-fresh flavor!

—**MARY JOHNSON** COLOMA, WI

PREP: 15 MIN. • **COOK:** 4 HOURS
MAKES: 6 SERVINGS

- 6 boneless pork loin chops (4 ounces each)
- 2 medium acorn squash, halved lengthwise, seeded and sliced
- ½ cup packed brown sugar
- 2 tablespoons butter, melted
- 1 tablespoon orange juice
- ¾ teaspoon salt
- ¾ teaspoon browning sauce, optional
- ½ teaspoon grated orange peel

Place pork chops in a 5-qt. slow cooker; add squash. In a small bowl, mix remaining ingredients; pour over squash. Cook, covered, on low 4-6 hours or until pork is tender.

SAUCY RANCH
PORK AND POTATOES

PORK CHOPS &
ACORN SQUASH

PORK WITH PEACH PICANTE SAUCE

LIGHT HAM TETRAZZINI

Pork with Peach Picante Sauce

When fresh peaches are in season, I cook these pork ribs up for family and friends. I love the recipe because I only need six ingredients, the slow cooker does most of the work for me and the ribs turn out tender and tasty every time.

—**CONNIE JENISTA** VALRICO, FL

PREP: 20 MIN. + CHILLING
COOK: 5½ HOURS
MAKES: 4 SERVINGS

- 2 **pounds boneless country-style pork ribs**
- 2 **tablespoons taco seasoning**
- ½ **cup mild salsa**
- ¼ **cup peach preserves**
- ¼ **cup barbecue sauce**
- 2 **cups chopped fresh peeled peaches or frozen unsweetened sliced peaches, thawed and chopped**

1. In a large bowl, toss ribs with taco seasoning. Cover and refrigerate overnight.

2. Place pork in a 3-qt. slow cooker. In a small bowl, combine the salsa, preserves and barbecue sauce. Pour over ribs. Cover and cook on low for 5-6 hours or until the meat is tender.

3. Add the peaches; cover and cook 30 minutes longer or until peaches are tender.

Light Ham Tetrazzini

This creamy pasta is an easy way to serve a hungry crowd. If you're bringing this tetrazzini to a potluck, cook and add the spaghetti to the slow cooker just before heading to the gathering.

—**SUSAN BLAIR** STERLING, MI

PREP: 15 MIN. • **COOK:** 4 HOURS
MAKES: 10 SERVINGS

- 2 **cans (10¾ ounces each) reduced-fat reduced-sodium condensed cream of mushroom soup, undiluted**
- 2 **cups sliced fresh mushrooms**
- 2 **cups cubed fully cooked ham**
- 1 **cup fat-free evaporated milk**

- ¼ **cup white wine or water**
- 2 **teaspoons prepared horseradish**
- 1 **package (14½ ounces) multigrain spaghetti**
- 1 **cup shredded Parmesan cheese**

1. In a 5-qt. slow cooker, mix the first six ingredients. Cook, covered, on low 4-5 hours until heated through.

2. To serve, cook spaghetti according to package directions; drain. Add spaghetti and cheese to soup mixture; toss to combine.

TOP TIP

Looking for a side dish for a ham entree? Whip up Light Ham Tetrazzini but leave out the cubed ham. The result will be a perfect pairing for your meaty main course.

Sweet & Sour Pork Wraps

What a great change of pace! We always make these Asian-inspired wraps at our family's annual party, and they're a true favorite. The cabbage and cilantro give them great texture and unbeatable flavor.

—**ANDREW DEVITO** HARTFORD, CT

PREP: 15 MIN. • **COOK:** 6 HOURS
MAKES: 8 SERVINGS (2 WRAPS EACH)

- 1 boneless pork shoulder butt roast (3 to 4 pounds)
- 1 medium onion, chopped
- 1 cup water
- 1 cup sweet-and-sour sauce
- ¼ cup sherry or chicken broth
- ¼ cup reduced-sodium soy sauce
- 1 envelope onion soup mix
- 1 tablespoon minced fresh gingerroot
- 3 garlic cloves, minced
- 16 flour tortillas (6 inches), warmed
- 4 cups shredded cabbage
- ¼ cup minced fresh cilantro

1. Place roast and onion in a 6-qt. slow cooker. In a small bowl, whisk water, sweet-and-sour sauce, sherry, soy sauce, soup mix, ginger and garlic until blended; pour over pork. Cook, covered, on low 6-8 hours or until meat is tender.

2. When cool enough to handle, shred pork with two forks. To serve, spoon about ⅓ cup pork mixture onto the center of each tortilla. Top with ¼ cup cabbage; sprinkle with cilantro. Fold bottom of tortilla over filling; fold both sides to close.

Country Ribs Dinner

This is my favorite recipe for a classic rib dinner. It's always a treat for my family when we I serve it.
—**ROSE INGALL** MANISTEE, MI

PREP: 10 MIN. • **COOK:** 6¼ HOURS
MAKES: 4 SERVINGS

- 2 pounds boneless country-style pork ribs
- ½ teaspoon salt
- ¼ teaspoon pepper
- 8 small red potatoes (about 1 pound), halved
- 4 medium carrots, cut into 1-inch pieces
- 3 celery ribs, cut into ½-inch pieces
- 1 medium onion, coarsely chopped
- ¾ cup water
- 1 garlic clove, crushed
- 1 can (10¾ ounces) condensed cream of mushroom soup, undiluted

1. Sprinkle ribs with salt and pepper; transfer to a 4-qt. slow cooker. Add potatoes, carrots, celery, onion, water and garlic. Cook, covered, on low 6-8 hours or until meat and vegetables are tender.
2. Remove meat and vegetables; skim fat from cooking juices. Whisk soup into cooking juices; return meat and vegetables to slow cooker. Cook, covered, 15-30 minutes longer or until heated through.

Pork Chili

My husband usually tries to avoid spending time in the kitchen, but he'll frequently offer to prepare a big batch of his chili. Of course, he always serves as his own taste-tester!
—**LINDA TEMPLE** ST. JOSEPH, MO

PREP: 15 MIN. • **COOK:** 6 HOURS
MAKES: 10-12 SERVINGS

- 2½ pounds boneless pork, cut into 1-inch cubes
- 2 tablespoons vegetable oil
- 1 can (28 ounce) diced tomatoes, undrained
- 1 can (16 ounces) chili beans, undrained
- 1 can (8 ounces) tomato sauce
- ¼ cup salsa
- ¼ cup chopped onion
- ¼ cup chopped green pepper
- 1 tablespoon chili powder
- 1 teaspoon minced jalapeno pepper
- ¼ teaspoon garlic powder
- ¼ teaspoon cayenne powder
- ¼ teaspoon pepper
- ¼ teaspoon salt

In a large skillet over medium-high heat, brown pork in oil; drain. Place in a 5-qt. slow cooker; add remaining ingredients. Cover and cook on high for 2 hours. Reduce heat to low and cook 4 hours longer.
NOTE *Wear disposable gloves when cutting hot peppers; the oils can burn skin. Avoid touching your face.*

Slow-Cooked Ham with Pineapple Sauce

This delightful dish is great any time of the year. That said, we usually serve it during the holidays because everyone is crazy about it.
—**TERRY ROBERTS** YORKTOWN, VA

PREP: 10 MIN. • **COOK:** 6 HOURS
MAKES: 12 SERVINGS

- 1 fully cooked boneless ham (4 to 5 pounds)
- 1 can (20 ounces) unsweetened crushed pineapple, undrained
- 1 cup packed brown sugar
- 1 tablespoon cornstarch
- ¼ teaspoon salt
- 2 tablespoons lemon juice
- 1 tablespoon yellow mustard

Place ham in a 5-qt. slow cooker. In a small saucepan, mix the remaining ingredients, stirring to dissolve cornstarch. Bring to a boil, stirring occasionally. Pour over ham, covering completely. Cover and cook on low for 6-8 hours.

COUNTRY RIBS DINNER

PORK CHILI

SLOW-COOKED HAM WITH PINEAPPLE SAUCE

READY IN ④

Pineapple-Dijon Ham Sandwiches

My kids like ham, but it's a challenge to come up with different ways to prepare it. I like combining ham and pineapple, so I decided to put them in the slow cooker. The result was amazing. Even my two youngest ones ate their sandwiches right up.

—**CAMILLE BECKSTRAND** LAYTON, UT

PREP: 20 MIN. • **COOK:** 3 HOURS
MAKES: 10 SERVINGS

- 2 **pounds fully cooked ham, cut into ½-inch cubes**
- 1 **can (20 ounces) crushed pineapple, undrained**
- 1 **medium green pepper, finely chopped**
- ¾ **cup packed brown sugar**
- ¼ **cup finely chopped onion**
- ¼ **cup Dijon mustard**
- 1 **tablespoon dried minced onion**
- 10 **hamburger buns, split**
- 10 **slices Swiss cheese**
  Additional Dijon mustard, optional

1. In a greased 4-qt. slow cooker, combine first seven ingredients. Cook, covered, on low 3-4 hours or until heated through.
2. Preheat broiler. Place bun bottoms and tops on baking sheets, cut side up. Using a slotted spoon, place ham mixture on bottoms; top with cheese. Broil 3-4 in. from heat 1-2 minutes or until cheese is melted and tops are toasted. Replace tops. If desired, serve with additional mustard.

PINEAPPLE-DIJON HAM SANDWICHES

Cranberry Pork & Sweet Potatoes

With tender pork chops straight from the slow cooker and sweet potatoes flavored with applesauce, cranberry sauce and brown sugar, this is a wonderful meal for the holiday season.

—**DORIS BRANHAM** KINGSTON, TN

PREP: 10 MIN. • **COOK:** 6 HOURS
MAKES: 6 SERVINGS

- 1⅔ cups sweetened applesauce (about 15 ounces)
- 3 pounds sweet potatoes (about 3 large), peeled and cut into 1-inch slices
- ¾ teaspoon salt, divided
- ¼ teaspoon pepper, divided
- ¼ cup packed brown sugar
- 6 bone-in pork loin chops (6 ounces each)
- 1 can (14 ounces) whole-berry cranberry sauce

1. Place applesauce in a 6-qt. slow cooker. Top with sweet potatoes; sprinkle with ¼ teaspoon salt, ⅛ teaspoon pepper and brown sugar.
2. Place pork chops over potatoes; sprinkle with remaining salt and pepper. Spoon cranberry sauce over pork. Cook, covered, on low 6-8 hours or until pork and sweet potatoes are tender.

Three Beans and Sausage

For a stick-to-your-ribs meal, try this hearty combination of beans and sausage. Because it calls for several canned items, it's easy to prepare and inexpensive to serve.

—**JUDY SUMNER** RIVERTON, UT

PREP: 15 MIN. • **COOK:** 4 HOURS
MAKES: 8 SERVINGS

- 1½ pounds smoked sausage, cut into 1-inch pieces
- 1 can (16 ounces) kidney beans, rinsed and drained
- 1 can (15½ ounces) great northern beans, rinsed and drained
- 1 can (15 ounces) black beans, rinsed and drained
- 1 cup chopped onion
- 1 cup water
- 1 can (8 ounces) tomato sauce
- ⅔ cup chopped celery
- 1 teaspoon chicken bouillon granules
- 1 teaspoon minced garlic
- 1 bay leaf
- ½ teaspoon pepper
- ¼ teaspoon dried oregano, optional
- ¼ teaspoon dried thyme, optional
  Hot cooked rice

In a 5-qt. slow cooker, combine the first 12 ingredients. Sprinkle with oregano and thyme if desired. Cover and cook on low for 4-5 hours or until heated through. Discard bay leaf. Serve with rice.

CRANBERRY PORK
& SWEET POTATOES

Sweet Sausage 'n' Beans

This slow-cooker version of the French dish cassoulet is sweet, saucy and chock-full of beans, smoked sausage and vegetables. Best of all, it only serves three, so you're not stuck with lots of leftovers.

—**TASTE OF HOME TEST KITCHEN**

PREP: 10 MIN. • **COOK:** 4 HOURS
MAKES: 3 SERVINGS

- ¼ cup thinly sliced carrot
- ¼ cup chopped onion
- 1 cup frozen lima beans, thawed
- 1 cup frozen cut green beans, thawed
- ½ pound smoked sausage, cut into ¼-inch slices
- ¾ cup baked beans
- ¼ cup ketchup
- 2 tablespoons brown sugar
- 1½ teaspoons cider vinegar
- ½ teaspoon prepared mustard

In a 1½-qt. slow cooker, layer the carrot, onion, lima beans, green beans, sausage and baked beans. In a small bowl, combine the ketchup, brown sugar, vinegar and mustard; pour over beans. Cover and cook on high for 4 hours or until vegetables are tender. Stir before serving.

Pulled Pork Sandwiches

Foolproof and wonderfully delicious describes my barbecue pork recipe. Just four ingredients and a slow cooker make a fabulous dish with hardly any effot. The extras freeze well for busy nights.

—**SARAH JOHNSON** CHICAGO, IL

PREP: 15 MIN. • **COOK:** 7 HOURS
MAKES: 6 SERVINGS

- 1 Hormel lemon-garlic pork loin filet (about 1⅓ pounds)
- 1 can (12 ounces) Dr Pepper
- 1 bottle (18 ounces) barbecue sauce
- 6 hamburger buns, split

1. Place pork in a 3-qt. slow cooker. Pour Dr Pepper over top. Cover and cook on low for 7-9 hours or until meat is tender.

2. Remove meat; cool slightly. Discard cooking juices. Shred meat with two forks and return to slow cooker. Stir in barbecue sauce; heat through. Serve on buns.

FREEZE OPTION *Place individual portions of cooled meat mixture and juice in freezer containers. To use, partially thaw in refrigerator overnight. Microwave, covered, on high in a microwave-safe dish until heated through, gently stirring and adding a little water if necessary.*

Peachy Baby Back Ribs

I took classic baby back ribs and added a sweet peach flavor. All my friends who love barbecue say this is a real winner!

—**MARY LOUISE BURK** ROME, GA

PREP: 15 MIN. • **COOK:** 6 HOURS
MAKES: 6 SERVINGS

- 2 bottles (18 ounces each) hickory smoke-flavored barbecue sauce
- 1 can (15 ounces) sliced peaches, drained and halved crosswise
- 1 medium onion, chopped
- ¾ cup jalapeno pepper jelly
- ½ cup pickled hot jalapeno slices
- 6 pounds pork baby back ribs, well-trimmed
- 1 teaspoon salt
- ½ teaspoon pepper
  Thinly sliced green onions

1. In a large bowl, mix the first five ingredients. Cut ribs into 3-rib portions; sprinkle with salt and pepper. Place half of the ribs in a 6-qt. slow cooker; pour half of the sauce mixture over ribs. Repeat layers. Cook, covered, on low 6-8 hours or until meat is tender.

2. Remove ribs from slow cooker; keep warm. Strain cooking juices, reserving peaches and vegetables. Skim fat from cooking juices; thicken if desired. Stir in reserved peaches and vegetables; serve with ribs. Sprinkle with green onions.

PULLED PORK SANDWICHES

PEACHY BABY BACK RIBS

GREEN CHILI SHREDDED PORK

EXPRESS PREP

Green Chili Shredded Pork

Slow cooker pork with green chilies always makes my hungry clan happy. Getting creative with the leftovers is part of the fun.
—**MARY SHIVERS** ADA, OK

PREP: 10 MIN. • **COOK:** 6 HOURS
MAKES: 8 SERVINGS

- 1 boneless pork loin roast (3 to 4 pounds)
- 1½ cups apple cider or juice
- 1 can (4 ounces) chopped green chilies, drained
- 3 garlic cloves, minced
- 1½ teaspoons salt
- 1½ teaspoons hot pepper sauce
- 1 teaspoon chili powder
- 1 teaspoon pepper
- ½ teaspoon ground cumin
- ½ teaspoon dried oregano
- 16 flour tortillas (8 inches)
  Optional toppings: chopped peeled mango, shredded lettuce, chopped fresh cilantro and lime wedges

1. Place pork in a 5- or 6-qt. slow cooker. In a small bowl, mix cider, green chilies, garlic, salt, pepper sauce, chili powder, pepper, cumin and oregano; pour over pork. Cook, covered, on low 6-8 hours or until meat is tender.

2. Remove roast; cool slightly. Shred pork with two forks. Return to slow cooker; heat through. Using tongs, serve pork in tortillas with toppings as desired.
FREEZE OPTION *Place shredded pork in freezer containers; top with cooking juices. Cool and freeze. To use, partially thaw in refrigerator overnight. Heat through in a saucepan, stirring occasionally.*

⑤INGREDIENTS

Apple-Dijon Pork Roast

This cold-weather favorite takes only a few minutes to assemble and is incredibly delicious. I like to serve the roast with rice, then use the tangy sauce as a gravy for both.
—**CINDY STEFFEN** CEDARBURG, WI

PREP: 15 MIN. • **COOK:** 4 HOURS
MAKES: 8 SERVINGS

- 1 boneless pork loin roast (2 to 3 pounds)
- 1 can (14½ ounces) chicken broth
- 1 cup unsweetened apple juice
- ½ cup Dijon mustard
- 6 tablespoons cornstarch
- 6 tablespoons cold water

1. Place roast in a 5-qt. slow cooker. In a small bowl, combine the broth, apple juice and mustard; pour over roast. Cover and cook on low for 4-5 hours or until tender. Remove roast and keep warm.
2. For gravy, strain cooking juices and skim fat. Pour juices into a small saucepan. Combine cornstarch and water until smooth; gradually stir into juices. Bring to a boil; cook and stir for 2 minutes or until thickened. Serve with pork.

SAUSAGE SPANISH RICE

Sausage Spanish Rice

My husband and I both work the midnight shift, so I'm always on the lookout for slow cooker recipes. This one couldn't be easier. We often enjoy it as a main course because it's so hearty, but it's also good as a side dish for Southwestern entrees.

—**MICHELLE MCKAY** GARDEN CITY, MI

PREP: 10 MIN. • **COOK:** 5 HOURS
MAKES: 6 SERVINGS

- 1 **pound smoked kielbasa or Polish sausage, sliced**
- 2 **cans (14½ ounces each) diced tomatoes, undrained**
- 2 **cup water**
- 1½ **cups uncooked converted rice**
- 1 **cup salsa**
- 1 **medium onion**
- ½ **cup chopped green pepper**
- ½ **cup chopped sweet red pepper**
- 1 **can (4 ounces) chopped green chilies**
- 1 **envelope taco seasoning**

In a 3- or 4-qt. slow cooker, combine all ingredients. Cover and cook on low for 5-6 hours or until rice is tender.

**SUPER EASY
COUNTRY-STYLE RIBS**

**BARBECUE BRATS
& PEPPERS**

**SLOW COOKER
BREAKFAST CASSEROLE**

Super Easy Country-Style Ribs

When we were growing up, our mom made these for us all the time, and we still can't get enough of them. I created this freeze-thaw-slow cook version to save me time on busy weeknights.

—**STEPHANIE LOAIZA** LAYTON, UT

PREP: 10 MIN. + FREEZING
COOK: 5 HOURS
MAKES: 4 SERVINGS

- 1½ cups ketchup
- ½ cup packed brown sugar
- ½ cup white vinegar
- 2 teaspoons seasoned salt
- ½ teaspoon liquid smoke, optional
- 2 pounds boneless country-style pork ribs

1. In a large resealable plastic freezer bag, combine ketchup, brown sugar, vinegar, seasoned salt and, if desired, liquid smoke. Add pork ribs; seal bag and freeze.
2. To use, place filled freezer bag in refrigerator 48 hours or until completely thawed. Transfer contents of bag to a 3-qt. slow cooker. Cook, covered, on low 5-6 hours or until meat is tender. Remove ribs to a serving platter. Skim fat from cooking liquid. If desired, transfer to a small saucepan. Bring to a boil; cook 12-15 minutes or until sauce is reduced to 1½ cups. Serve with the ribs.

Barbecue Brats & Peppers

We live in brat country, and this barbecue-style recipe feeds a crowd. The sauce makes it a welcome change from the same old grilled brat.

—**MARIA ZRUCKY** KRONENWETTER, WI

PREP: 15 MIN. • **COOK:** 6 HOURS
MAKES: 10 SERVINGS

- 2 bottles (12 ounces each) beer or nonalcoholic beer
- 1 bottle (18 ounces) barbecue sauce
- ½ cup ketchup
- 1 large sweet onion, halved and sliced
- 1 large sweet yellow pepper, cut into strips
- 1 large sweet orange pepper, cut into strips
- 1 jalapeno pepper, thinly sliced
- 1 serrano pepper, thinly sliced
- 10 uncooked bratwurst links
- 10 brat or hot dog buns, split

1. Place the first eight ingredients in a 5-qt. slow cooker; stir to combine. In a large skillet, brown bratwurst on all sides over medium-high heat; transfer to slow cooker.
2. Cook, covered, on low 6-8 hours or until sausages are cooked through and vegetables are tender. Using tongs, serve bratwurst and pepper mixture on buns.

Slow Cooker Breakfast Casserole

I love this breakfast casserole because I can make it the night before and it's ready early in the morning. It's ideal for camping or when I have weekend guests.

—**ELLIE STUTHEIT** LAS VEGAS, NV

PREP: 25 MIN. • **COOK:** 7 HOURS
MAKES: 12 SERVINGS

- 1 package (30 ounces) frozen shredded hash brown potatoes
- 1 pound bulk pork sausage, cooked and drained
- 1 medium onion, chopped
- 1 can (4 ounces) chopped green chilies
- 1½ cups (6 ounces) shredded cheddar cheese
- 12 large eggs
- 1 cup 2% milk
- ½ teaspoon salt
- ½ teaspoon pepper

In a greased 5- or 6-qt. slow cooker, layer half of the potatoes, sausage, onion, chilies and cheese. Repeat layers. In a large bowl, whisk the eggs, milk, salt and pepper; pour over top. Cover and cook on low for 7-9 hours or until eggs are set.

TOP TIP

The next time you bring your slow cooker to a potluck, reunion or other large get-together, bring an extension cord, too. This way, you can rest assured that your dish will stay hot on the buffet table.

EXPRESS PREP
Ham Barbecue

We have used this recipe for family gatherings and birthday parties countless times. The juicy, full-flavored sandwiches are so easy to make, and they taste great. I usually double the recipe so I have leftovers for lunches during the week.

—JENNIFER MIDDLEKAUFF
NEW HOLLAND, PA

PREP: 10 MIN. • **COOK:** 4 HOURS
MAKES: 12 SERVINGS

- 2 **pounds thinly sliced deli ham**
- 1 **cup water**
- 1 **cup ketchup**
- ¼ **cup packed brown sugar**
- ¼ **cup Worcestershire sauce**
- 2 **tablespoons white vinegar**
- 2 **teaspoons prepared mustard**
- 12 **hamburger buns, split and toasted**

Place the ham in a greased 3-qt. slow cooker. In a large bowl, combine the water, ketchup, brown sugar, Worcestershire sauce, vinegar and mustard; pour over ham and stir well. Cover and cook on low for 4-5 hours or until heated through. Serve on buns.

Peachy Pork Chops

Here's a slow-cooked dish that serves two! I played around with many variations of this recipe until I came up with one that was just right. The warm peaches make an excellent side dish for the pork.

—BONNIE MORROW SPENCERPORT, NY

PREP: 15 MIN. • **COOK:** 5 HOURS
MAKES: 2 SERVINGS

- 2 **bone-in center-cut pork loin chops (7 ounces each)**
- 2 **teaspoons canola oil**
- 1 **can (8¼ ounces) sliced peaches**
- 1 **can (8 ounces) tomato sauce**
- ½ **cup water**
- 1 **teaspoon reduced-sodium soy sauce**
- ⅛ **teaspoon dried rosemary, crushed**
- ⅛ **teaspoon dried thyme**
- ⅛ **teaspoon dried basil**
  Dash to ⅛ teaspoon cayenne pepper

1. In a small skillet, brown pork chops in oil; drain. Transfer to a 1½-qt. slow cooker.
2. Drain peaches, reserving juice. In a bowl, combine the tomato sauce, water, soy sauce, rosemary, thyme, basil, cayenne and reserved peach juice; pour over pork. Top with peaches. Cover and cook on low for 5 hours or until pork is tender.

EXPRESS PREP
Beer Brat Chili

My husband and I love this chili because it smells so good as it simmers all day. I can't think of a better way to use leftover brats.

—KATRINA KRUMM APPLE VALLEY, MN

PREP: 10 MIN. • **COOK:** 5 HOURS
MAKES: 8 SERVINGS (2½ QUARTS)

- 1 **can (15 ounces) white kidney or cannellini beans, rinsed and drained**
- 1 **can (15 ounces) pinto beans, rinsed and drained**
- 1 **can (15 ounces) Southwestern black beans, undrained**
- 1 **can (14½ ounces) Italian diced tomatoes, undrained**
- 1 **can (10 ounces) diced tomatoes and green chilies, undrained**
- 1 **package (14 ounces) fully cooked beer bratwurst links, sliced**
- 1½ **cups frozen corn**
- 1 **medium sweet red pepper, chopped**
- 1 **medium onion, finely chopped**
- ¼ **cup chili seasoning mix**
- 1 **garlic clove, minced**

In a 5-qt. slow cooker, combine all ingredients. Cook, covered, on low 5-6 hours.

Teriyaki Pork Roast

I'm always looking for no-fuss recipes, so I was thrilled to find this one. The tender teriyaki pork roast has become an all-time favorite.

—ROXANNE HULSEY GAINESVILLE, GA

PREP: 10 MIN. • **COOK:** 7 HOURS
MAKES: 8 SERVINGS

- ¾ cup unsweetened apple juice
- 2 tablespoons sugar
- 2 tablespoons reduced-sodium soy sauce
- 1 tablespoon white vinegar
- 1 teaspoon ground ginger
- ¼ teaspoon garlic powder
- ⅛ teaspoon pepper
- 1 boneless pork loin roast (about 3 pounds), halved
- 7½ teaspoons cornstarch
- 3 tablespoons cold water

1. In a greased 3-qt. slow cooker, combine the first seven ingredients. Add roast and turn to coat. Cover and cook on low for 7-8 hours or until meat is tender.

2. Remove pork to a serving platter; keep warm. Skim fat from cooking juices; transfer to a small saucepan. Bring liquid to a boil. Combine cornstarch and water until smooth. Gradually stir into the pan. Bring to a boil; cook and stir for 2 minutes or until thickened. Serve with meat.

BEER BRAT CHILI

TERIYAKI PORK ROAST

SLOW COOKER TROPICAL PORK CHOPS

PORK AND BEEF BARBECUE

READY IN ④

Slow Cooker Tropical Pork Chops

Pork and fruit go nicely together. When you add fresh herbs, you get a light and lively main dish that everyone loves.

—**ROXANNE CHAN** ALBANY, CA

PREP: 15 MIN. • **COOK:** 3 HOURS
MAKES: 4 SERVINGS

- 2 jars (23½ ounces each) mixed tropical fruit, drained and chopped
- ¾ cup thawed limeade concentrate
- ¼ cup sweet chili sauce
- 1 garlic clove, minced
- 1 teaspoon minced fresh gingerroot
- 4 bone-in pork loin chops (¾ inch thick and 5 ounces each)
- 1 green onion, finely chopped
- 2 tablespoons minced fresh cilantro
- 2 tablespoons minced fresh mint
- 2 tablespoons slivered almonds, toasted
- 2 tablespoons finely chopped crystallized ginger, optional
- ½ teaspoon grated lime peel

1. In a 3-qt. slow cooker, combine the first five ingredients. Add pork, arranging chops to sit snugly in fruit mixture. Cook, covered, on low 3-4 hours or until meat is tender (a thermometer inserted in pork should read at least 145°).
2. In a small bowl, mix remaining ingredients. To serve, remove pork chops from slow cooker. Using a slotted spoon, serve fruit over pork. Sprinkle with herb mixture.
NOTE *To toast nuts, place in a dry nonstick skillet and heat over low heat until lightly browned, stirring occasionally.*

Pork and Beef Barbecue

It's the combination of beef stew meat and tender pork that keep my friends and family asking about these tangy sandwiches. Add a little lettuce and tomato for a crisp contrast.

—**CORBIN DETGEN** BUCHANAN, MI

PREP: 15 MIN. • **COOK:** 6 HOURS
MAKES: 12 SERVINGS

- 1 can (6 ounces) tomato paste
- ½ cup packed brown sugar
- ¼ cup chili powder
- ¼ cup cider vinegar
- 2 teaspoons Worcestershire sauce
- 1 teaspoon salt
- 1½ pounds beef stew meat, cut into ¾-inch cubes
- 1½ pounds pork chop suey meat or pork tenderloin, cut into ¾-inch cubes
- 3 medium green peppers, chopped
- 2 large onions, chopped
- 12 sandwich buns, split
  Lettuce and tomatoes, optional

1. In a 5-qt. slow cooker, combine the first six ingredients. Stir in beef, pork, green peppers and onions. Cover and cook on low for 6-8 hours or until meat is tender.
2. Shred meat with two forks. Serve on buns with lettuce and tomatoes if desired.

Pork Carnitas

I often use this recipe when entertaining. I set out all the toppings, and folks have fun assembling their own carnitas. Because I can prepare everything in advance, I get to spend more time with my guests.

—**TRACY BYERS** CORVALLIS, OR

PREP: 15 MIN. • **COOK:** 9 HOURS
MAKES: 12 SERVINGS

- 1 boneless pork shoulder butt roast or pork loin roast (2 to 3 pounds), cut into 3-inch cubes
- ½ cup lime juice
- 1 teaspoon salt
- ½ teaspoon pepper
- ½ teaspoon crushed red pepper flakes
- 12 flour tortillas (6 inches), warmed
- 2 cups (8 ounces) shredded cheddar or Monterey Jack cheese
- 2 medium avocados, peeled and diced
- 2 medium tomatoes, diced
- 1 medium onion, diced
  Shredded lettuce
  Minced fresh cilantro, optional
  Salsa

1. In a 3-qt. slow cooker, combine pork, lime juice, salt, pepper and pepper flakes. Cover and cook on high for 1 hour; stir. Reduce heat to low and cook 8-10 hours longer or until meat is tender.

2. Shred pork with two forks. Spoon about ⅓ cup pork mixture down the center of each tortilla. Top with cheese, avocados, tomatoes, onion, lettuce and, if desired, cilantro. Fold in bottom and sides of tortillas. Serve with salsa.

FREEZE OPTION *Before adding toppings, freeze cooled shredded meat mixture in freezer containers. To use, partially thaw in refrigerator overnight. Heat through in a saucepan, stirring occasionally and adding a little broth or water if necessary. Serve as directed.*

(5)INGREDIENTS EXPRESS PREP

Zesty Ham

This tasty five-ingredient ham cooks on its own in the slow cooker, making it perfect for company. Leftovers are delicious in casseroles.

—**HEATHER SPRING**
SHEPPARD AIR FORCE BASE, TX

PREP: 5 MIN. • **COOK:** 6 HOURS
MAKES: 15-20 SERVINGS

- ½ cup packed brown sugar
- 1 teaspoon ground mustard
- 1 teaspoon prepared horseradish
- 2 tablespoons plus ¼ cup cola, divided
- 1 fully cooked boneless ham (5 to 6 pounds), cut in half

In a small bowl, combine the brown sugar, mustard, horseradish and 2 tablespoons cola. Rub over ham. Transfer to a 5-qt. slow cooker; add remaining cola to slow cooker. Cover and cook on low for 6-8 hours or until a thermometer reads 140°.

PORK CARNITAS

READY IN (4)
Slow Cooker BBQ Ham Sandwiches

Friends love these barbecue sandwiches and often ask me to make them. Since they're always a hit, we double the recipe and serve them at potlucks and other large gatherings.
—**DANA KNOX** BUTLER, PA

PREP: 20 MIN. • **COOK:** 2 HOURS
MAKES: 16 SERVINGS

- 3 cups ketchup
- ¾ cup chopped onion
- ¾ cup chopped green pepper
- ¾ cup packed brown sugar
- ½ cup lemon juice
- ⅓ cup Worcestershire sauce
- 1 tablespoon prepared mustard
- 1¼ teaspoons ground allspice
- 1½ teaspoons liquid smoke, optional
- 3 pounds thinly sliced deli ham
- 16 kaiser or ciabatta rolls, split

1. In a large saucepan, combine the first eight ingredients; if desired, stir in liquid smoke. Bring to a boil. Reduce heat; simmer, uncovered, 5 minutes, stirring occasionally.
2. Place ham in a 5- or 6-qt. slow cooker. Add sauce; stir gently to combine. Cook, covered, on low 2-3 hours or until heated through. Serve on rolls.

DID YOU KNOW?

Depending on the recipe, pork and ham dishes can be tasty options if you're counting calories or fat grams. Slow Cooker BBQ Ham Sandwiches, for instance, have 348 calories each with 4 grams of fat and just a trace of saturated fat.

READY IN (4)
Hash Browns with Ham

Convenient grocery store items such as frozen hash browns and canned chicken soup make this an easy-to-fix meal. Both kids and adults love it because it's super tasty and chock-full of cheese.
—**LIGHTNINGBUG**
TASTEOFHOME.COM

PREP: 15 MIN. • **COOK:** 3¼ HOURS
MAKES: 8 SERVINGS

- 1 package (32 ounces) frozen cubed hash brown potatoes, thawed
- 1 cup cubed fully cooked ham
- 1 small onion, chopped
- 2 cups (8 ounces) shredded cheddar cheese, divided
- 1 can (14¾ ounces) condensed cream of chicken soup, undiluted
- ½ cup butter, melted
- 1 cup (8 ounces) sour cream

1. In a 3-qt. slow cooker, combine the potatoes, ham, onion and 1 cup cheese. Combine soup and butter; pour over potato mixture. Cover and cook on low for 3-4 hours or until potatoes are tender.
2. Stir in sour cream. Sprinkle with remaining cheese. Cover and cook for 15 minutes or until cheese is melted.

Italian Shredded Pork Stew

Need a warm meal for a blustery night? Throw together this slow-cooked stew loaded with nutritious sweet potatoes and kale. The shredded pork is so savory and tender that you'll want to make the recipe often.
—**ROBIN JUNGERS** CAMPBELLSPORT, WI

PREP: 20 MIN. • **COOK:** 8 HOURS
MAKES: 9 SERVINGS (3½ QUARTS)

- 2 medium sweet potatoes, peeled and cubed
- 2 cups chopped fresh kale
- 1 large onion, chopped
- 3 garlic cloves, minced
- 1 boneless pork shoulder butt roast (2½-3½ pounds)
- 1 can (14 ounces) white kidney or cannellini beans, rinsed and drained
- 1½ teaspoons Italian seasoning
- ½ teaspoon salt
- ½ teaspoon pepper
- 3 cans (14½ ounces each) chicken broth
  Sour cream, optional

1. Place the sweet potatoes, kale, onion and garlic in a 5-qt. slow cooker. Place roast on vegetables. Add the beans and seasonings. Pour broth over top. Cover and cook on low for 8-10 hours or until meat is tender.
2. Remove meat; cool slightly. Skim fat from cooking juices. Shred pork with two forks and return to slow cooker; heat through. Garnish servings with sour cream if desired.

SLOW COOKER BBQ
HAM SANDWICHES

HASH BROWNS
WITH HAM

ITALIAN SHREDDED
PORK STEW

CAROLINA CHEESE SHRIMP AND GRITS

READY IN ④

Carolina Cheese Shrimp and Grits

Shrimp and grits are a favorite in my house, if only we could agree on a recipe! I stirred things up with cheddar and Cajun seasoning and created a winning version!

—**CHARLOTTE PRICE** RALEIGH, NC

PREP: 15 MIN. • **COOK:** 2¾ HOURS
MAKES: 6 SERVINGS

- 1 cup uncooked stone-ground grits
- 1 large garlic clove, minced
- ½ teaspoon salt
- ¼ teaspoon pepper
- 4 cups water
- 2 cups (8 ounces) shredded cheddar cheese
- ¼ cup butter, cubed
- 1 pound peeled and deveined cooked shrimp (31-40 per pound)
- 2 medium tomatoes, seeded and finely chopped
- 4 green onions, finely chopped
- 2 tablespoons chopped fresh parsley
- 4 teaspoons lemon juice
- 2 to 3 teaspoons Cajun seasoning

1. Place the first five ingredients in a 3-qt. slow cooker; stir to combine. Cook, covered, on high 2½-3 hours or until water is absorbed and grits are tender, stirring every 45 minutes.
2. Stir in cheese and butter until melted. Stir in remaining ingredients; cook, covered, on high 15-30 minutes or until heated through.

Meaty Slow-Cooked Jambalaya

Sure makes life easy having this wonderful, flavorful dish stashed away in the freezer! Another plus, you throw it all in the slow cooker. No skillet necessary.

—DIANE SMITH PINE MOUNTAIN, GA

PREP: 25 MIN. • **COOK:** 7¼ HOURS
MAKES: 12 SERVINGS (3½ QUARTS)

- 1   can (28 ounces) diced tomatoes, undrained
- 1   cup reduced-sodium chicken broth
- 1   large green pepper, chopped
- 1   medium onion, chopped
- 2   celery ribs, sliced
- ½   cup white wine or additional reduced-sodium chicken broth
- 4   garlic cloves, minced
- 2   teaspoons Cajun seasoning
- 2   teaspoons dried parsley flakes
- 1   teaspoon dried basil
- 1   teaspoon dried oregano
- ¾   teaspoon salt
- ½   to 1 teaspoon cayenne pepper
- 2   pounds boneless skinless chicken thighs, cut into 1-inch pieces
- 1   package (12 ounces) fully cooked andouille or other spicy chicken sausage links
- 2   pounds uncooked medium shrimp, peeled and deveined
- 8   cups hot cooked brown rice

1. In a large bowl, combine the first 13 ingredients. Place chicken and sausage in a 6-qt. slow cooker. Pour tomato mixture over top. Cook, covered, on low 7-9 hours or until chicken is tender.

2. Stir in shrimp. Cook, covered, 15-20 minutes longer or until shrimp turn pink. Serve with rice.

READY IN ④

Trout Chowder

This hearty chowder cooks conveniently on its own so I can spend more time fishing. Broccoli adds a fresh taste and a lively color to the rich cheesy broth.

—LINDA KESSELRING CORNING, NY

PREP: 15 MIN. • **COOK:** 1½ HOURS
MAKES: 6 SERVINGS

- 1   medium onion, chopped
- 1   tablespoon butter
- 2   cups whole milk
- 1   cup ranch salad dressing
- 1   pound boneless trout fillets, skin removed
- 1   package (9 ounces) frozen broccoli cuts, thawed
- 1   cup cubed or shredded cheddar cheese
- 1   cup cubed or shredded Monterey Jack cheese
- ¼   teaspoon garlic powder
     Paprika, optional

1. In a large skillet, saute onion in butter until tender. Transfer to a 3-qt. slow cooker; add the milk, dressing, fish, broccoli, cheeses and garlic powder.

2. Cover and cook on high for 1-2 hours or until soup is bubbly and fish flakes easily with a fork. Sprinkle with paprika if desired.

MEATY SLOW-COOKED JAMBALAYA

Shrimp Marinara

This marinara sauce simmers nicely on its own. For a faster version, omit the uncooked shrimp and add cooked shrimp, which merely requires heating through, shortly before mealtime. Serve it all over spaghetti for a delicious, dressed-up main dish.
—**SUE MACKEY** JACKSON, WI

PREP: 30 MIN. • **COOK:** 3 HOURS 20 MIN.
MAKES: 6 SERVINGS

- 1 can (14½ ounces) Italian diced tomatoes, undrained
- 1 can (6 ounces) tomato paste
- ½ to 1 cup water
- 2 garlic cloves, minced
- 2 tablespoons minced fresh parsley
- 1 teaspoon salt
- 1 teaspoon dried oregano
- ½ teaspoon dried basil
- ¼ teaspoon pepper
- 1 pound uncooked medium shrimp, peeled and deveined
- ¾ pound spaghetti, cooked and drained
  Shredded Parmesan cheese, optional

1. In a 3-qt. slow cooker, combine the first nine ingredients. Cover and cook on low for 3-4 hours.
2. Stir in shrimp. Cover and cook 20 minutes longer or just until shrimp turn pink. Serve with spaghetti. Sprinkle with cheese if desired.

Marty's Bean Burger Chili

My husband and I met while working the dinner shift at a homeless shelter, where they served my chili. Since then, I've updated the recipe, using veggie bean burgers.
—**MRS. MARTY NICKERSON**
ELLINGTON, CT

PREP: 15 MIN. • **COOK:** 7 HOURS
MAKES: 6 SERVINGS

- 2 cans (14½ ounces each) no-salt-added diced tomatoes, drained
- 1 can (14½ ounces) diced tomatoes, drained
- 1 can (16 ounces) kidney beans, undrained
- 1 can (15 ounces) black beans, undrained
- 1 can (15 ounces) garbanzo beans or chickpeas, rinsed and drained
- 4 frozen spicy black bean veggie burgers, thawed and coarsely chopped
- 1 large onion, finely chopped
- 1 large sweet red or green pepper, chopped
- 2 tablespoons chili powder
- 1 tablespoon Worcestershire sauce
- 3 teaspoons dried basil
- 3 teaspoons dried oregano
- 2 teaspoons hot pepper sauce
- 2 garlic cloves, minced

Place all ingredients in a 5- or 6-qt. slow cooker; stir to combine. Cook, covered, on low 7-9 hours to allow flavors to blend.

Slow Cooker Mac n Cheese

This all-time classic is a rich and cheesy meatless main dish. I've never met anyone who didn't ask for second helpings.
—**BERNICE GLASCOE** ROXBORO, NC

PREP: 15 MIN. • **COOK:** 3¾ HOURS
MAKES: 10 SERVINGS

- 1 package (16 ounces) elbow macaroni
- ½ cup butter, melted
- 4 cups (16 ounces) shredded cheddar cheese, divided
- 1 can (12 ounces) evaporated milk
- 1 can (10¾ ounces) condensed cheddar cheese soup, undiluted
- 1 cup 2% milk
- 2 large eggs, beaten
- ⅛ teaspoon paprika

1. Cook macaroni according to package directions; drain. Place in a 5-qt. slow cooker; add butter.
2. In a large bowl, mix 3 cups cheese, evaporated milk, condensed soup, 2% milk and eggs. Pour over macaroni mixture; stir to combine. Cook, covered, on low 3½-4 hours or until a thermometer reads at least 160°.
3. Sprinkle with remaining cheese. Cook, covered, on low 15-20 minutes longer or until cheese is melted. Sprinkle with paprika.

MARTY'S BEAN
BURGER CHILI

SLOW COOKER MAC N CHEESE

**CHILI & CHEESE
CRUSTLESS QUICHE**

READY IN ④

Chili & Cheese Crustless Quiche

This hearty Tex-Mex egg casserole is great for any meal of the day. I add a salad and dinner is served.

—**GAIL WATKINS** NORWALK, CA

PREP: 15 MIN.
COOK: 3 HOURS + STANDING
MAKES: 6 SERVINGS

- 3 **corn tortillas (6 inches)**
- 2 **cans (4 ounces each) whole green chilies**
- 1 **can (15 ounces) chili con carne**
- 1½ **cups (6 ounces) shredded cheddar cheese, divided**
- 4 **large eggs**
- 1½ **cups 2% milk**
- 1 **cup biscuit/baking mix**
- ¼ **teaspoon salt**
- ¼ **teaspoon pepper**
- 1 **teaspoon hot pepper sauce, optional**
- 1 **can (4 ounces) chopped green chilies**
- 2 **medium tomatoes, sliced**
  Sour cream, optional

1. In a greased 4- or 5-qt. slow cooker, layer tortillas, whole green chilies, chili con carne and 1 cup cheese.

2. In a small bowl, whisk eggs, milk, biscuit mix, salt, pepper and, if desired, pepper sauce until blended; pour into slow cooker. Top with chopped green chilies and tomatoes.

3. Cook, covered, on low 3-4 hours or until a thermometer reads 160°, sprinkling with remaining cheese during the last 30 minutes of cooking. Turn off slow cooker; remove insert. Let stand 15 minutes before serving. If desired, top with sour cream.

TOP TIP

Have a second slow cooker? Need a slow-cooked side dish to serve with this quiche? Consider Comforting Cheesy Potatoes (p. 56), Green Chili Creamed Corn (p. 59) or Easy Beans with Potatoes and Bacon (p. 63).

BARBECUE COBB SALAD

Barbecue Cobb Salad

One night, I already had some barbecue chicken in the slow cooker, but wanted to figure out how to get all my daily vegetable servings in one sitting. I decided to turn our chicken dinner into a salad. It was the perfect way to make sure my family ate all of their veggies.

—CAMILLE BECKSTRAND LAYTON, UT

PREP: 30 MIN. • **COOK:** 3 HOURS
MAKES: 6 SERVINGS

- 1 bottle (18 ounces) barbecue sauce
- 2 tablespoons brown sugar
- ½ teaspoon garlic powder
- ¼ teaspoon paprika
- 1½ pounds boneless skinless chicken breasts
- 12 cups chopped romaine
- 3 plum tomatoes, chopped
- 2 avocados, peeled and chopped
- 2 small carrots, thinly sliced
- 1 medium sweet red or green pepper, chopped
- 3 hard-cooked large eggs, chopped
- 6 bacon strips, cooked and crumbled
- 1½ cups (6 ounces) shredded cheddar cheese
  Salad dressing of your choice

1. In a greased 3-qt. slow cooker, mix barbecue sauce, brown sugar, garlic powder and paprika. Add chicken; turn to coat. Cook, covered, on low 3-4 hours or until chicken is tender (a thermometer should read at least 165°).
2. Remove chicken from slow cooker; cut into bite-size pieces. In a bowl, toss chicken with 1 cup barbecue sauce mixture. Place romaine on a large serving platter; arrange chicken, vegetables, eggs, bacon and cheese over romaine. Drizzle with dressing.

½ teaspoon salt
1½ cups vegetable or chicken broth
1 can (10¾ ounces) condensed cream of celery soup, undiluted
½ cup white wine or additional vegetable broth
1 pound cod fillets, cut into 1-inch pieces
1 can (14½ ounces) diced tomatoes, undrained
1 can (12 ounces) fat-free evaporated milk

1. In a 5-qt. slow cooker, combine the first 15 ingredients. Cook, covered, on low 6-8 hours or until potatoes are tender.
2. Remove bay leaf. Stir in cod, tomatoes and milk; cook, covered, 30-35 minutes longer or until fish just begins to flake easily with a fork.

TOP TIP

When buying fresh fish, avoid fillets that have a strong, fishy odor. Fillets and steaks should have firm flesh that has a moist look and is springy to the touch.

SLOW-COOKED FISH STEW

Slow-Cooked Fish Stew

I love fish and chowder, so this stew is a favorite of mine. It's made without cream or whole milk for a healthier take. Feel free to top servings with a little grated cheddar.
—JANE WHITTAKER PENSACOLA, FL

PREP: 25 MIN. • **COOK:** 6½ HOURS
MAKES: 8 SERVINGS (3 QUARTS)

1 pound potatoes (about 2 medium), peeled and finely chopped
1 package (10 ounces) frozen corn, thawed
1½ cups frozen lima beans, thawed
1 large onion, finely chopped
1 celery rib, finely chopped
1 medium carrot, finely chopped
4 garlic cloves, minced
1 bay leaf
1 teaspoon lemon-pepper seasoning
1 teaspoon dried parsley flakes
1 teaspoon dried rosemary, crushed

SLOW-COOKED STUFFED PEPPERS

Slow-Cooked Stuffed Peppers

I use the slow cooker more than anyone I know. I love the convenience of walking in the door and having a meal ready to go. My stuffed peppers are a favorite because they're healthy and easy: no need to parboil the peppers, as with many other recipes.
—**MICHELLE GURNSEY** LINCOLN, NE

PREP: 15 MIN. • **COOK:** 3 HOURS
MAKES: 4 SERVINGS

- 4 medium sweet red peppers
- 1 can (15 ounces) black beans, rinsed and drained
- 1 cup (4 ounces) shredded pepper jack cheese
- ¾ cup salsa
- 1 small onion, chopped
- ½ cup frozen corn
- ⅓ cup uncooked converted long grain rice
- 1¼ teaspoons chili powder
- ½ teaspoon ground cumin
  Reduced-fat sour cream, optional

1. Cut and discard tops from peppers; remove seeds. In a large bowl, mix beans, cheese, salsa, onion, corn, rice, chili powder and cumin; spoon into peppers. Place in a 5-qt. slow cooker coated with cooking spray.

2. Cook, covered, on low 3-4 hours or until peppers are tender and filling is heated through. If desired, serve with sour cream.

BREAKFAST-FOR-DINNER BAKE

CHUNKY PASTA SAUCE

LAMB WITH ORZO

Breakfast-for-Dinner Bake

I slice the potatoes for this meal-in-one the night before, but frozen potatoes work, too, for extra convenience. Of course, this recipe is great for breakfast as well. Simply let it simmer overnight.

—KIMBERLY CLARK-THIRY
MOORCROFT, WY

PREP: 15 MIN. • **COOK:** 7 HOURS
MAKES: 8 SERVINGS

- 4 pounds potatoes, peeled and thinly sliced (about 8 cups)
- 1 medium green pepper, finely chopped
- 1 package (10 ounces) frozen chopped spinach, thawed and squeezed dry
- 1 cup sliced fresh mushrooms
- 1 medium onion, finely chopped
- 8 large eggs
- 1 cup water
- 1 cup 2% milk
- 1¼ teaspoons salt
- ¼ teaspoon pepper
- 2 cups (8 ounces) shredded cheddar cheese

1. In a greased 6-qt. slow cooker, layer the first five ingredients. In a large bowl, whisk eggs, water, milk, salt and pepper; pour over top. Sprinkle with cheese.
2. Cook, covered, on low 7-9 hours or until potatoes are tender and eggs are set.

Chunky Pasta Sauce

Your kitchen will smell heavenly when you make this hearty meal. The sauce is loaded with beef, pork and lots of veggies. If you prefer a thinner sauce, add another ½ cup of water.

—CHRISTY HINRICHS PARKVILLE, MO

PREP: 25 MIN. • **COOK:** 6 HOURS
MAKES: 8 SERVINGS

- 1 pound ground beef
- ½ pound ground pork
- 2 cans (28 ounces each) diced tomatoes, undrained
- ½ to 1 cup water
- 1 can (6 ounces) tomato paste
- 1 cup chopped carrots
- 1 medium onion, cut into wedges
- 1 medium sweet red pepper, cut into 1-inch pieces
- 2 tablespoons sugar
- 2 teaspoons minced garlic
- 1 teaspoon salt
- 1 teaspoon dried basil
- 1 teaspoon dried oregano
- 1 teaspoon pepper
  Hot cooked bow tie pasta

1. In a large skillet, cook beef and pork over medium heat until no longer pink; drain.
2. Transfer to a 3-qt. slow cooker. Stir in the tomatoes, water, tomato paste, vegetables, sugar, garlic and seasonings.
3. Cover and cook on low for 6-8 hours or until vegetables are tender. Serve with pasta.

Lamb with Orzo

Looking to switch up your slow-cooker staples? Consider this lamb entree! A terrific meal-in-one, it certainly adds flair to dinnertime doldrums. Lemon juice and zesty lemon peel complement the flavors of fresh spinach and feta cheese.

—DAN KELMENSON
WEST BLOOMFIELD, MI

PREP: 30 MIN. • **COOK:** 8 -10 HOURS
MAKES: 9 SERVINGS

- 1 boneless lamb shoulder roast (3 pounds)
- 3 tablespoons lemon juice
- 3 garlic cloves, minced
- 2 teaspoons dried oregano
- 2 teaspoons grated lemon peel
- ¼ teaspoon salt
- 1 package (16 ounces) orzo pasta
- 2 packages (9 ounces each) fresh spinach, torn divided
- 1 cup (4 ounces) crumbled feta cheese, divided

1. Cut roast in half. Place in a 5-qt. slow cooker. Drizzle with lemon juice. Sprinkle with the garlic, oregano, lemon peel and salt. Cover and cook on low for 8-10 hours or until meat is tender.
2. Cook orzo according to package directions. Remove lamb from slow cooker. Shred meat with two forks; set aside and keep warm.
3. Skim fat from cooking juices if necessary; return 1 cup cooking juices to slow cooker. Add one package of spinach. Cook on high for 5-10 minutes or until spinach is wilted. Drain orzo; add to spinach mixture. Stir in reserved meat and ½ cup feta cheese.
4. To serve, arrange remaining fresh spinach on nine individual plates. Top with lamb mixture. Sprinkle each with remaining feta cheese.

Buffalo Shrimp Mac & Cheese

READY IN ④

For a rich, creamy and slightly spicy shrimp and pasta recipe, you can't beat this crowd-pleasing slow cooker dish. It's a nice new twist on popular Buffalo chicken dishes.

—**ROBIN HAAS** CRANSTON, RI

PREP: 15 MIN. • **COOK:** 3½ HOURS
MAKES: 6 SERVINGS

- 2 cups 2% milk
- 1 cup half-and-half cream
- 2 tablespoons Louisiana-style hot sauce
- 1 tablespoon butter
- 1 teaspoon ground mustard
- ½ teaspoon onion powder
- ¼ teaspoon white pepper
- ¼ teaspoon ground nutmeg
- 2 cups (8 ounces) finely shredded cheddar cheese
- 1 cup (4 ounces) shredded Gouda or Swiss cheese
- 1½ cups uncooked elbow macaroni
- ¾ pound frozen cooked salad shrimp, thawed
- 1 cup (4 ounces) crumbled blue cheese
- 2 tablespoons minced fresh chives
- 2 tablespoons minced fresh parsley
   Additional Louisiana-style hot sauce, optional

1. In a 3-qt. slow cooker, combine the first eight ingredients; stir in shredded cheeses and macaroni. Cook, covered, on low 3 to 3½ hours or until macaroni is almost tender.
2. Stir in shrimp and blue cheese; cook, covered, 30-35 minutes longer or until heated through. Just before serving, stir in chives, parsley and, if desired, additional hot sauce.

Simple Poached Salmon

EXPRESS PREP READY IN ④

I love this recipe because it's healthy and almost effortless. The salmon always cooks to perfection!

—**ERIN CHILCOAT** CENTRAL ISLIP, NY

PREP: 10 MIN. • **COOK:** 1½ HOURS
MAKES: 4 SERVINGS

- 2 cups water
- 1 cup white wine
- 1 medium onion, sliced
- 1 celery rib, sliced
- 1 medium carrot, sliced
- 2 tablespoons lemon juice
- 3 fresh thyme sprigs
- 1 fresh rosemary sprig
- 1 bay leaf
- ½ teaspoon salt
- ¼ teaspoon pepper
- 4 salmon fillets (1¼ inches thick and 6 ounces each)
   Lemon wedges

1. In a 3-qt. slow cooker, combine the first 11 ingredients. Cook, covered, on low 45 minutes.
2. Carefully place fillets in liquid; add additional warm water (120° to 130°) to cover if needed. Cook, covered, 45-55 minutes or just until fish flakes easily with a fork (a thermometer inserted in fish should read at least 145°). Remove fish from cooking liquid. Serve warm or cold with lemon wedges.

Slow Cooker Ham & Eggs

READY IN ④

This dish is great anytime of the year, but I love serving it on holiday mornings. It's basically a hands-free recipe that helps me create a fun meal for family.

—**ANDREA SCHAAK** JORDAN, MN

PREP: 15 MIN. • **COOK:** 3 HOURS
MAKES: 6 SERVINGS

- 6 large eggs
- 1 cup biscuit/baking mix
- ⅔ cup 2% milk
- ⅓ cup sour cream
- 2 tablespoons minced fresh parsley
- 2 garlic cloves, minced
- ½ teaspoon salt
- ½ teaspoon pepper
- 1 cup cubed fully cooked ham
- 1 cup (4 ounces) shredded Swiss cheese
- 1 small onion, finely chopped
- ⅓ cup shredded Parmesan cheese

1. In a large bowl, whisk the first eight ingredients until blended; stir in remaining ingredients. Pour into a greased 3- or 4-qt. slow cooker.
2. Cook, covered, on low 3-4 hours or until eggs are set. Cut into wedges.

BUFFALO SHRIMP
MAC & CHEESE

SIMPLE POACHED SALMON

SLOW COOKER
HAM & EGGS

GULF COAST JAMBALAYA RICE

READY IN ④

Gulf Coast Jambalaya Rice

As the stew of the South, jambalaya is a definite staple. For ages, home cooks have been making their own versions of the traditional recipe. This slow-cooked rendition is my personal favorite.

—JUDY BATSON TAMPA, FL

PREP: 20 MIN. • **COOK:** 3¼ HOURS
MAKES: 8 SERVINGS

- 1 **pound boneless skinless chicken breasts, cut into 1-inch cubes**
- 1 **pound smoked kielbasa, cut into ¼-inch slices**
- 2 **cups chicken stock**
- 1 **large green pepper, chopped**
- 1 **cup chopped sweet onion**
- 2 **celery ribs, chopped**
- 2 **garlic cloves, minced**
- 2 **teaspoons Creole seasoning**
- 1 **teaspoon seafood seasoning**
- 1 **teaspoon pepper**
- 1 **pound uncooked medium shrimp, peeled and deveined**
- 2 **cups uncooked instant rice**

1. Place the first 10 ingredients in a 5-qt. slow cooker. Cook, covered, on low 3-4 hours or until the chicken is tender.

2. Stir in shrimp and rice. Cook, covered, 15-20 minutes longer or until the shrimp turn pink and the rice is tender.

NOTE *The following spices may be substituted for 1 teaspoon Creole seasoning ¼ teaspoon each salt, garlic powder and paprika; and a pinch each of dried thyme, ground cumin and cayenne pepper.*

Vegetarian Red Bean Chili

For an easy vegetarian idea that even meat lovers will like, give this chili a try! I top bowls with shredded cheddar cheese.

—**CONNIE BARNETT** ATHENS, GA

PREP: 10 MIN. • **COOK:** 5 HOURS
MAKES: 6 SERVINGS (2 QUARTS)

- 1 can (16 ounces) red beans, rinsed and drained
- 2 cans (8 ounces each) no-salt-added tomato sauce
- 2 cups water
- 1 can (14½ ounces) diced tomatoes, undrained
- 1 package (12 ounces) frozen vegetarian meat crumbles
- 1 large onion, chopped
- 1 to 2 tablespoons chili powder
- 1 tablespoon ground cumin
- 2 garlic cloves, minced
- 1 teaspoon pepper
- ½ teaspoon salt
- ½ teaspoon cayenne pepper
  Sour cream and shredded cheddar cheese, optional

In a 4-qt. slow cooker, combine all ingredients. Cover and cook on low for 5-6 hours or until heated through. Serve with sour cream and cheddar cheese if desired.

NOTE *Vegetarian meat crumbles are a nutritious protein source made from soy. Look for them in the natural foods freezer section.*

Posole Verde

With fresh tomatillos, green chilies and hominy, this hearty, healthy soup nods to authentic Mexican fare. Family and friends frequently request it when they're invited for dinner.

—**GAYLE EHRENMAN** WHITE PLAINS, NY

PREP: 30 MIN. • **COOK:** 7 HOURS
MAKES: 8 SERVINGS (3 QUARTS)

- 1 pork tenderloin (1 pound), cubed
- 1 package (12 ounces) fully cooked spicy chicken sausage links, sliced
- 8 tomatillos, husks removed and cut into 1-inch pieces
- 2 cans (14 ounces each) hominy, rinsed and drained
- 1 can (16 ounces) kidney beans, rinsed and drained
- 1 can (14½ ounces) chicken broth
- 3 cans (4 ounces each) chopped green chilies
- 1 large red onion, quartered and sliced
- 2 tablespoons brown sugar
- 3 garlic cloves, minced
- 1 tablespoon ground cumin
- 1 tablespoon chili powder
- 1 teaspoon dried oregano
  Minced fresh cilantro, optional

In a 6-qt. slow cooker, combine the first 13 ingredients. Cover and cook on low for 8-10 hours or until pork is tender. Sprinkle with cilantro if desired.

VEGETARIAN RED BEAN CHILI

Slow Cook Lamb Chops

This is my favorite recipe for lamb. It's great for people who are trying lamb for the first time, since the meat turns out very tender and oh-so delicious. I decided to wrap the chops in bacon because that's how I prepare venison. I think it really enhances the flavor.

—SANDY MCKENZIE BRAHAM, MN

PREP: 10 MIN. • **COOK:** 5½ HOURS
MAKES: 4 SERVINGS

- 4 bacon strips
- 4 lamb shoulder blade chops, trimmed
- 2¼ cups thinly sliced peeled potatoes
- 1 cup thinly sliced carrots
- ½ teaspoon dried rosemary, crushed
- ¼ teaspoon garlic powder
- ¼ teaspoon salt
- ¼ teaspoon pepper
- ¼ cup chopped onion
- 2 garlic cloves, minced
- 1 can (10¾ ounces) condensed cream of mushroom soup, undiluted
- ⅓ cup 2% milk
- 1 jar (4½ ounces) sliced mushrooms, drained

1. Wrap bacon around lamb chops; secure with toothpicks. Place in a 3-qt. slow cooker. Cover and cook on high for 1½ hours.

2. Remove chops; discard toothpicks and bacon. Drain liquid from slow cooker. Add potatoes and carrots; top with lamb chops. Sprinkle with the rosemary, garlic powder, salt, pepper, onion and garlic.

3. In a small bowl, combine soup and milk. Add mushrooms. Pour over the chops. Cover and cook on low for 4-6 hours or until meat and vegetables are tender.

Deluxe Walking Nachos

This slow-cooker chili makes an awesome filling for a handheld bag of walk-around nachos. Cut the bag longways to make it easier to load up your fork.

—MALLORY LYNCH MADISON, WI

PREP: 20 MIN. • **COOK:** 6 HOURS
MAKES: 18 SERVINGS

- 1 pound lean ground beef (90% lean)
- 1 large sweet onion, chopped
- 3 garlic cloves, minced
- 2 cans (14½ ounces each) diced tomatoes with mild green chilies
- 2 cans (15 ounces each) pinto beans, rinsed and drained
- 2 cans (15 ounces each) black beans, rinsed and drained
- 2 to 3 tablespoons chili powder
- 2 teaspoons ground cumin
- ½ teaspoon salt
- 18 packages (1 ounce each) nacho-flavored tortilla chips
  Optional toppings: shredded cheddar cheese, sour cream, chopped tomatoes and pickled jalapeno slices

1. In a large skillet, cook beef, onion and garlic over medium heat 6-8 minutes or until beef is no longer pink, breaking up beef into crumbles; drain.

2. Transfer beef mixture to a 5-qt. slow cooker. Drain one can tomatoes, discarding liquid; add to slow cooker. Stir in beans, chili powder, cumin, salt and remaining tomatoes. Cook, covered, on low 6-8 hours to allow flavors to blend. Mash beans to desired consistency.

3. Just before serving, cut open tortilla chip bags. Divide chili among bags; add toppings as desired.

FREEZE OPTION *Freeze cooled chili in a freezer container. To use, partially thaw in refrigerator overnight. Heat through in a saucepan, stirring occasionally and adding a little water if necessary.*

TOP TIP

Deluxe Walking Nachos are great for camping trips, picnics, little league games and other outdoor events such as watching concerts or fireworks. Simplify the fun by heating up a can of chili, then pile on the toppings you like.

DELUXE WALKING NACHOS

SOUTHWEST ENTREE SALAD

1 **small red onion, chopped**
1 **cup fresh or frozen corn**
1 **cup (4 ounces) crumbled cotija or shredded part-skim mozzarella cheese**
Salad dressing of your choice

1. Place pork in a 5- or 6-qt. slow cooker. In a small bowl, mix cider, green chilies, garlic, salt, pepper sauce, chili powder, pepper, cumin and oregano; pour over pork. Cook, covered, on low 6-8 hours or until meat is tender.

2. Remove roast from slow cooker; discard cooking juices. Shred pork with two forks. Arrange salad greens on a large serving platter. Top with pork, black beans, tomatoes, onion, corn and cheese. Serve with salad dressing.

FREEZE OPTION *Place shredded pork in a freezer container; top with cooking juices. Cool and freeze. To use, partially thaw in refrigerator overnight. Heat through in a saucepan, stirring occasionally.*

TOP TIP

When a recipe calls for a small amount of apple juice, turn to juice boxes. Unlike a large bottle of open juice, the extra boxes store nicely in the pantry and don't take up room in the refrigerator. You'll have juice on hand for future recipes.

Southwest Entree Salad

I make a knockout shredded pork, served in tortillas. Sometimes, however, I like to turn it into a hearty salad of pork, greens, black beans and other Southwestern sprinklings.
—**MARY SHIVERS** ADA, OK

PREP: 20 MIN. • **COOK:** 6 HOURS
MAKES: 12 SERVINGS

1 **boneless pork loin roast (3 to 4 pounds)**
1½ **cups apple cider or juice**
1 **can (4 ounces) chopped green chilies, drained**
3 **garlic cloves, minced**
1½ **teaspoons salt**
1½ **teaspoons hot pepper sauce**
1 **teaspoon chili powder**
1 **teaspoon pepper**
½ **teaspoon ground cumin**
½ **teaspoon dried oregano**
12 **cups torn mixed salad greens**
1 **can (15 ounces) black beans, rinsed and drained**
2 **medium tomatoes, chopped**

Easy Slow Cooker Mac & Cheese

My sons always cheer, "You're the best mom in the world!" whenever I make this creamy mac and cheese perfection. You just can't beat a response like that!

—**HEIDI FLEEK** HAMBURG, PA

PREP: 25 MIN. • **COOK:** 1 HOUR
MAKES: 8 SERVINGS

- 2 cups uncooked elbow macaroni
- 1 can (10¾ ounces) condensed cheddar cheese soup, undiluted
- 1 cup 2% milk
- ½ cup sour cream
- ¼ cup butter, cubed
- ½ teaspoon onion powder
- ¼ teaspoon white pepper
- ⅛ teaspoon salt
- 1 cup (4 ounces) shredded cheddar cheese
- 1 cup (4 ounces) shredded fontina cheese
- 1 cup (4 ounces) shredded provolone cheese

1. Cook macaroni according to package directions for al dente. Meanwhile, in a large saucepan, combine soup, milk, sour cream, butter and seasonings; cook and stir over medium-low heat until blended. Stir in the cheeses until well melted.
2. Drain macaroni; transfer to a greased 3-qt. slow cooker. Stir in cheese mixture. Cook, covered, on low 1-2 hours or until heated through.

EASY SLOW COOKER MAC & CHEESE

EYE-OPENING BURRITOS

PASTA E FAGIOLI

CREAMY MUSHROOMS & POTATOES

Eye-Opening Burritos

When I serve my hearty burritos, I like to use a second slow cooker to keep the tortillas warm and pliable. Just place a clean wet cloth in the bottom, then cover it with foil and add your tortillas.
—**BETH OSBURN** LEVELLAND, TX

PREP: 30 MIN. • **COOK:** 4 HOURS
MAKES: 10 SERVINGS

- 1 pound bulk pork sausage, cooked and drained
- ½ pound bacon strips, cooked and crumbled
- 18 large eggs, lightly beaten
- 2 cups frozen shredded hash brown potatoes, thawed
- 1 large onion, chopped
- 1 can (10¾ ounces) condensed cheddar cheese soup, undiluted
- 1 can (4 ounces) chopped green chilies
- 1 teaspoon garlic powder
- ½ teaspoon pepper
- 2 cups (8 ounces) shredded cheddar cheese
- 10 flour tortillas (10 inches), warmed
    Optional toppings: jalapeno peppers, salsa or hot pepper sauce

1. In a large bowl, combine the first nine ingredients. Pour half of the egg mixture into a 4- or 5-qt. slow cooker coated with cooking spray. Top with half of the cheese. Repeat layers.
2. Cook, covered, on low 4-5 hours or until center is set and a thermometer reads 160°.
3. Spoon ¾ cup egg mixture across center of each tortilla. Fold bottom and sides of tortilla over filling and roll up. Add toppings of your choice.

Pasta e Fagioli

This is my favorite soup because it's hearty, healthy and full of flavor. It always turns out thick and delicious.
—**PENNY NOVY** BUFFALO GROVE, IL

PREP: 30 MIN. • **COOK:** 7½ HOURS
MAKES: 8 SERVINGS (2½ QUARTS)

- 1 pound ground beef
- 1 medium onion, chopped
- 1 carton (32 ounces) chicken broth
- 2 cans (14½ ounces each) diced tomatoes, undrained
- 1 can (15 ounces) white kidney or cannellini beans, rinsed and drained
- 2 medium carrots, chopped
- 1½ cups finely chopped cabbage
- 1 celery rib, chopped
- 2 tablespoons minced fresh basil or 2 teaspoons dried basil
- 2 garlic cloves, minced
- ½ teaspoon salt
- ½ teaspoon pepper
- 1 cup ditalini or other small pasta
    Grated Parmesan cheese, optional

1. In a large skillet, cook beef and onion over medium heat until beef is no longer pink and onion is tender; drain.
2. Transfer to a 4- or 5-qt. slow cooker. Stir in the broth, tomatoes, beans, carrots, cabbage, celery, basil, garlic, salt and pepper. Cover and cook on low for 7-8 hours or until vegetables are tender.
3. Stir in pasta. Cover and cook on high 30 minutes longer or until pasta is tender. Sprinkle with cheese if desired.

Creamy Mushrooms & Potatoes

I like this comforting main dish because it uses only a handful of ingredients and simmers on its own in the slow cooker. Best of all, folks always come back for seconds!
—**TRACI MEADOWS** MONETT, MO

PREP: 25 MIN. • **COOK:** 4 HOURS
MAKES: 4 SERVINGS

- 1 can (10¾ ounces) condensed cream of mushroom soup, undiluted
- ½ cup 2% milk
- 1 tablespoon dried parsley flakes
- 6 medium potatoes, peeled and thinly sliced
- 1 small onion, chopped
- 1½ cups cubed fully cooked ham
- 6 slices process American cheese

In a small bowl, combine the soup, milk and parsley. In a greased 3-qt. slow cooker, layer half of the potatoes, onion, ham, cheese and soup mixture. Repeat layers. Cover and cook on low for 4-5 hours or until potatoes are tender.

AFRICAN PEANUT
SWEET POTATO STEW

African Peanut Sweet Potato Stew

When I was in college, my mom made an amazing sweet potato stew. I shared it with friends, and now all of us serve it to our own kids. They all love it as well!

—**ALEXIS SCATCHELL** NILES, IL

PREP: 20 MIN. • **COOK:** 6 HOURS
MAKES: 8 SERVINGS (2½ QUARTS)

- 1 **can (28 ounces) diced tomatoes, undrained**
- 1 **cup fresh cilantro leaves**
- ½ **cup chunky peanut butter**
- 3 **garlic cloves, halved**
- 2 **teaspoons ground cumin**
- 1 **teaspoon salt**
- ½ **teaspoon ground cinnamon**
- ¼ **teaspoon smoked paprika**
- 3 **pounds sweet potatoes (about 6 medium), peeled and cut into 1-inch pieces**
- 1 **can (15 ounces) garbanzo beans or chickpeas, rinsed and drained**
- 1 **cup water**
- 8 **cups chopped fresh kale Chopped peanuts and additional cilantro leaves, optional**

1. Place the first eight ingredients in a food processor; process until pureed. Transfer to a 5-qt. slow cooker; stir in sweet potatoes, beans and water.

2. Cook, covered, on low 6-8 hours or until potatoes are tender, adding kale during the last 30 minutes. If desired, top each serving with chopped peanuts and additional cilantro.

TOP TIP

Select sweet potatoes that are firm with no cracks or bruises. If stored in a cool, dark, well-ventilated place, they'll remain fresh for about 2 weeks. If the temperature is above 60°, they'll sprout sooner or become woody. Once cooked, sweet potatoes can be stored for up to 1 week in the refrigerator.

ITALIAN SHRIMP 'N' PASTA

Italian Shrimp 'n' Pasta

I love this change-of-pace dinner. The shrimp, orzo, tomatoes and cayenne pepper remind me of a Creole dish, but the Italian seasoning adds a different twist. The strips of chicken thighs stay nice and moist during the slow cooking.

—KAREN EDWARDS SANFORD, ME

PREP: 10 MIN. • **COOK:** 7⅓ HOURS
MAKES: 6-8 SERVINGS

- 1 **pound boneless skinless chicken thighs, cut into 2x1-in. strips**
- 2 **tablespoons canola oil**
- 1 **can (28 ounces) crushed tomatoes**
- 2 **celery ribs, chopped**
- 1 **medium green pepper, cut into 1-inch pieces**
- 1 **medium onion, coarsely chopped**
- 2 **garlic cloves, minced**
- 1 **tablespoon sugar**
- ½ **teaspoon salt**
- ½ **teaspoon Italian seasoning**
- ⅛ to ¼ **teaspoon cayenne pepper**
- 1 **bay leaf**
- ½ **cup uncooked orzo pasta or other small pasta**
- 1 **pound cooked medium shrimp, peeled and deveined**

1. In a large skillet, brown chicken in oil; transfer to a 3-qt. slow cooker. Stir in the next 10 ingredients. Cover and cook on low for 7-8 hours or until chicken is no longer pink.

2. Discard bay leaf. Stir in pasta; cover and cook on high for 15 minutes or until pasta is tender. Stir in shrimp; cover and cook for 5 minutes longer or until heated through.

Autumn Pumpkin Chili

I've prepared this chili often, and everyone loves it, even my most finicky grandchildren. It's earned thumbs up with family and friends, so it's a definite "keeper" in my book!

—**KIMBERLY NAGY** PORT HADLOCK, WA

PREP: 20 MIN. • **COOK:** 7 HOURS
MAKES: 4 SERVINGS

- 1 **medium onion, chopped**
- 1 **small green pepper, chopped**
- 1 **small sweet yellow pepper, chopped**
- 1 **tablespoon canola oil**
- 1 **garlic clove, minced**
- 1 **pound ground turkey**
- 1 **can (15 ounces) solid-pack pumpkin**
- 1 **can (14½ ounces) diced tomatoes, undrained**
- 4½ **teaspoons chili powder**
- ¼ **teaspoon pepper**
- ¼ **teaspoon salt**
    Optional toppings: shredded cheddar cheese, sour cream and sliced green onions

1. Saute the onion and green and yellow peppers in oil in a large skillet until tender. Add garlic; cook 1 minute longer. Crumble turkey into skillet. Cook over medium heat until meat is no longer pink.
2. Transfer to a 3-qt. slow cooker. Stir in the pumpkin, tomatoes, chili powder, pepper and salt. Cover and cook on low for 7-9 hours. Serve with toppings.

Spicy Seafood Stew

This zippy stew is very easy and quick to prepare. The hardest part is peeling and dicing the potatoes, and even that can be done the night before. Place peeled potatoes in water and store them in the fridge.

—**BONNIE MARLOW** OTTOVILLE, OH

PREP: 30 MIN. • **COOK:** 4¾ HOURS
MAKES: 9 SERVINGS

- 2 **pounds potatoes, peeled and diced**
- 1 **pound carrots, sliced**
- 1 **jar (26 ounces) spaghetti sauce**
- 2 **jars (6 ounces each) sliced mushrooms, drained**
- 1½ **teaspoons ground turmeric**
- 1½ **teaspoons minced garlic**
- 1 **teaspoon cayenne pepper**
- ¾ **teaspoon salt**
- 1½ **cups water**
- 1 **pound sea scallops**
- 1 **pound uncooked medium shrimp, peeled and deveined**

1. In a 5-qt. slow cooker, combine the first eight ingredients. Cover and cook on low for 4½-5 hours or until potatoes are tender.
2. Stir in the water, scallops and shrimp. Cover and cook for 15-20 minutes or until scallops are opaque and shrimp turn pink.

Spicy Hash Brown Supper

I love to develop my own recipes. My family and our friends from church are my favorite and most honest critics, and they love this meal!

—**ANGELA SHERIDAN** OPDYKE, IL

PREP: 15 MIN. • **COOK:** 5 HOURS
MAKES: 9 SERVINGS

- 1 **pound bulk spicy pork sausage**
- 1 **package (30 ounces) frozen shredded hash brown potatoes, thawed**
- 2 **cups (16 ounces) sour cream**
- 1 **jar (16 ounces) double-cheddar cheese sauce**
- 2 **cans (4 ounces each) chopped green chilies**
- ½ **teaspoon crushed red pepper flakes**

In a large skillet, cook sausage over medium heat until no longer pink; drain. Transfer to a 4-qt. slow cooker. Stir in the remaining ingredients. Cover and cook on low for 5-6 hours or until heated through.
NOTE *This recipe was tested with Ragu double-cheddar cheese sauce.*

DID YOU KNOW?

A stew is defined by the cooking technique, not the ingredients. Any dish prepared by simmering food in liquid in a covered pot for a long period of time is considered stew. The term usually refers to a main dish that contains meat, vegetables and a thick broth made from the cooking juices. Goulash, for instance, is a Hungarian stew made with meat and vegetables, and seasoned with paprika.

AUTUMN PUMPKIN CHILI

SPICY SEAFOOD STEW

SPICY HASH BROWN SUPPER

Cheesy Tater Tot Dinner

This slow-cooker meal pays homage to my favorite style of pizza, Hawaiian with bacon and pineapple. The Tater Tots make it kid-friendly.

—**LISA RENSHAW** KANSAS CITY, MO

PREP: 15 MIN.
COOK: 4 HOURS + STANDING
MAKES: 8 SERVINGS

- 1 package (32 ounces) frozen Tater Tots, thawed
- 8 ounces Canadian bacon, chopped
- 1 cup frozen pepper strips, thawed and chopped
- 1 medium onion, finely chopped
- 1 can (8 ounces) pineapple tidbits, drained
- 2 large eggs
- 3 cans (5 ounces each) evaporated milk
- 1 can (15 ounces) pizza sauce
- 1 cup (4 ounces) shredded provolone cheese
- ½ cup grated Parmesan cheese, optional

1. Place half of the Tater Tots in a greased 5-qt. slow cooker. Layer with Canadian bacon, peppers, onion and pineapple. Top with remaining Tater Tots. In a large bowl, whisk eggs, milk and pizza sauce; pour over top. Sprinkle with provolone cheese.

2. Cook, covered, on low 4-5 hours or until heated through. If desired, sprinkle with Parmesan cheese; let stand, covered, 20 minutes.

EXPRESS PREP **READY IN ④**

Tangy Venison Stroganoff

A silky sour cream sauce tops tender chunks of venison and chopped onion in this delightful change-of-pace dish, ideal for an autumn dinner.

—**ELLEN SPES** CARO, MI

PREP: 10 MIN. • **COOK:** 3¾ HOURS
MAKES: 4 SERVINGS

- 1½ pounds boneless venison steak, cubed
- 1 medium onion, sliced
- 1 can (10½ ounces) condensed beef broth, undiluted
- 1 tablespoon Worcestershire sauce
- 1 tablespoon ketchup
- 1 teaspoon curry powder
- ½ teaspoon ground ginger
- ½ teaspoon salt
- ¼ teaspoon pepper
- 4½ teaspoons cornstarch
- ½ cup sour cream
- 2 tablespoons prepared horseradish
  Hot cooked noodles

1. Place venison and onion in a 3-qt. slow cooker. Combine the next seven ingredients; pour over venison. Cover and cook on high for 3 to 3½ hours or until meat is tender.

2. In a small bowl, combine the cornstarch, sour cream and horseradish. Gradually stir into venison mixture. Cover and cook 15 minutes longer or until sauce is thickened. Serve with noodles.

EXPRESS PREP

Slow Cooker Salmon Loaf

I'm always looking for quick, easy recipes that can be prepared ahead of time. I also don't like to heat up my oven during our hot Georgia summers. I adapted this recipe from one I found in an old slow-cooker book of my grandma's. I serve it with macaroni and cheese and no-fuss pinto beans.

—**KELLY RITTER** DOUGLASVILLE, GA

PREP: 10 MIN. • **COOK:** 4 HOURS
MAKES: 6 SERVINGS

- 2 large eggs, lightly beaten
- 2 cups seasoned stuffing croutons
- 1 cup chicken broth
- 1 cup grated Parmesan cheese
- ¼ teaspoon ground mustard
- 1 can (14¾ ounces) salmon, drained, bones and skin removed

1. Cut three 20x3-in. strips of heavy duty foil; crisscross so they resemble spokes of a wheel. Place strips on the bottom and up the sides of a 3-qt. slow cooker coated with cooking spray.

2. In a large bowl, combine the first five ingredients. Add salmon and mix well. Gently shape mixture into a round loaf. Place in the center of the strips.

3. Cover and cook on low for 4-6 hours or until a thermometer reads 160°. Using foil strips as handles, remove the loaf to a platter.

CINNAMON–RAISIN BANANA BREAD PUDDING, 208

210

202

190

Swift Sweets

It's easy to surprise your family with a weekday dessert when you let the slow cooker do the work. Loaded with lip-smacking appeal, these luscious treats will be on the menu time and again.

MOLTEN MOCHA CAKE, 193

CINNAMON-APPLE
BROWN BETTY

READY IN ④

Cinnamon-Apple Brown Betty

If I had to define the "Betty" of Apple Brown Betty, she'd be a smart and thrifty Southern gal with a knack for creating simple, soul-comforting desserts. In this sweet dish, spiced apples are slow-cooked between layers of cinnamon-raisin bread cubes for a wonderful twist on the traditional oven-baked classic.

—HEATHER DEMERITTE
SCOTTSDALE, AZ

PREP: 15 MIN. • **COOK:** 2 HOURS
MAKES: 6 SERVINGS

- 5 medium tart apples, cubed
- 2 tablespoons lemon juice
- 1 cup packed brown sugar
- 1 teaspoon ground cinnamon
- ¼ teaspoon ground nutmeg
- 6 cups cubed day-old cinnamon-raisin bread (about 10 slices)
- 6 tablespoons butter, melted
  Sweetened whipped cream, optional

1. In a large bowl, toss apples with lemon juice. In a small bowl, mix brown sugar, cinnamon and nutmeg; add to apple mixture and toss to coat. In a large bowl, drizzle butter over bread cubes; toss to coat.

2. Place 2 cups bread cubes in a greased 3- or 4-qt. slow cooker. Layer with half of the apple mixture and 2 cups bread cubes. Repeat layers. Cook, covered, on low 2-3 hours or until apples are tender. Stir before serving. If desired, top with whipped cream.

Pumpkin Pie Pudding

My husband loves anything pumpkin, and this creamy, comforting dessert is one of his favorites. Although we make the super-easy pudding all year long, it's especially nice in the fall.

—**ANDREA SCHAAK** BLOOMINGTON, MN

PREP: 10 MIN. • **COOK:** 6 HOURS
MAKES: 6 SERVINGS

- 1 can (15 ounces) solid-pack pumpkin
- 1 can (12 ounces) evaporated milk
- ¾ cup sugar
- ½ cup biscuit/baking mix
- 2 large eggs, beaten
- 2 tablespoons butter, melted
- 2½ teaspoons pumpkin pie spice
- 2 teaspoons vanilla extract
  Whipped topping, optional

1. In a large bowl, combine the first eight ingredients. Transfer to a 3-qt. slow cooker coated with cooking spray.
2. Cover and cook on low for 6-7 hours or until a thermometer reads 160°. Serve in bowls with whipped topping if desired.

Crunchy Candy Clusters

Before I retired, I took these yummy peanut butter bites to work for special occasions. I still make them for holidays because my family looks forward to the coated cereal and marshmallow treats.

—**FAYE O'BRYAN** OWENSBORO, KY

PREP: 15 MIN. • **COOK:** 1 HOUR
MAKES: 6½ DOZEN

- 2 pounds white candy coating, coarsely chopped
- 1½ cups peanut butter
- ½ teaspoon almond extract, optional
- 4 cups Cap'n Crunch cereal
- 4 cups crisp rice cereal
- 4 cups miniature marshmallows

1. Place candy coating in a 5-qt. slow cooker. Cover and cook on high for 1 hour. Add peanut butter. Stir in extract if desired.
2. In a large bowl, combine the cereals and marshmallows. Stir in the peanut butter mixture until well coated.
3. Drop by tablespoonfuls onto waxed paper. Let stand until set. Store at room temperature.

PUMPKIN PIE PUDDING

EXPRESS PREP | READY IN ④
Chocolate Pecan Fondue

When our kids have sleepovers, I like to surprise them with this chocolate treat. Our favorite dippers include fruit, marshmallows, cookies and pound cake.
—**SUZANNE MCKINLEY** LYONS, GA

START TO FINISH: 15 MIN.
MAKES: 1⅓ CUPS

- ½ cup half-and-half cream
- 2 tablespoons honey
- 9 ounces semisweet chocolate, broken into small pieces
- ¼ cup finely chopped pecans
- 1 teaspoon vanilla extract
  Fresh fruit and shortbread cookies

1. In a heavy saucepan over low heat, combine cream and honey; heat until warm. Add chocolate; stir until melted. Stir in pecans and vanilla.
2. Transfer to a fondue pot or a 1½-qt. slow cooker and keep warm. Serve with fruit and cookies.

Hot Caramel Apples

Who ever thought you could make such a delicious dessert in a slow cooker? This old-time favorite goes together quickly, and it's such a treat to come home to the comforting aroma of cinnamon baked apples.
—**PAT SPARKS** ST. CHARLES, MO

PREP: 15 MIN. • **COOK:** 4 HOURS
MAKES: 4 SERVINGS

- 4 large tart apples, cored
- ½ cup apple juice
- ½ cup packed brown sugar
- 12 Red Hots
- ¼ cup butter
- 8 caramels
- ¼ teaspoon ground cinnamon
  Whipped cream, optional

1. Peel about ¾ in. off the top of each apple; place in a 3-qt. slow cooker. Pour juice over apples. Fill the center of each apple with 2 tablespoons of sugar, three Red Hots, 1 tablespoon butter and two caramels. Sprinkle with cinnamon.
2. Cover and cook on low for 4-6 hours or until the apples are tender. Serve immediately with whipped cream if desired.

DID YOU KNOW?

If the word "chopped" comes before the ingredient when listed in a recipe, then chop the ingredient before measuring. If the word "chopped" comes after the ingredient, then chop after measuring. Using the example of "¼ cup chopped nuts," you should chop the nuts first, and then measure out ¼ cup.

EXPRESS PREP | READY IN ④
Burgundy Pears

These warm spiced pears elevate slow cooking to a new level of elegance, yet they're incredibly easy to make. Your friends won't believe this fancy-looking dessert came from a slow cooker.
—**ELIZABETH HANES** PERALTA, NM

PREP: 10 MIN. • **COOK:** 3 HOURS
MAKES: 6 SERVINGS

- 6 medium ripe pears
- ⅓ cup sugar
- ⅓ cup Burgundy wine or grape juice
- 3 tablespoons orange marmalade
- 1 tablespoon lemon juice
- ¼ teaspoon ground cinnamon
- ¼ teaspoon ground nutmeg
  Dash salt
  Vanilla ice cream

1. Peel pears, leaving stems intact. Core from the bottom. Stand pears upright in a 5-qt. slow cooker. In a small bowl, combine the sugar, wine or grape juice, marmalade, lemon juice, cinnamon, nutmeg and salt. Carefully pour over pears.
2. Cover and cook on low for 3-4 hours or until tender. To serve, drizzle pears with sauce and garnish with vanilla ice cream.

HOT CARAMEL APPLES

BURGUNDY PEARS

**CHOCOLATE
PEANUT DROPS**

**APPLE-NUT BREAD
PUDDING**

(5) INGREDIENTS READY IN (4)

Chocolate Peanut Drops

I was surprised these chocolate candies came from a slow cooker. You can get several dozen candies from one batch, making them ideal for gift-giving.

—ANITA BELL HERMITAGE, TN

PREP: 20 MIN.
COOK: 1½ HOURS + STANDING
MAKES: ABOUT 11 DOZEN

- 4 ounces German sweet chocolate, chopped
- 1 package (12 ounces) semisweet chocolate chips
- 4 packages (10 to 12 ounces each) white baking chips
- 2 jars (16 ounces each) lightly salted dry roasted peanuts

1. In a 6-qt. slow cooker, layer ingredients in order listed (do not stir). Cover and cook on low for 1½ hours. Stir to combine. (If chocolate is not melted, cover and cook 15 minutes longer; stir. Repeat in 15-minute increments until chocolate is melted.)

2. Drop mixture by rounded tablespoonfuls onto waxed paper. Let stand until set. Store in an airtight container at room temperature.

CHOCOLATE PEANUT BARK *Cook chocolate mixture as directed; spread into two 15x10x1-in. waxed paper-lined baking pans. Refrigerate 30 minutes or until firm. Cut into bite-sized pieces.*

EXPRESS PREP READY IN (4)

Apple-Nut Bread Pudding

Traditional bread pudding gives way to autumn's influences in this comforting dessert. I add apples and pecans to my slow-cooked version, then top warm servings with a little bit of vanilla ice cream.

—LORI FOX MENOMONEE FALLS, WI

PREP: 10 MIN. • **COOK:** 3 HOURS
MAKES: 6-8 SERVINGS

- 8 slices cinnamon-raisin bread, cubed
- 2 medium tart apples, peeled and sliced
- 1 cup chopped pecans, toasted
- 1 cup sugar
- 1 teaspoon ground cinnamon
- ½ teaspoon ground nutmeg
- 3 large eggs, lightly beaten
- 2 cups half-and-half cream
- ¼ cup apple juice
- ¼ cup butter, melted
  Vanilla ice cream

Place bread cubes, apples and pecans in a greased 3-qt. slow cooker. In a bowl, combine the sugar, cinnamon and nutmeg. Add the eggs, cream, apple juice and butter; mix well. Pour over bread mixture. Cover and cook on low for 3-4 hours or until a knife inserted in the center comes out clean. Serve with ice cream.

CHOCOLATE
PUDDING CAKE

Chocolate Pudding Cake

For a rich, fudgy dessert that's a cross between pudding and cake, try this. I like to serve it warm with a scoop of vanilla ice cream.

—**PAIGE ARNETTE** LAWRENCEVILLE, GA

PREP: 10 MIN. • **COOK:** 6 HOURS
MAKES: 10-12 SERVINGS

- 1 **package chocolate cake mix (regular size)**
- 1 **package (3.9 ounces) instant chocolate pudding mix**
- 2 **cups (16 ounces) sour cream**
- 4 **large eggs**
- 1 **cup water**
- ¾ **cup canola oil**
- 1 **cup (6 ounces) semisweet chocolate chips**
  Whipped cream or ice cream, optional

1. In a large bowl, combine the first six ingredients; beat on low speed for 30 seconds. Beat on medium for 2 minutes. Stir in chocolate chips. Pour into a greased 5-qt. slow cooker.
2. Cover and cook on low for 6-8 hours or until a toothpick inserted near the center comes out with moist crumbs. Serve in bowls with whipped cream or ice cream if desired.

MOLTEN
MOCHA CAKE

APPLE-PEAR
COMPOTE

CLASSIC
BANANAS
FOSTER

Molten Mocha Cake

My daughter says this cake is one of her favorite desserts. I once shared the cake with my neighbor's son. He liked it so much that he ate the whole thing without telling anyone about it!

—**AIMEE FORTNEY** FAIRVIEW, TN

PREP: 10 MIN. • **COOK:** 2½ HOURS
MAKES: 4 SERVINGS

- 4 **large eggs**
- 1½ **cups sugar**
- ½ **cup butter, melted**
- 3 **teaspoons vanilla extract**
- 1 **cup all-purpose flour**
- ½ **cup baking cocoa**
- 1 **tablespoon instant coffee granules**
- ¼ **teaspoon salt**
  Fresh raspberries or sliced fresh strawberries and vanilla ice cream, optional

1. In a large bowl, beat eggs, sugar, butter and vanilla until blended. In another bowl, whisk flour, cocoa, coffee granules and salt; gradually beat into egg mixture.

2. Transfer to greased 1½-qt. slow cooker. Cook, covered, on low 2½-3 hours or until a toothpick comes out with moist crumbs. If desired, serve warm cake with berries and ice cream.

Apple-Pear Compote

Apples and pears are popular fruits, so this treat is great for brunch buffets. For a tasty addition, I like to add raisins or chopped nuts to the compote. Sometimes I even stir in 1/3 cup brandy or rum.

—**NANCY HEISHMAN** LAS VEGAS, NV

PREP: 20 MIN. • **COOK:** 3¼ HOURS
MAKES: 8 CUPS

- 5 **medium apples, peeled and chopped**
- 3 **medium pears, chopped**
- 1 **medium orange, thinly sliced**
- ½ **cup dried cranberries**
- ½ **cup packed brown sugar**
- ½ **cup maple syrup**
- ⅓ **cup butter, cubed**
- 2 **tablespoons lemon juice**
- 2 **teaspoons ground cinnamon**
- 1 **teaspoon ground ginger**
- 5 **tablespoons orange juice, divided**
- 4 **teaspoons cornstarch**
  Sweetened whipped cream and toasted chopped pecans, optional

1. In a 4- or 5-qt. slow cooker, combine the first 10 ingredients. Stir in 2 tablespoons orange juice. Cook, covered, on low 3-4 hours or until fruit is tender.

2. In a small bowl, mix cornstarch and remaining orange juice until smooth; gradually stir into fruit mixture. Cook, covered, on high 15-20 minutes longer or until sauce is thickened. If desired, top with whipped cream and pecans.

FREEZE OPTION *Freeze cooled compote in freezer containers. To use, partially thaw in refrigerator overnight. Heat through in a saucepan, stirring occasionally and adding a little orange juice if necessary.*

Classic Bananas Foster

The flavors of caramel, rum and walnut naturally complement fresh bananas in this classic dessert made easy! It's my go-to choice for any family get-together.

—**CRYSTAL JO BRUNS** ILIFF, CO

PREP: 10 MIN. • **COOK:** 2 HOURS
MAKES: 5 SERVINGS

- 5 **medium firm bananas**
- 1 **cup packed brown sugar**
- ¼ **cup butter, melted**
- ¼ **cup rum**
- 1 **teaspoon vanilla extract**
- ½ **teaspoon ground cinnamon**
- ⅓ **cup chopped walnuts**
- ⅓ **cup flaked coconut**
  Vanilla ice cream or sliced pound cake

1. Cut bananas in half lengthwise, then widthwise; layer in the bottom of a 1½-qt. slow cooker.

2. Combine the brown sugar, butter, rum, vanilla and cinnamon; pour over bananas. Cover and cook on low for 1½ hours or until heated through.

3. Sprinkle with walnuts and coconut; cook 30 minutes longer. Serve with ice cream or pound cake.

**SLOW-COOKER
BREAD PUDDING**

Fruit Dessert Topping

You'll quickly warm up to the old-fashioned taste of this fruit topping! I like to spoon it over vanilla ice cream or slices of pound cake.
—**DORIS HEATH** FRANKLIN, NC

PREP: 10 MIN. • **COOK:** 3½ HOURS
MAKES: ABOUT 6 CUPS

- 3 **medium tart apples, peeled and sliced**
- 3 **medium pears, peeled and sliced**
- 1 **tablespoon lemon juice**
- ½ **cup packed brown sugar**
- ½ **cup maple syrup**
- ¼ **cup butter, melted**
- ½ **cup chopped pecans**
- ¼ **cup raisins**
- 2 **cinnamon sticks (3 inches)**
- 1 **tablespoon cornstarch**
- 2 **tablespoons cold water**
  Pound cake or ice cream

1. In a 3-qt. slow cooker, toss apples and pears with lemon juice. Combine the brown sugar, maple syrup and butter; pour over fruit. Stir in the pecans, raisins and cinnamon sticks. Cover and cook on low for 3-4 hours.

2. Combine cornstarch and water until smooth; gradually stir into slow cooker. Cover and cook on high for 30-40 minutes or until thickened. Discard cinnamon sticks. Serve with pound cake or ice cream.

Slow-Cooker Bread Pudding

A slow cooker turns day-old cinnamon rolls into a comforting, old-fashioned dessert. It tastes wonderful topped with lemon or vanilla sauce or whipped cream.
—**EDNA HOFFMAN** HEBRON, IN

PREP: 15 MIN. • **COOK:** 3 HOURS
MAKES: 6 SERVINGS

- 8 **cups cubed day-old unfrosted cinnamon rolls**
- 4 **large eggs**
- 2 **cups milk**
- ¼ **cup sugar**
- ¼ **cup butter, melted**
- ½ **teaspoon vanilla extract**
- ¼ **teaspoon ground nutmeg**
- 1 **cup raisins**

Place cubed cinnamon rolls in a 3-qt. slow cooker. In a small bowl, whisk the eggs, milk, sugar, butter, vanilla and nutmeg. Stir in raisins. Pour over cinnamon rolls; stir gently. Cover and cook on low for 3 hours or until a knife inserted near the center comes out clean.
NOTE *8 slices of cinnamon or white bread, cut into 1-inch cubes, may be substituted for the cinnamon rolls.*

Strawberry Rhubarb Sauce

This tart and tangy fruit sauce is excellent over pound cake or ice cream. I've served this rosy-colored mixture many times and gotten rave reviews from friends and family.

—JUDITH WASMAN
HARKERS ISLAND, NC

PREP: 10 MIN. • **COOK:** 6 HOURS
MAKES: 10 SERVINGS

- 6 **cups chopped rhubarb (½-inch pieces)**
- 1 **cup sugar**
- ½ **teaspoon grated orange peel**
- ½ **teaspoon ground ginger**
- 1 **cinnamon stick (3 inches)**
- ½ **cup white grape juice**
- 2 **cups halved unsweetened strawberries**
  Angel food cake, pound cake or vanilla ice cream

1. Place rhubarb in a 3-qt. slow cooker. Combine sugar, orange peel and ginger; sprinkle over rhubarb. Add cinnamon stick and grape juice. Cover and cook on low for 5-6 hours or until rhubarb is tender.

2. Stir in strawberries; cook 1 hour longer. Discard cinnamon stick. Serve with cake or ice cream.

STRAWBERRY RHUBARB SAUCE

WARM STRAWBERRY FONDUE

Glazed Cinnamon Apples

If you are seeking comfort food on the sweet side, this warm and yummy apple dessert made with cinnamon and nutmeg fits the bill.

—MEGAN MAZE OAK CREEK, WI

PREP: 20 MIN. • **COOK:** 3 HOURS
MAKES: 7 SERVINGS

- 6 **large tart apples**
- 2 **tablespoons lemon juice**
- ½ **cup packed brown sugar**
- ½ **cup sugar**
- 2 **tablespoons all-purpose flour**
- 1 **teaspoon ground cinnamon**
- ¼ **teaspoon ground nutmeg**
- 6 **tablespoons butter, melted**
  Vanilla ice cream

1. Peel, core and cut each apple into eight wedges; transfer to a 3-qt. slow cooker. Drizzle with lemon juice. Combine the sugars, flour, cinnamon and nutmeg; sprinkle over apples. Drizzle with butter.

2. Cover and cook on low for 3-4 hours or until apples are tender. Serve in dessert dishes with ice cream.

TOP TIP

When cooking apples in a slow cooker, look for those that hold their shape with a firm flesh. Varieties such as Empire, Fuji, Golden Delicious, Jonagold, Rome Beauty and Royal Gala are good choices.

---

⑤ **INGREDIENTS** *EXPRESS* PREP
READY IN ④

Warm Strawberry Fondue

You only need a handful of ingredients to fix this refreshing fondue. Use grapes, bananas, strawberries and angel food cake cubes as dippers.

—SHARON MENSING GREENFIELD, IA

START TO FINISH: 15 MIN.
MAKES: 1½ CUPS

- 1 **package (10 ounces) frozen sweetened sliced strawberries, thawed**
- ¼ **cup half-and-half cream**
- 1 **teaspoon cornstarch**
- ½ **teaspoon lemon juice**
  Angel food cake cubes and fresh fruit

1. In a food processor, combine the strawberries, cream, cornstarch and lemon juice; cover and process until smooth.

2. Pour into saucepan. Bring to a boil; cook and stir for 2 minutes or until slightly thickened. Transfer to a fondue pot or 1½-qt. slow cooker; keep warm. Serve with cake and fruit.

Gooey Peanut Butter-Chocolate Cake

Here in Wisconsin, winter weather is extreme. A hot dessert is just the thing to warm us up. This chocolaty delight gets its crunch from a sprinkling of peanuts.

—LISA ERICKSON RIPON, WI

PREP: 20 MIN. • **COOK:** 2 HOURS
MAKES: 8 SERVINGS

- 1¾ cups sugar, divided
- 1 cup 2% milk
- ¾ cup creamy peanut butter
- 3 tablespoons canola oil
- 2 cups all-purpose flour
- ¾ cup baking cocoa, divided
- 3 teaspoons baking powder
- 2 cups boiling water
  Chopped salted peanuts, optional

1. In a large bowl, beat 1 cup sugar, milk, peanut butter and oil until well blended. In another bowl, whisk flour, ½ cup cocoa and baking powder; gradually beat into peanut butter mixture (batter will be thick). Transfer to a greased 5-qt. slow cooker.

2. In a small bowl, mix the remaining sugar and cocoa. Stir in water. Pour over the batter (do not stir).

3. Cook, covered, on high 2 to 2½ hours or until a toothpick inserted in cake portion comes out with moist crumbs. If desired, sprinkle with peanuts. Serve warm.

GLAZED CINNAMON APPLES

GOOEY PEANUT BUTTER-CHOCOLATE CAKE

Butterscotch-Pecan Bread Pudding

Bread pudding fans just might hoard this tasty treat. Toppings like whipped cream and a butterscotch drizzle make the dessert irresistible.

—**LISA VARNER** EL PASO, TX

PREP: 15 MIN. • **COOK:** 3 HOURS
MAKES: 8 SERVINGS

- 9 **cups cubed day-old white bread (about 8 slices)**
- ½ **cup chopped pecans**
- ½ **cup butterscotch chips**
- 4 **large eggs**
- 2 **cups half-and-half cream**
- ½ **cup packed brown sugar**
- ½ **cup butter, melted**
- 1 **teaspoon vanilla extract**
  Whipped cream and butterscotch ice cream topping

1. Place bread, pecans and butterscotch chips in a greased 4-qt. slow cooker. In a large bowl, whisk eggs, cream, brown sugar, melted butter and vanilla until blended. Pour over bread mixture; stir gently to combine.
2. Cook, covered, on low 3-4 hours or until a knife inserted in center comes out clean. Serve warm with whipped cream and butterscotch topping.

Slow Cooker Baked Apples

Coming home to this irresistible dessert on a dreary day is just wonderful; it's slow-cooker easy.

—**EVANGELINE BRADFORD**
ERLANGER, KY

PREP: 25 MIN. • **COOK:** 4 HOURS
MAKES: 6 SERVINGS

- 6 **medium tart apples**
- ½ **cup raisins**
- ⅓ **cup packed brown sugar**
- 1 **tablespoon grated orange peel**
- 1 **cup water**
- 3 **tablespoons thawed orange juice concentrate**
- 2 **tablespoons butter**

1. Core apples and peel the top third of each if desired. Combine the raisins, brown sugar and orange peel; spoon into apples. Place in a 5-qt. slow cooker.
2. Pour water around apples. Drizzle with orange juice concentrate. Dot with butter. Cover and cook on low for 4-5 hours or until apples are tender.

Blueberry Cobbler

This simple-to-make dessert comes together in a jiffy. If you like, you can substitute the blueberry pie filling with other flavors, such as apple or cherry.

—**NELDA CRONBAUGH** BELLE PLAINE, IA

PREP: 10 MIN. • **COOK:** 3 HOURS
MAKES: 6 SERVINGS

- 1 **can (21 ounces) blueberry pie filling**
- 1 **package (9 ounces) yellow cake mix**
- ¼ **cup chopped pecans**
- ¼ **cup butter, melted**
  Vanilla ice cream, optional

Place pie filling in a greased 1½-qt. slow cooker. Sprinkle with cake mix and pecans. Drizzle with butter. Cover and cook on high for 3 hours or until topping is golden brown. Serve warm with ice cream if desired.

DID YOU KNOW?

There is a difference between a cobbler and a crisp. Cobblers have biscuit toppings over the fruit. The topping can be either in a single layer or dropped over the fruit to give a cobblestone effect. Crisps have a crumb topping over the fruit. The topping has flour, sugar and butter and may or may not have oats, nuts and spices.

BUTTERSCOTCH-PECAN
BREAD PUDDING

SLOW COOKER
BAKED APPLES

BLUEBERRY
COBBLER

**CHOCOLATE
PEANUT CLUSTERS**

READY IN ④

Chocolate Peanut Clusters

I turn to my slow cooker to prepare these convenient chocolate treats. Making candies couldn't be any easier and cleanup is a snap!
—**PAM POSEY** WATERLOO, SC

PREP: 25 MIN.
COOK: 2 HOURS + STANDING
MAKES: 6½ POUNDS

- 1 **jar (16 ounces) salted dry roasted peanuts**
- 1 **jar (16 ounces) unsalted dry roasted peanuts**
- 1 **package (11½ ounces) milk chocolate chips**
- 1 **package (10 ounces) peanut butter chips**
- 3 **packages (10 to 12 ounces each) white baking chips**
- 2 **packages (10 ounces each) 60% cacao bittersweet chocolate baking chips**

1. In a 6-qt. slow cooker, combine peanuts. Layer with the remaining ingredients in order given (do not stir). Cover and cook on low for 2 to 2½ hours or until chips are melted, stirring halfway through cooking.
2. Stir to combine. Drop by tablespoonfuls onto waxed paper. Refrigerate until set. Store in an airtight container at room temperature.

Pear-Blueberry Granola

Oatmeal fans will love this dish. It's a delicious dessert when served with vanilla ice cream, but the pears, blueberries and granola make a beautiful breakfast item, too.

—LISA WORKMAN BOONES MILL, VA

PREP: 15 MIN. • **COOK:** 3 HOURS
MAKES: 10 SERVINGS

- 5 medium pears, peeled and thinly sliced
- 2 cups fresh or frozen unsweetened blueberries
- ½ cup packed brown sugar
- ⅓ cup apple cider or unsweetend apple juice
- 1 tablespoon all-purpose flour
- 1 tablespoon lemon juice
- 2 teaspoons ground cinnamon
- 2 tablespoons butter
- 3 cups granola without raisins

In a 4-qt. slow cooker, combine the first seven ingredients. Dot with butter. Sprinkle granola over top. Cover and cook on low for 3-4 hours or until fruit is tender.

Warm Apple-Cranberry Dessert

Served with ice cream, this heartwarming dessert promises to become a favorite in your house! I love that on nights when we have this, dessert practically makes itself.

—MARY JANE JONES ATHENS, OH

PREP: 20 MIN. • **COOK:** 2 HOURS
MAKES: 10 SERVINGS

- 5 large apples, peeled and sliced
- 1 cup fresh or frozen cranberries, thawed
- ¾ cup packed brown sugar, divided
- 2 tablespoons lemon juice
- ½ cup all-purpose flour
  Dash salt
- ⅓ cup cold butter
  Vanilla ice cream
  Toasted chopped pecans

1. In a greased 5-qt. slow cooker, combine apples, cranberries, ¼ cup brown sugar and lemon juice. In a small bowl, mix flour, salt and remaining brown sugar; cut in butter until crumbly. Sprinkle over fruit mixture.
2. Cook, covered, on high 2 to 2½ hours or until apples are tender. Serve with ice cream and pecans.

PEAR-BLUEBERRY GRANOLA

Butterscotch Pears

This grand finale simmers during dinner and impresses as soon as you bring it to the table. Serve as is or with a slice of pound cake. Leftover pear nectar is heavenly when added to sparkling wine or enjoyed on ice with breakfast.

—**THERESA KREYCHE** TUSTIN, CA

PREP: 20 MIN. • **COOK:** 2 HOURS
MAKES: 8 SERVINGS

- 4 large firm pears
- 1 tablespoon lemon juice
- ¼ cup packed brown sugar
- 3 tablespoons butter, softened
- 2 tablespoons all-purpose flour
- ½ teaspoon ground cinnamon
- ¼ teaspoon salt
- ½ cup chopped pecans
- ½ cup pear nectar
- 2 tablespoons honey

1. Cut pears in half lengthwise; remove cores. Brush pears with lemon juice. In a small bowl, combine the brown sugar, butter, flour, cinnamon and salt; stir in pecans. Spoon into pears; place in 4-qt. slow cooker.
2. Combine pear nectar and honey; drizzle over pears. Cover and cook on low for 2-3 hours or until heated through. Serve warm.

Caramel-Pecan Stuffed Apples

This irresistible dessert is slow-cooker easy. Warm and comforting, the tender apples are filled with chewy pecans and a yummy caramel topping.

—**PAMELA JANE KAISER**
MANSFIELD, MO

PREP: 20 MIN. • **COOK:** 3 HOURS
MAKES: 6 SERVINGS

- 6 large tart apples
- 2 teaspoons lemon juice
- ⅓ cup chopped pecans
- ¼ cup chopped dried apricots
- ¼ cup packed brown sugar
- 3 tablespoons butter, melted
- ¾ teaspoon ground cinnamon
- ¼ teaspoon ground nutmeg
  Granola and caramel ice cream topping, optional

1. Core apples and peel top third of each; brush peeled portions with lemon juice. Place in a 6-qt. slow cooker.
2. Combine the pecans, apricots, brown sugar, butter, cinnamon and nutmeg. Place a heaping tablespoonful of mixture in each apple. Pour 2 cups water around apples.
3. Cover and cook on low for 3-4 hours or until apples are tender. Serve with granola and caramel topping if desired.

Elvis' Pudding Cake

I love the flavors of peanut butter and banana together, and this slow-cooker pudding cake is just like eating an Elvis sandwich...only sweeter! Banana chips add a surprisingly crunchy texture. Find them near the dried fruit in the grocery store.

—**LISA RENSHAW** KANSAS CITY, MO

PREP: 10 MIN.
COOK: 3 HOURS + STANDING
MAKES: 12 SERVINGS

- 3 cups cold 2% milk
- 1 package (3.4 ounces) instant banana cream pudding mix
- 1 package banana cake mix (regular size)
- ½ cup creamy peanut butter
- 2 cups peanut butter chips
- 1 cup chopped dried banana chips

1. In a small bowl, whisk milk and pudding mix for 2 minutes. Let stand for 2 minutes or until soft-set. Transfer to a greased 5-qt. slow cooker.
2. Prepare cake mix batter according to package directions, adding peanut butter before mixing. Pour over pudding. Cover and cook on low for 3 to 3½ hours or until a toothpick inserted near the center comes out with moist crumbs.
3. Sprinkle with peanut butter chips; cover and let stand for 15-20 minutes or until partially melted. Top with banana chips.

CARAMEL-PECAN STUFFED APPLES

ELVIS' PUDDING CAKE

FRUIT SALSA

Apple Granola Dessert

I would be lost without my slow cooker. In addition to using it to prepare our evening meal, I often make desserts in it, including these tender apples that get a tasty treatment from granola cereal.

—**JANIS LAWRENCE** CHILDRESS, TX

PREP: 10 MIN. • **COOK:** 6 HOURS
MAKES: 4-6 SERVINGS

- 4 **medium tart apples, peeled and sliced**
- 2 **cups granola cereal with fruit and nuts**
- ¼ **cup honey**
- 2 **tablespoons butter, melted**
- 1 **teaspoon ground cinnamon**
- ½ **teaspoon ground nutmeg**
  Whipped topping, optional

In a 1½-qt. slow cooker, combine apples and cereal. In a small bowl, combine the honey, butter, cinnamon and nutmeg; pour over apple mixture and mix well. Cover and cook on low for 6-8 hours. Serve with whipped topping if desired.

DID YOU KNOW?

Crystallization is the natural process by which liquid honey becomes solid. Heating honey is the only way to dissolve the crystals. Place honey in warm water and stir until the crystals dissolve. Or set it in a microwave-safe container and microwave on high, stirring every 30 seconds, until the crystals dissolve.

Fruit Salsa

Serve this fruity salsa anywhere you'd use ordinary salsa. My son and I experimented with different ingredients to find the combination we liked best. Preparing it in a slow cooker minimizes prep time and maximizes flavor.

—**FLORENCE BUCHKOWSKY**
PRINCE ALBERT, SK

PREP: 10 MIN. • **COOK:** 2 HOURS
MAKES: 4 CUPS

- 3 **tablespoons cornstarch**
- 4 **teaspoons white vinegar**
- 1 **can (11 ounces) mandarin oranges, undrained**
- 1 **can (8½ ounces) sliced peaches, undrained**
- ¾ **cup pineapple tidbits**
- 1 **medium onion, chopped**
- ½ **each medium green, sweet red and yellow peppers, chopped**
- 3 **garlic cloves, minced**
  Tortilla chips

1. In a 3-qt. slow cooker, combine cornstarch and vinegar until smooth. Stir in the fruits, onion, peppers and garlic.
2. Cover and cook on high for 2-3 hours or until thickened and heated through, stirring occasionally. Serve with the tortilla chips.

Chocolate Bread Pudding

I love chocolate and I love berries, so I was thrilled to come across a recipe that combines the two. I use egg bread when making this dessert.
—**BECKY FOSTER** UNION, OR

PREP: 10 MIN. • **COOK:** 2¼ HOURS
MAKES: 6-8 SERVINGS

- 6 cups cubed day-old bread (¾-inch cubes)
- 1½ cups semisweet chocolate chips
- 1 cup fresh raspberries
- 4 large eggs
- ½ cup heavy whipping cream
- ½ cup milk
- ¼ cup sugar
- 1 teaspoon vanilla extract
  Whipped cream and additional raspberries, optional

1. In a greased 3-qt. slow cooker, layer half of the bread cubes, chocolate chips and raspberries. Repeat layers. In a bowl, whisk the eggs, cream, milk, sugar and vanilla. Pour over bread mixture.
2. Cover and cook on high for 2¼-2½ hours or until a thermometer reads 160°. Let stand for 5-10 minutes. Serve with whipped cream and additional raspberries if desired.

**CHOCOLATE
BREAD PUDDING**

BUTTERSCOTCH APPLE CRISP

FRUIT COMPOTE DESSERT

SLOW COOKER RHUBARB STRAWBERRY SAUCE

Butterscotch Apple Crisp

Here's a cozy way to warm up winter nights. Apple crisp gets a sweet surprise with the addition of butterscotch. Your house will smell marvelous as this dessert simmers on its own all afternoon!

—JOLANTHE ERB HARRISONBURG, VA

PREP: 10 MIN. • **COOK:** 5 HOURS
MAKES: 6 SERVINGS

- 6 cups sliced peeled tart apples (about 5 large)
- ¾ cup packed brown sugar
- ½ cup all-purpose flour
- ½ cup quick-cooking oats
- 1 package (3½ ounces) cook-and-serve butterscotch pudding mix
- 1 teaspoon ground cinnamon
- ½ cup cold butter, cubed
  Vanilla ice cream, optional

1. Place apples in a 3-qt. slow cooker. In a large bowl, combine the brown sugar, flour, oats, pudding mix and cinnamon. Cut in butter until mixture resembles coarse crumbs. Sprinkle over the apples.
2. Cover and cook on low for 5-6 hours or until apples are tender. Serve with ice cream if desired.

Fruit Compote Dessert

This is one of the first desserts I learned to make in the slow cooker, and it's the one guests still enjoy the most. It tastes like it came from a fancy restaurant.

—LAURA BRYANT GERMAN
WEST WARREN, MA

PREP: 15 MIN. • **COOK:** 3 HOURS
MAKES: 8 SERVINGS

- 2 medium tart apples, peeled
- 2 medium peaches, peeled and cubed
- 2 cups unsweetened pineapple chunks
- 1¼ cups unsweetened pineapple juice
- ¼ cup honey
- 2 lemon slices (¼ inch)
- 1 cinnamon stick (3½ inches)
- 1 medium firm banana, thinly sliced
  Whipped cream, sliced almonds and maraschino cherries, optional

1. Cut apples into ¼-in. slices and then in half; place in a 3-qt. slow cooker. Add the peaches, pineapple, pineapple juice, honey, lemon and cinnamon. Cover and cook on low for 3-4 hours.
2. Just before serving, stir in banana slices. Serve with a slotted spoon if desired. Garnish with whipped cream, almonds and cherries if desired.

Slow Cooker Rhubarb Strawberry Sauce

We recently started growing our own rhubarb, and we live in a part of Oregon where strawberries are plentiful. I created this to use up those ingredients. I drizzle some of the sauce over ice cream, and I fill a crisp with the rest.

—KIM BANICK SALEM, OR

PREP: 15 MIN. • **COOK:** 4½ HOURS
MAKES: 5 CUPS

- 4 cups sliced fresh or frozen rhubarb, thawed (about 10 stalks)
- 4 cups fresh strawberries (about 1¼ pounds), halved
- 1½ cups sugar
- ¼ cup water
- 3 tablespoons butter
- 1 teaspoon vanilla extract
- ¼ cup cornstarch
- 3 tablespoons cold water
  Vanilla ice cream

1. In a 3-qt. slow cooker, combine the first six ingredients. Cook, covered, on low 4-5 hours or until rhubarb is tender.
2. In a small bowl, mix cornstarch and cold water until smooth; gradually stir into sauce. Cook, covered, on low 30 minutes longer or until thickened. Serve with ice cream.
NOTE *If using frozen rhubarb, measure rhubarb while still frozen, then thaw completely. Drain in a colander, but do not press liquid out.*

APPLE PIE OATMEAL DESSERT

2. Transfer to a greased 3-qt. slow cooker. Cook, covered, on low 4-5 hours or until apples are tender and top is set.

3. Stir in remaining milk. Serve warm or cold with ice cream if desired.

EXPRESS PREP | READY IN 4

Cinnamon-Raisin Banana Bread Pudding

My family likes to change the toppings for this luscious dessert. We use berries, chopped nuts or fruits, ice cream, whipped cream or caramel topping. If I'm making the dessert for adults only, I love to add a little rum to the milk mixture to give the pudding extra flavor.
—**AYSHA SCHURMAN** AMMON, ID

PREP: 10 MIN. • **COOK:** 2½ HOURS
MAKES: 8 SERVINGS

> 4 **large eggs**
> 2¼ **cups 2% milk**
> ¾ **cup mashed ripe banana (about 1 large)**
> ¼ **cup packed brown sugar**
> ⅓ **cup butter, melted**
> 1 **teaspoon vanilla extract**
> 1 **loaf (1 pound) cinnamon-raisin bread, cut into 1-inch cubes**
> ½ **cup chopped pecans, toasted**
>   **Vanilla ice cream, optional**

1. In a large bowl, whisk the first six ingredients. Stir in bread and pecans. Transfer to a greased 4-qt. slow cooker.

2. Cook, covered, on low 2½-3 hours or until a knife inserted near the center comes out clean. Serve warm with ice cream if desired.

Apple Pie Oatmeal Dessert

This warm and comforting dessert brings back memories of time spent with my family around the kitchen table. I serve the dish with sweetened whipped cream as a topper.
—**CAROL GREER** EARLVILLE, IL

PREP: 15 MIN. • **COOK:** 4 HOURS
MAKES: 6 SERVINGS

> 1 **cup quick-cooking oats**
> ½ **cup all-purpose flour**
> ⅓ **cup packed brown sugar**
> 2 **teaspoons baking powder**
> 1½ **teaspoons apple pie spice**
> ¼ **teaspoon salt**
> 3 **large eggs**
> 1⅔ **cups 2% milk, divided**
> 1½ **teaspoons vanilla extract**
> 3 **medium apples, peeled and finely chopped**
>   **Vanilla ice cream, optional**

1. In a large bowl, whisk oats, flour, brown sugar, baking powder, pie spice and salt. In a small bowl, whisk eggs, 1 cup milk and vanilla until blended. Add to oat mixture, stirring just until moistened. Fold in apples.

Tropical Compote Dessert

Enjoy a taste of summer throughout the year! To make a more adult version of this recipe, use a bit of brandy instead of the extra tropical fruit juice.

—TASTE OF HOME TEST KITCHEN

PREP: 15 MIN. • **COOK:** 2¼ HOURS
MAKES: 6 SERVINGS

- 1 jar (23½ ounces) mixed tropical fruit
- 1 jalapeno pepper, seeded and chopped
- ¼ cup sugar
- 1 tablespoon chopped crystallized ginger
- ¼ teaspoon ground cinnamon
- 1 can (15 ounces) mandarin oranges, drained
- 1 jar (6 ounces) maraschino cherries, drained
- 1 medium firm banana, sliced
- 6 individual round sponge cakes
- 6 tablespoons flaked coconut, toasted

1. Drain tropical fruit, reserving ¼ cup liquid. Combine tropical fruit and jalapeno in a 1½-qt. slow cooker. Combine the sugar, ginger, cinnamon and reserved juice; pour over fruit. Cover and cook on low for 2 hours. Stir in the mandarin oranges, cherries and banana; cook 15 minutes longer.

2. Place sponge cakes on dessert plates; top with compote. Sprinkle with coconut.

NOTE *Wear disposable gloves when cutting hot peppers; the oils can burn skin. Avoid touching your face.*

CINNAMON-RAISIN BANANA BREAD PUDDING

TROPICAL COMPOTE DESSERT

SLOW COOKER
CHERRY BUCKLE

MINTY HOT FUDGE
SUNDAE CAKE

EXPRESS PREP **READY IN** ④

Slow Cooker Cherry Buckle

I saw this recipe on a cooking show and came up with my own version. When the comforting aroma of this homey dessert drifts around the house, it's hard not to take a peek inside the slow cooker.

—**SHERRI MELOTIK** OAK CREEK, WI

PREP: 10 MIN. • **COOK:** 3 HOURS
MAKES: 6 SERVINGS

- 2 cans (15 ounces each) sliced pears, drained
- 1 can (21 ounces) cherry pie filling
- ¼ teaspoon almond extract
- 1 package yellow cake mix (regular size)
- ¼ cup old-fashioned oats
- ¼ cup sliced almonds
- 1 tablespoon brown sugar
- ½ cup butter, melted
  Vanilla ice cream, optional

1. In a greased 5-qt. slow cooker, combine pears and pie filling; stir in extract. In a large bowl, combine cake mix, oats, almonds and brown sugar; stir in melted butter. Sprinkle over fruit.
2. Cook, covered, on low 3-4 hours or until topping is golden brown. If desired, serve with ice cream.

Minty Hot Fudge Sundae Cake

The best part about dessert from the slow cooker is that when dinner's done, a hot treat is ready to serve. In this case, it's a chocolaty, gooey, minty treat!

—**TERRI MCKITRICK** DELAFIELD, WI

PREP: 15 MIN. • **COOK:** 4 HOURS
MAKES: 12 SERVINGS

- 1¾ cups packed brown sugar, divided
- 1 cup all-purpose flour
- 5 tablespoons baking cocoa, divided
- 2 teaspoons baking powder
- ½ teaspoon salt
- ½ cup evaporated milk
- 2 tablespoons butter, melted
- ½ teaspoon vanilla extract
- ⅛ teaspoon almond extract
- 1 package (4.67 ounces) mint Andes candies
- 1¾ cups boiling water
- 4 teaspoons instant coffee granules
  Vanilla ice cream, whipped cream and maraschino cherries

1. In a large bowl, combine 1 cup brown sugar, flour, 3 tablespoons cocoa, baking powder and salt. In another bowl, combine the milk, butter and extracts. Stir into dry ingredients just until moistened. Transfer to a 3-qt. slow cooker coated with cooking spray. Sprinkle with candies.
2. Combine the water, coffee granules and remaining brown sugar and cocoa; pour over batter (do not stir). Cover and cook on high for 4 to 4½ hours or until a toothpick inserted near the center of the cake comes out clean. Serve with ice cream, whipped cream and cherries.

CHERRY & SPICE RICE PUDDING

Cherry & Spice Rice Pudding

Cinnamon and cherries sweeten the deal in this dessert. If you've never tried rice pudding, this is an excellent place to start.

—DEB PERRY TRAVERSE CITY, MI

PREP: 10 MIN. • **COOK:** 2 HOURS
MAKES: 12 SERVINGS

- 4 **cups cooked long grain rice**
- 1 **can (12 ounces) evaporated milk**
- 1 **cup 2% milk**
- ⅓ **cup sugar**
- ¼ **cup water**
- ¾ **cup dried cherries**
- 3 **tablespoons butter, softened**
- 2 **teaspoons vanilla extract**
- ½ **teaspoon ground cinnamon**
- ¼ **teaspoon ground nutmeg**

1. In a large bowl, combine the rice, evaporated milk, milk, sugar and water. Stir in the remaining ingredients. Transfer to a 3-qt. slow cooker coated with cooking spray.

2. Cover and cook on low for 2-3 hours or until mixture is thickened. Stir lightly before serving. Serve warm or cold. Refrigerate leftovers.

TARRAGON ASPARAGUS, 225

216

226

221

BONUS: No-Fuss Salads & Sides

Complete your slow-cooked entree with a garden-fresh salad or quick-as-can-be side dish. These bonus recipes may not use a slow cooker, but they'll help you set a complete meal on the table in a flash.

JEWELED ENDIVE SALAD, 221

Fruited Rice Pilaf

I'm always trying to get fruit into our menus. I stirred some into plain rice pilaf one night, and it was a hit!

—**LUCILLE GENDRON** PELHAM, NH

START TO FINISH: 15 MIN.
MAKES: 4 SERVINGS

- 1 **package (6 ounces) rice pilaf**
- 2 **tablespoons butter, softened**
- ½ **cup pineapple chunks**
- ½ **cup raisins**
- ¼ **cup prepared Italian salad dressing**
  Toasted coconut, optional

Cook the rice pilaf according to package directions. Stir in the butter until melted. Add the pineapple, raisins and salad dressing. Top with toasted coconut if desired.

Pea Pods and Peppers

This is a modification of a recipe I found in a cookbook. I now make it about once a month. It's an easy, yet well-flavored, side that goes well with a variety of main courses.

—**CASSANDRA GOURLEY** WILLIAMS, AZ

START TO FINISH: 15 MIN.
MAKES: 4 SERVINGS

- ¾ **pound fresh snow peas**
- 1 **medium sweet red pepper, julienned**
- ½ **small onion, sliced**
- ¼ **teaspoon garlic salt**
- ⅛ **teaspoon pepper**
- 1 **tablespoon canola oil**
- 1 **tablespoon butter**

In a large skillet, saute the snow peas, red pepper, onion, garlic salt and pepper in oil and butter until vegetables are tender.

Cajun Spiced Broccoli

I usually make this without the Creole seasoning, but a few weeks ago, I decided to try adding a different spice just to see what would happen. I loved it!

—**KRISTA FRANK** RHODODENDRON, OR

START TO FINISH: 15 MIN.
MAKES: 4 SERVINGS

- 1 **bunch broccoli, cut into florets**
- 2 **tablespoons canola oil**
- 2 **large garlic cloves, minced**
- ¾ **teaspoon Creole seasoning**

In a large nonstick skillet coated with cooking spray, saute broccoli in oil until crisp-tender, adding the garlic and Creole seasoning during the last 2 minutes of cooking.

NOTE *The following spices may be substituted for 1 teaspoon Creole seasoning: ¼ teaspoon each salt, garlic powder and paprika; and a pinch each of dried thyme, ground cumin and cayenne pepper.*

Sauteed Corn with Cheddar

My husband only likes this kind of corn, so I make this about once a week. Plus, it's so easy that anyone could make this in a jiffy!

—**SARAH COPE** DUNDEE, NY

START TO FINISH: 10 MIN.
MAKES: 2 SERVINGS

- 1½ **cups frozen corn, thawed**
- ⅛ **teaspoon salt**
- ⅛ **teaspoon pepper**
- 1 **tablespoon butter**
- ¾ **cup shredded cheddar cheese**

In a small skillet, saute the corn, salt and pepper in butter until tender. Stir in cheese.

Mixed Greens with Lemon Champagne Vinaigrette

You've got crunch from the walnuts, sweet pomegranate seeds, all kinds of greens and a dressing that's smooth but has just enough zing. And it's simple, too.

—**RAY UYEDA** MOUNTAIN VIEW, CA

START TO FINISH: 15 MIN.
MAKES: 10 SERVINGS

- 2 **tablespoons champagne vinegar**
- 2 **teaspoons lemon juice**
- 1 **teaspoon Dijon mustard**
- 1 **shallot, finely chopped**
- ½ **cup olive oil**
- 4 **cups torn leaf lettuce**
- 4 **cups fresh spinach**
- 2 **cups fresh arugula**
- ¾ **cup chopped walnuts, toasted**
- ½ **cup pomegranate seeds**

1. In a small bowl, whisk vinegar, lemon juice, mustard and shallot. Gradually whisk in oil.

2. In a large bowl, combine the lettuce, spinach and arugula. Pour vinaigrette over salad; toss to coat. Top with the walnuts and the pomegranate seeds. Serve immediately.

NOTE *To toast nuts, bake in a shallow pan in a 350° oven for 5-10 minutes or cook in a skillet over low heat until lightly browned, stirring occasionally.*

SAUTEED CORN WITH CHEDDAR

MIXED GREENS WITH LEMON CHAMPAGNE VINAIGRETTE

**BRUSSELS SPROUTS
WITH LEEKS**

**ROSEMARY
POLENTA**

---

(5) INGREDIENTS *EXPRESS* PREP
READY IN (4)

Brussels Sprouts with Leeks

Since my husband and I both love Brussels sprouts, I often experiment with different combinations to enhance the flavor. We found leeks give the sprouts a special taste.
—**PATRICIA MICKELSON** SAN JOSE, CA

START TO FINISH: 15 MIN.
MAKES: 2 SERVINGS

- 10 **Brussels sprouts, trimmed and halved**
- 1 **medium leek (white portion only), thinly sliced**
- 1 **tablespoon butter**
  Dash salt

1. In a large saucepan, bring 1 in. of water and Brussels sprouts to a boil. Reduce heat; cover and simmer for 8 minutes.
2. Add the leek; cover and simmer for 2-4 minutes longer or until the vegetables are tender. Drain; stir in butter and salt.

---

(5) INGREDIENTS *EXPRESS* PREP
READY IN (4)

Rosemary Polenta

Bring a bit of Italian flair to dinner by quickly dressing up polenta. Using the purchased variety lets you get this dish to the table pronto.
—**CASANDRA RITTENHOUSE**
NORTH HOLLYWOOD, CA

START TO FINISH: 10 MIN.
MAKES: 4 SERVINGS

- 1 **tube (1 pound) polenta**
- ½ **cup grated Parmesan cheese**
- ¼ **teaspoon dried rosemary, crushed**
- ⅓ to ½ **cup water**
  Butter, minced fresh parsley and coarsely ground pepper, optional

Prepare the polenta according to package directions for soft polenta, stirring in cheese, rosemary and enough water to achieve desired consistency. Top with butter, parsley and pepper if desired.
NOTE *This recipe was tested in a 1,100-watt microwave.*

EXPRESS PREP READY IN (4)

Green Salad with Tangy Basil Vinaigrette

A tart and tangy dressing turns a basic salad into something special. It works for weeknight dining but is special enough for company and pairs perfectly with anything.
—**KRISTIN RIMKUS** SNOHOMISH, WA

START TO FINISH: 15 MIN.
MAKES: 4 SERVINGS

- 3 **tablespoons white wine vinegar**
- 4½ **teaspoons minced fresh basil**
- 4½ **teaspoons olive oil**
- 1½ **teaspoons honey**
- ¼ **teaspoon salt**
- ⅛ **teaspoon pepper**
- 6 **cups torn mixed salad greens**
- 1 **cup cherry tomatoes, halved**
- 2 **tablespoons shredded Parmesan cheese**

In a small bowl, whisk the first six ingredients until blended. In a large bowl, combine salad greens and tomatoes. Drizzle with the vinaigrette; toss to coat. Sprinkle with cheese.

Potluck Antipasto Salad

I take this fresh-tasting, colorful salad to potluck dinners throughout the year, since everyone who tries it loves it. The pasta, garbanzo beans and pepperoni make it a hearty dish.

—**AGNES BULKLEY** HICKSVILLE, NY

PREP: 15 MIN. + CHILLING
MAKES: 12-16 SERVINGS

- 1 **package (16 ounces) spiral pasta**
- 1 **can (15 ounces) garbanzo beans or chickpeas, rinsed and drained**
- 1 **package (3½ ounces) sliced pepperoni, halved**
- 1 **can (2¼ ounces) sliced ripe olives, drained**
- ½ **cup diced sweet red pepper**
- ½ **cup diced green pepper**
- 4 **medium fresh mushrooms, sliced**
- 2 **garlic cloves, minced**
- 2 **tablespoons minced fresh basil or 2 teaspoons dried basil**
- 2 **teaspoons salt**
- 1½ **teaspoons minced fresh oregano or ½ teaspoon dried oregano**
- ½ **teaspoon pepper**
- ¼ **teaspoon cayenne pepper**
- 1 **cup olive oil**
- ⅔ **cup lemon juice**

1. Cook the pasta according to package directions; drain and rinse in cold water. Place in a large salad bowl. Stir in the next 12 ingredients.

2. In a small bowl, whisk oil and lemon juice. Pour over salad and toss to coat. Cover and refrigerate 6 hours or overnight. Stir salad before serving.

EXPRESS *PREP* **READY IN** ④

Mixed Greens with Orange Juice Vinaigrette

Like a string of pearls on a little black dress, a vinaigrette is a classic way to dress a salad. A little oil, a little vinegar, a tangy infusion of orange juice and a sprinkle of orange peel are just enough—and not too much.

—**KRISTIN BATAILLE** STAMFORD, CT

START TO FINISH: 10 MIN.
MAKES: 6 SERVINGS

- 2 **tablespoons olive oil**
- 2 **tablespoons orange juice**
- 1 **tablespoon cider vinegar**
- 1 **teaspoon grated orange peel**
  Dash salt
  Dash pepper
- 1 **package (5 ounces) spring mix salad greens**

In a small bowl, whisk the first six ingredients. Place salad greens in a large bowl. Drizzle greens with vinaigrette; toss to coat.

DID YOU KNOW?

Cider vinegar, made from apples, has a faint fruity flavor and is used in recipes where a slightly milder vinegar flavor is preferred. White vinegar has a sharp, harsh flavor and is generally used for pickling and in recipes where a clean, strong taste is desired.

POTLUCK ANTIPASTO SALAD

Summertime Squash

Everyone knows the best-tasting vegetables come from a country garden. I use my garden-grown veggies to create this colorful, nutritious dish.

—GWENDOLYN LAMBERT
FRISCO CITY, AL

START TO FINISH: 15 MIN.
MAKES: 2 SERVINGS

- 1 teaspoon cornstarch
- ⅛ teaspoon salt
- ¼ cup vegetable broth
- 1 small zucchini, cut into ¼-inch slices
- 1 small yellow summer squash, cut into ¼-inch slices
- ½ small sweet red pepper, cut into strips
- 1½ teaspoons canola oil
- ½ teaspoon butter
- 1 garlic clove, minced

In a small bowl, combine the cornstarch, salt and broth until smooth; set aside. In a large skillet, saute the zucchini, squash and red pepper in oil and butter until tender. Add garlic; saute 1 minute longer. Stir cornstarch mixture and add to the pan. Bring to a boil; cook and stir for 2 minutes or until thickened.

Sicilian Salad

Loaded with fabulous flavor, this hearty salad comes together in no time. Chop the tomatoes and celery and cube the mozzarella before guests arrive, and you'll have this ready in moments.

—BETH BURGMEIER EAST DUBUQUE, IL

START TO FINISH: 15 MIN.
MAKES: 10 SERVINGS

- 1 package (9 ounces) iceberg lettuce blend
- 1 jar (16 ounces) pickled banana peppers, drained and sliced
- 1 jar (5¾ ounces) sliced green olives with pimientos, drained
- 3 plum tomatoes, chopped
- 4 celery ribs, chopped
- 1 cup chopped pepperoni
- ½ cup cubed part-skim mozzarella cheese
- ½ cup Italian salad dressing

In a large bowl, combine the first seven ingredients. Drizzle with dressing and toss to coat.

Easy Lemon-Pepper Green Beans

I plant a garden every year, and I always have a lot of green beans to use. My family loves the beans prepared this way.

—PAULA BROADWAY-JONES
CAMBRIDGE, NE

START TO FINISH: 15 MIN.
MAKES: 4 SERVINGS

- 1 garlic clove, minced
- 1 tablespoon olive oil
- 1 package (16 ounces) frozen cut green beans
- ½ cup chicken broth
- ¾ teaspoon lemon-pepper seasoning
- ½ teaspoon dried parsley flakes
- ¼ teaspoon salt

Saute garlic in oil in a large skillet for 1 minute. Add the beans, broth, lemon-pepper, parsley and salt. Bring to a boil. Reduce heat; simmer, uncovered, for 4-5 minutes or until beans are tender.

Spiral Pasta Salad

I use convenient purchased dressing to give a simple salad a big flavor boost. I suggest that you make larger batches of this speedy dish to take to potlucks and picnics.

—MYLINDA AUXTER GRAYTOWN, OH

START TO FINISH: 15 MIN.
MAKES: 2 SERVINGS

- 1 cup cooked spiral pasta
- ⅓ cup halved grape tomatoes
- ¼ cup quartered sliced cucumber
- ¼ cup quartered sliced sweet onion
- ¼ cup sliced ripe olives
- 3 tablespoons grated Parmesan cheese
- ¼ cup ranch salad dressing

In a bowl, combine the first six ingredients. Add dressing and toss to coat. Cover salad and refrigerate until serving.

TOP TIP

Vidalia and other sweet, mild-flavored onions are high in sugar and water content and low in tear-inducing sulfur compounds. Because of those properties, these onions are not suited for long-term storage, so you should use them within several weeks after buying them.

Vermicelli Pasta Salad

I started making this salad because it's loaded with peppers, my husband's favorite. Don't be surprised when there are no leftovers to take home after the family reunion, picnic or church potluck.

—JANIE COLLE HUTCHINSON, KS

PREP: 20 MIN. + CHILLING
MAKES: 10 SERVINGS

- 12 **ounces uncooked vermicelli**
- 1 **bottle (16 ounces) creamy Italian salad dressing**
- 1 **small green pepper, chopped**
- 1 **small sweet red pepper, chopped**
- 6 **green onions, chopped**
- 1 **teaspoon dill seed**
- 1 **teaspoon caraway seeds**
- 1 **teaspoon poppy seeds**

Cook the vermicelli according to package directions. Drain; transfer to a large bowl. Add the remaining ingredients; toss pasta to coat. Refrigerate until cold.

VERMICELLI PASTA SALAD

Pear & Blue Cheese Salad

Build your ideal salad with ingredients you find at your local grocery salad bar. Look for fresh fruit and strong-flavored cheeses.

—TASTE OF HOME TEST KITCHEN

START TO FINISH: 10 MIN.
MAKES: 10 SERVINGS

- 12 **cups torn romaine**
- ⅔ **cup balsamic vinaigrette**
- 2 **medium pears, sliced**
- ⅔ **cup crumbled blue cheese**
- ⅔ **cup glazed pecans**

Place romaine in a large bowl. Drizzle with vinaigrette; toss to coat. Top with pears, cheese and pecans. Serve immediately.

PEAR & BLUE CHEESE SALAD

JEWELED
ENDIVE SALAD

LEMON DATE
COUSCOUS

WALNUT ZUCCHINI SAUTE

Jeweled Endive Salad

My friends have a huge potluck party every Christmas. I wanted to bring something unique, so I topped off endive and watercress with jewel-toned pomegranate seeds.

—ALYSHA BRAUN ST. CATHARINES, ON

START TO FINISH: 15 MIN.
MAKES: 8 SERVINGS

- 1 **bunch watercress (4 ounces)**
- 2 **heads endive, halved lengthwise and thinly sliced**
- 1 **cup pomegranate seeds (about 1 pomegranate)**
- 1 **shallot, thinly sliced**

DRESSING
- ⅓ **cup olive oil**
- 3 **tablespoons lemon juice**
- 2 **teaspoons grated lemon peel**
- ¼ **teaspoon salt**
- ⅛ **teaspoon pepper**

1. In a large bowl, combine the watercress, endive, pomegranate seeds and shallot.
2. In a small bowl, whisk the dressing ingredients. Drizzle over salad; toss to coat.

EXPRESS PREP READY IN 4

Lemon Date Couscous

Couscous is a perfect way to highlight bold flavors, and it goes with many main dishes.

—ROXANNE CHAN ALBANY, CA

START TO FINISH: 10 MIN.
MAKES: 4 SERVINGS

- ¾ **cup uncooked couscous**
- ½ **cup fresh baby spinach**
- ½ **cup shredded carrots**
- ¼ **cup chopped dates**
- 2 **tablespoons sliced almonds**
- 1 **teaspoon lemon juice**
- ¼ **teaspoon grated lemon peel**
- ⅛ **teaspoon salt**
- ⅛ **teaspoon lemon-pepper seasoning**
    Thinly sliced green onions

1. Cook couscous according to package directions.
2. Meanwhile, in a small bowl, combine the spinach, carrots, dates, almonds, lemon juice, lemon peel, salt and lemon-pepper. Stir in couscous. Garnish with green onions.

5 INGREDIENTS EXPRESS PREP READY IN 4

Walnut Zucchini Saute

This recipe is special to me because I can get my family to eat their veggies when I serve it.

—ANGELA STEWART WEST SENECA, NY

START TO FINISH: 15 MIN.
MAKES: 4 SERVINGS

- 2 **medium zucchini, cut into ¼-inch slices**
- ⅓ **cup chopped walnuts**
- 2 **teaspoons olive oil**
- 1 **teaspoon butter**
- 3 **garlic cloves, minced**
- ¼ **teaspoon salt**
- ¼ **teaspoon pepper**

Saute zucchini and walnuts in oil and butter in a large skillet until zucchini is tender. Add the garlic, salt and pepper; cook and stir for 1 minute.

5 INGREDIENTS EXPRESS PREP READY IN 4

Creamed Spinach and Mushrooms

Once when my family was snowed in, we had to make do with what was on hand. After looking through the fridge, I was able to put this warm side dish together. It is very versatile and takes only 10 minutes from start to finish.

—MICHELLE FERRARIO IJAMSVILLE, MD

START TO FINISH: 10 MIN.
MAKES: 2 SERVINGS

- 1½ **cups sliced fresh mushrooms**
- 2 **tablespoons olive oil**
- ½ **teaspoon butter**
- 1 **package (6 ounces) fresh baby spinach**
- 3 **ounces reduced-fat cream cheese, cubed**
- ¼ **teaspoon salt**
- ⅛ **teaspoon pepper**

1. In a small skillet, saute the mushrooms in oil and butter until tender. Add spinach; cover and cook for 1 minute or until wilted.
2. Stir in the cream cheese, salt and pepper. Serve immediately.

READY IN 4

Supreme Spaghetti Salad

I use bottled salad dressing to perk up the pasta and fresh vegetables in this swift and cheap salad. It's a delicious addition to any meal or picnic.

—WENDY BYRD SALEM, VA

PREP: 15 MIN. + CHILLING
MAKES: 12 SERVINGS

- 1 **package (1 pound) spaghetti, broken into 4-inch pieces**
- 1 **bottle (16 ounces) zesty Italian salad dressing**
- 1 **large cucumber, diced**
- 1 **large tomato, seeded and diced**
- 1½ **cups fresh broccoli florets**
- 2 **tablespoons shredded Parmesan cheese**
- 2 **teaspoons Salad Supreme Seasoning**

Cook spaghetti according to the package directions. Drain and rinse in cold water. Place spaghetti in a large serving bowl. Add the remaining ingredients; toss to coat. Cover and refrigerate for at least 45 minutes.
NOTE *This recipe was tested with McCormick's Salad Supreme Seasoning. Look for it in the spice aisle.*

EXPRESS PREP READY IN ④

Grilled Romaine with Swiss

Lovely to look at and crazy good, this fast and easy veggie dish is something you won't want to stop eating.

—TASTE OF HOME TEST KITCHEN

START TO FINISH: 15 MIN.
MAKES: 4 SERVINGS

- 2 romaine hearts, halved lengthwise
- 1 tablespoon olive oil
- ⅛ teaspoon salt
- ⅛ teaspoon pepper
- ⅓ cup prepared raspberry vinaigrette
- ½ cup shredded Swiss cheese
- ½ cup dried cherries
- ⅓ cup chopped walnuts

1. Brush romaine with oil and sprinkle with salt and pepper.
2. Moisten a paper towel with cooking oil; using long-handled tongs, rub on the grill rack to coat. Grill the romaine, covered, over medium heat for 30 seconds on each side or until heated through. Transfer to a platter; drizzle with vinaigrette. Sprinkle with cheese, cherries and walnuts.

⑤ INGREDIENTS EXPRESS PREP
READY IN ④

Broccoli Side Dish

With just a few ingredients, this makes a special side that kids of all ages will enjoy. A touch of brown sugar makes it an easy option for parents trying to get the kids to eat more veggies!

—TASTE OF HOME TEST KITCHEN

START TO FINISH: 10 MIN.
MAKES: 4 SERVINGS

- 5 cups fresh broccoli florets
- 2 tablespoons butter, melted
- 4 teaspoons soy sauce
- 2 teaspoons brown sugar
- ½ teaspoon minced garlic

Place the broccoli in a large microwave-safe bowl. Combine the remaining ingredients; pour over broccoli. Cover and microwave on high for 3-4 minutes or until tender. Serve with a slotted spoon. **NOTE** *This recipe was tested in a 1,100-watt microwave.*

EXPRESS PREP READY IN ④

Greek Pasta Salad

My mother-in-law gave me this recipe, and I have made it many times. I've taken it to church picnics and potlucks, and someone always asks for the recipe.

—LAURA FREEMAN RUFFIN, NC

START TO FINISH: 20 MIN.
MAKES: 4 SERVINGS

- 1½ cups uncooked penne pasta
- ½ cup cubed cooked turkey or chicken
- 1 can (3.8 ounces) sliced ripe olives, drained
- ¼ cup chopped green pepper
- ¼ cup chopped sweet red pepper
- ¼ cup crumbled feta cheese
- ⅓ cup creamy Caesar salad dressing

Cook pasta according to package directions; drain and rinse in cold water. In a serving bowl, combine the pasta, turkey, olives, peppers and feta cheese. Drizzle with the dressing and toss to coat. Cover and refrigerate until serving. **NOTE** *You may substitute 1½ cups of tricolor spiral pasta for the penne. Proceed as directed.*

⑤ INGREDIENTS EXPRESS PREP
READY IN ④

Dill Potato Wedges

These are my absolute favorites. I've been making them for years!

—JEANNIE KLUGH LANCASTER, PA

START TO FINISH: 15 MIN.
MAKES: 4 SERVINGS

- 1 tablespoon olive oil
- 1 package (20 ounces) refrigerated red potato wedges
- ½ teaspoon salt
- ½ teaspoon pepper
- 2 tablespoons grated Parmesan cheese
- 1 teaspoon snipped fresh dill or ¼ teaspoon dill weed

In a large skillet, heat oil over medium heat. Add potato wedges; sprinkle with the salt and pepper. Cook for 10-12 minutes or until tender and golden brown, stirring occasionally. Remove from the heat; sprinkle with cheese and dill.

⑤ INGREDIENTS EXPRESS PREP
READY IN ④

Easy Tossed Salad

Apples, almonds and cranberries provide amazing crunch, color and nutrition galore in this easy five-ingredient salad.

—KATHERINE WOLLGAST
FLORISSANT, MO

START TO FINISH: 10 MIN.
MAKES: 4 SERVINGS

- 8 cups torn mixed salad greens
- 1 large apple, sliced
- ½ cup sliced almonds, toasted
- ½ cup dried cranberries
- ½ cup fat-free poppy seed salad dressing

In a salad bowl, combine the salad greens, apple, almonds and the cranberries. Drizzle with dressing; toss to coat. Serve immediately.

GREEK
PASTA SALAD

DILL POTATO WEDGES

Lemon Green Beans

These green beans dress up any entree with their vibrant color. Best of all, they're so simple. Just microwave them, throw in your seasoning and "poof," they're done! I've also made this on the stovetop with canned beans.
—**TERRI WETZEL** ROSEBURG, OR

START TO FINISH: 10 MIN.
MAKES: 4 SERVINGS

- 1 package (16 ounces) frozen cut green beans, thawed
- 2 tablespoons water
- 1½ teaspoons dried minced onion
- 1 tablespoon lemon juice
- 1½ teaspoons real bacon bits
- ¼ teaspoon salt
- ¼ teaspoon pepper

Place the beans, water and onion in a 1-qt. microwave-safe dish. Cover and microwave on high for 4-5 minutes or until beans are crisp-tender; drain. Stir in the remaining ingredients.
NOTE *This recipe was tested in a 1,100-watt microwave.*

Southwest Black Bean Pasta

I created this recipe by combining some of my all-time favorite flavors and textures. It's great with crunchy tortilla chips, too!
—**DENISE RAMEY** FRANCESVILLE, IN

START TO FINISH: 15 MIN.
MAKES: 2 SERVINGS

- ½ cup uncooked spiral pasta
- ⅓ cup shredded cheddar cheese
- ⅓ cup frozen corn, thawed
- ⅓ cup black beans, rinsed and drained
- ¼ cup chopped celery
- ¼ cup chopped carrot
- ¼ cup salsa

- ¼ cup Western salad dressing
- 2 tablespoons sliced ripe olives
- 1 jalapeno pepper, seeded and finely chopped

Cook pasta according to package directions. Meanwhile, in a small bowl, combine the remaining ingredients. Drain pasta and rinse in cold water. Stir into bean mixture. Chill until serving.
NOTE *Wear disposable gloves when cutting hot peppers; the oils can burn skin. Avoid touching your face.*

Classy Carrots

Toasted pecans add a sweet crunch to this buttery side.
—**TASTE OF HOME** TEST KITCHEN

START TO FINISH: 15 MIN.
MAKES: 4 SERVINGS

- 1 package (16 ounces) frozen sliced carrots
- 2 tablespoons water
- 2 green onions, thinly sliced
- 2 tablespoons butter, cubed
- ½ teaspoon dried oregano
- ¼ teaspoon garlic salt
- ¼ teaspoon pepper
- 2 tablespoons chopped pecans, toasted

Place carrots and water in a large microwave-safe bowl. Cover and microwave on high for 5 minutes. Stir in the onions, butter, oregano, garlic salt and pepper. Cover and cook 2-3 minutes longer or until carrots are crisp-tender. Sprinkle with pecans.
NOTE *This recipe was tested in a 1,100-watt microwave.*

Easy Spanish Rice

With less sodium and fewer calories, this homemade Spanish rice rivals any store-bought brand. Plus, it goes from start to finish in a fast 15 minutes.
—**SUSAN LEBRUN** SULPHUR, LA

START TO FINISH: 15 MIN.
MAKES: 4 SERVINGS

- 2 cups water
- 2 cups instant brown rice
- 1 envelope enchilada sauce mix
- 1 cup picante sauce

In a large saucepan, bring water to a boil; stir in rice and sauce mix. Return to a boil. Reduce heat; cover and simmer for 5 minutes. Remove from the heat; stir in the picante sauce. Let rice stand for 5 minutes before serving.

DID YOU KNOW?

Brown rice is rice that has had the husk removed but not the bran layer. The bran layer retains more vitamin, mineral and fiber content than white rice. When cooked, the grains stay separate and offer a chewy texture.

Tarragon Asparagus

I grow purple asparagus, so I'm always looking for new ways to prepare it. Recently, my husband and I discovered how wonderful any color asparagus tastes when it's grilled.

—SUE GRONHOLZ (FIELD EDITOR)
BEAVER DAM, WI

START TO FINISH: 15 MIN.
MAKES: 8 SERVINGS

- 2 **pounds fresh asparagus, trimmed**
- 2 **tablespoons olive oil**
- 1 **teaspoon salt**
- ½ **teaspoon pepper**
- ¼ **cup honey**
- 2 **to 4 tablespoons minced fresh tarragon**

On a large plate, toss asparagus with oil, salt and pepper. Grill, covered, over medium heat for 6-8 minutes or until crisp-tender, turning occasionally and basting frequently with honey during the last 3 minutes. Sprinkle with fresh tarragon.

TARRAGON ASPARAGUS

APPLE & CHEDDAR SALAD

Apple & Cheddar Salad

Cheddar cheese is the perfect complement to the apples in this simple salad.

—TASTE OF HOME TEST KITCHEN

START TO FINISH: 10 MIN.
MAKES: 10 SERVINGS

- 12 **cups fresh baby spinach**
- ⅔ **cup honey Dijon vinaigrette**
- 1 **large apple, thinly sliced**
- ⅔ **cup salad croutons**
- ⅔ **cup shredded cheddar cheese**

Place spinach in a large bowl. Drizzle with vinaigrette; toss to coat. Top with apple, croutons and cheese. Serve immediately.

BROCCOLI WITH ORANGE
BROWNED BUTTER

CUCUMBER AND
RED ONION SALAD

---

(5) INGREDIENTS *EXPRESS PREP*
READY IN (4)

Broccoli with Orange Browned Butter

This easy butter sauce with orange peel, salt and nutmeg will turn everyone into broccoli lovers!

—**CHRISTINE BERGMAN** SUWANEE, GA

START TO FINISH: 15 MIN.
MAKES: 4 SERVINGS

- 1 package (12 ounces) frozen broccoli cuts
- 2 tablespoons butter
- 1 teaspoon grated orange peel
- ¼ teaspoon salt
  Dash ground nutmeg

1. Cook broccoli according to package directions. Meanwhile, in a small heavy saucepan, cook butter over medium heat for 3-4 minutes or until golden brown. Stir in the orange peel, salt and nutmeg.
2. Drain broccoli. Add to the saucepan and toss to coat.

READY IN (4)

Cucumber and Red Onion Salad

This is one of the first recipes I created myself. It's a great salad for picnics or potlucks. I always come home with an empty bowl!

—**BRYNN STECKMAN** WESTERVILLE, OH

PREP: 15 MIN. + CHILLING
MAKES: 4 SERVINGS

- 2 small seedless cucumbers, thinly sliced
- 1 cup thinly sliced red onion
- 1 tablespoon white vinegar
- 1 tablespoon white wine vinegar
- 1 tablespoon rice vinegar
- ¼ teaspoon salt
- ¼ teaspoon pepper
- ¼ teaspoon sesame oil

In a small bowl, combine the cucumbers and red onion. In a small bowl, whisk the vinegars, salt, pepper and oil. Pour over cucumber mixture; toss to coat. Cover and refrigerate for at least 1 hour. Serve with a slotted spoon.

EXPRESS PREP **READY IN (4)**

Asparagus, Mushrooms and Peas

Crisp-tender vegetables are tossed in a tangy dressing that has just a hint of sweetness from maple syrup. The fresh spring medley complements any meat entree.

—**KRISTY WILLIAMS** WEMBLEY, AB

START TO FINISH: 15 MIN.
MAKES: 6 SERVINGS

- ½ pound fresh asparagus, cut into 2-inch pieces
- ½ pound sliced fresh mushrooms
- 1 cup fresh or frozen peas
- 1 tablespoon olive oil
- ¼ cup balsamic vinegar
- ¼ cup maple syrup
- 2 teaspoons snipped fresh dill

In a large skillet, saute the asparagus, mushrooms and peas in oil until tender. Add the vinegar, syrup and dill; heat through. Serve with a slotted spoon.

Blueberry Spinach Salad

I came up with this summer recipe while trying to use up blueberries that I didn't want to go to waste. The combo of flavors and textures is simply delightful.

—**JAN LYSAK-RUIZ** YUCAIPA, CA

START TO FINISH: 10 MIN.
MAKES: 8 SERVINGS

- ½ cup olive oil
- ¼ cup white balsamic vinegar
- 2 teaspoons Dijon mustard
- 1 teaspoon sugar
- ¼ teaspoon salt
- 1 package (10 ounces) fresh spinach, trimmed
- 1 cup (4 ounces) crumbled feta cheese
- 1 cup fresh blueberries
- ½ cup pine nuts, toasted

1. Place the first five ingredients in a jar with a tight-fitting lid; shake well. Refrigerate dressing until serving.
2. In a large bowl, combine the spinach, cheese, blueberries and nuts. Just before serving, shake dressing and drizzle over salad; toss to coat.

BLUEBERRY SPINACH SALAD

Fiesta Side Salad

Perfect for a buffet, picnic or potluck, this colorful side can be served at room temperature. You'll want to make extra because the flavors will only get better the second day.

—**MICHELLE CHICOINE** APO, AE

PREP: 30 MIN. + CHILLING
MAKES: 8 SERVINGS

- ⅔ cup uncooked long grain rice
- 2 cups frozen corn, thawed
- 1 can (15 ounces) black beans, rinsed and drained
- 6 green onions, sliced
- ¼ cup pickled jalapeno slices, chopped
- ¼ cup canola oil
- 2 tablespoons cider vinegar
- 1 tablespoon lime juice
- 1 teaspoon chili powder
- 1 teaspoon molasses
- ½ teaspoon salt
- ½ teaspoon cumin seeds, toasted and ground

1. Cook rice according to package directions. Meanwhile, in a large bowl, combine the corn, beans, onions and jalapenos. In a jar with a tight-fitting lid, combine the remaining ingredients; shake well.
2. Stir rice into corn mixture. Add dressing and toss to coat. Cover and refrigerate for at least 2 hours.

TOP TIP

Toasting whole cumin seeds and then grinding them adds extra flavor to foods. If you don't have whole cumin seeds, substitute ¼ teaspoon of ground cumin but don't toast it.

Glazed Pearl Onions

These onions were served at a restaurant I visited in Florida, and the chef's assistant shared the recipe with me. They make a unique side to many entrees.
—**DIXIE TERRY** GOREVILLE, IL

START TO FINISH: 15 MIN.
MAKES: 6 SERVINGS

- 1 **package (16 ounces) frozen pearl onions, thawed**
- 2 **tablespoons butter**
- 2 **tablespoons plus 1½ teaspoons brown sugar**
- 1 **tablespoon Dijon mustard**
- 2 **tablespoons minced fresh parsley**

In a large skillet, saute onions in butter until tender. Add brown sugar and mustard; cook 2 minutes longer. Sprinkle with parsley.

Spinach & Feta Saute

With just the right level of garlic and a pleasant mix of cheese and almonds, this quick side will brighten any plate. You could also try it stuffed in a filet.
—**SHARON DELANEY-CHRONIS**
SOUTH MILWAUKEE, WI

START TO FINISH: 10 MIN.
MAKES: 2 SERVINGS

- 2 **garlic cloves, minced**
- 2 **tablespoons olive oil**
- 1 **package (6 ounces) fresh baby spinach**
- ¼ **cup slivered almonds**
- ½ **cup crumbled feta cheese**

In a large skillet, saute garlic in oil for 1 minute. Add the spinach and almonds; saute 2 minutes longer or just until the spinach is wilted. Sprinkle with cheese.

Pizza Salad

I love taking this fun summer dish to parties. It's a great change of pace that looks as good as it tastes. Its wonderfully zesty flavor really complements barbecued entrees!
—**DEBBIE TERENZINI-WILKERSON**
LUSBY, MD

PREP: 15 MIN. + CHILLING
MAKES: 16 SERVINGS

- 1 **pound spiral macaroni, cooked and drained**
- 3 **medium tomatoes, diced and seeded**
- 16 **ounces cheddar cheese, cubed**
- 1 **to 2 bunches green onions, sliced**
- 3 **ounces sliced pepperoni**
- ¾ **cup canola oil**
- ⅔ **cup grated Parmesan cheese**
- ½ **cup red wine vinegar**
- 2 **teaspoons dried oregano**
- 1 **teaspoon garlic powder**
- 1 **teaspoon salt**
- ¼ **teaspoon pepper**
  Croutons, optional

In a large bowl, combine macaroni, tomatoes, cheddar cheese, green onions and pepperoni. In a small bowl, combine oil, Parmesan cheese, vinegar and seasonings. Pour over macaroni mixture; toss to coat. Cover and refrigerate for several hours. Top with croutons just before serving if desired.

Sesame Tossed Salad

Crisp, crunchy and slightly sweet, this nutritious salad is simply delightful. Feel free to double up on any of your favorite toss-ins.
—**ELIZABETH PERKINS**
SOUTH RIDING, VA

START TO FINISH: 10 MIN.
MAKES: 4 SERVINGS

- 1 **package (5 ounces) spring mix salad greens**
- ½ **cup sliced fresh mushrooms**
- ½ **cup chopped cucumber**
- ½ **cup canned mandarin oranges**
- ¼ **cup sliced almonds, toasted**
- ¼ **cup shredded carrots**
- 2 **green onions, chopped**
- ⅓ **cup reduced-fat Asian toasted sesame salad dressing**

Combine the first seven salad ingredients in a large bowl. Drizzle with dressing; toss to coat. Serve immediately.

Curry Rice Pilaf

Salted cashews add a nice crunch to this simple rice dish flavored with curry and turmeric.
—**KATIE ROSE** PEWAUKEE, WI

START TO FINISH: 10 MIN.
MAKES: 5 SERVINGS

- 2 **packages (8½ ounces each) ready-to-serve jasmine rice**
- 2 **tablespoons butter**
- 1 **cup salted whole cashews**
- 2 **green onions, sliced**
- ½ **teaspoon curry powder**
- ¼ **teaspoon salt**
- ¼ **teaspoon ground turmeric**
- ¼ **teaspoon pepper**

Heat rice according to package directions. Meanwhile, in a small skillet, melt butter over medium heat. Add the cashews, onions and seasonings; cook and stir for 2-3 minutes or until onions are tender. Add rice; toss to coat.

PIZZA SALAD

SESAME TOSSED SALAD

CURRY RICE PILAF

PASSOVER POPOVERS, 234

233

232

242

BONUS:
Quick Breads

Nothing complements a comforting slow-cooked entree like a golden loaf of bread or buttery biscuits. Treat loved ones to any of these freshly baked sensations for a meal everyone is sure to remember.

CHIMICHURRI MONKEY BREAD, 244

SAVORY BISCUIT-
BREADSTICKS

Savory Biscuit-Breadsticks

I love to experiment in the kitchen with simple ingredients. Made with convenient refrigerated biscuits, these super-fast breadsticks are always a big hit.

—**BILLY HENSLEY** MOUNT CARMEL, TN

START TO FINISH: 20 MIN.
MAKES: 10 BREADSTICKS

- ½ cup grated Parmesan cheese
- 2 teaspoons dried minced garlic
- ¼ teaspoon crushed red pepper flakes
- 1 tube (12 ounces) refrigerated buttermilk biscuits
- 2 tablespoons olive oil

Preheat oven to 400°. In a shallow bowl, mix cheese, garlic and pepper flakes. Roll each biscuit into a 6-in. rope. Brush lightly with oil; roll in cheese mixture. Place on a greased baking sheet. Bake 8-10 minutes or until golden brown.

TOP TIP

The recipe for Savory Biscuit-Breadsticks is a snap to customize. If you're not wild about spice, leave out the red pepper flakes. Toss in a dash of dried basil or oregano leaves instead. You can make things easy with a little Italian seasoning or even a pinch of dried thyme.

Tamale Cakes

I wanted my kids to have something other than peanut butter and jelly for their lunches. These muffin tamales have all of the flavor without the fuss. Try them alongside slow-cooked chili!

—SUZANNE CLARK PHOENIX, AZ

PREP: 25 MIN. • **BAKE:** 20 MIN.
MAKES: 2 DOZEN

- **2 packages (8½ ounces each) corn bread/muffin mix**
- **1 can (14¾ ounces) cream-style corn**
- **2 large eggs, lightly beaten**
- **1½ cups (6 ounces) shredded reduced-fat Mexican cheese blend, divided**
- **1½ cups chopped cooked chicken breast**
- **¾ cup red enchilada sauce**

1. Preheat oven to 400°. In a large bowl, combine muffin mix, corn and eggs; stir just until moistened. Stir in 1 cup cheese. In another bowl, toss the chicken with the enchilada sauce.

2. Fill each of 24 foil-lined muffin cups with 2 tablespoons batter. Place 1 tablespoon chicken mixture into center of each; cover with about 1 tablespoon batter.

3. Bake 13-15 minutes or until golden brown. Sprinkle the tops with remaining cheese. Bake for 3-5 minutes longer or until cheese is melted. Cool 5 minutes before removing from pan to wire racks. Serve warm. Refrigerate leftovers.

⑤ INGREDIENTS **READY IN** ④

Sweet Onion Bread Skillet

Because there are just a few ingredients in this recipe, you will get the best results if you use the finest-quality ingredients, such as fresh Vidalia onions and aged Parmesan cheese.

—MARY LISA SPEER PALM BEACH, FL

PREP: 25 MIN. • **BAKE:** 10 MIN.
MAKES: 4 SERVINGS

- **1 large sweet onion, thinly sliced**
- **2 tablespoons butter**
- **2 tablespoons olive oil, divided**
- **1 can (13.8 ounces) refrigerated pizza crust**
- **¼ cup grated Parmesan cheese**

1. In a large skillet, saute onion in butter and 1 tablespoon oil until softened. Reduce heat to medium-low; cook, stirring occasionally, for 15-20 minutes or until golden brown. Set aside.

2. Brush bottom and sides of a 10-in. ovenproof skillet with the remaining oil. Unroll dough into skillet; flatten dough and build up edge slightly. Top with the onion mixture and cheese. Bake at 450° for 10-12 minutes or until golden brown. Cut into wedges.

TAMALE CAKES

Parmesan-Herb Dinner Rolls

I teach special needs students and have designed a culinary program for them. These tasty rolls are easy to do and often requested.

—CHRISTINA HASELMAN
MILLER CITY, OH

PREP: 10 MIN. + RISING • **BAKE:** 15 MIN.
MAKES: 1 DOZEN

- 12 frozen bread dough dinner rolls
- ½ cup grated Parmesan cheese
- 2 garlic cloves, minced
- 1½ teaspoons Italian seasoning
- ¼ teaspoon dill weed
- ¼ cup butter, melted

1. Place rolls on a greased baking sheet; thaw, covered, in the refrigerator overnight or at room temperature for 2 hours.

2. In a small bowl, mix cheese, garlic, Italian seasoning and dill. Brush rolls with butter; sprinkle with cheese mixture. Cover loosely with plastic wrap; let rise in a warm place until doubled, about 1 hour.

3. Preheat oven to 350°. Bake 15-20 minutes or until golden brown. Remove from pan to a wire rack; serve warm.

Marina's Golden Corn Fritters

Just one bite of these fritters takes me back to when my kids were young. They're all grown up now, but the tradition lives on at get-togethers, where I sometimes need to triple the recipe. Serve fritters with maple syrup or agave nectar. They're great alongside Southwestern entrees, too.

—MARINA CASTLE
CANYON COUNTRY, CA

START TO FINISH: 30 MIN.
MAKES: 32 FRITTERS

- 2½ cups all-purpose flour
- 3 teaspoons baking powder
- 2 teaspoons dried parsley flakes
- 1 teaspoon salt
- 2 large eggs
- ¾ cup 2% milk
- 2 tablespoons butter, melted
- 2 teaspoons grated onion
- 1 can (15¼ ounces) whole kernel corn, drained
  Oil for deep-fat frying

1. In a large bowl, whisk the flour, baking powder, parsley and salt. In another bowl, whisk the eggs, milk, melted butter and onion until blended. Add to dry ingredients, stirring just until moistened. Fold in corn.

2. In an electric skillet or deep fryer, heat oil to 375°. Drop batter by tablespoonfuls, several at a time, into hot oil. Fry 2-3 minutes on each side or until golden brown. Drain on paper towels.

Passover Popovers

Popovers have an important role at the table, substituting for bread. When puffed and golden brown, they're ready to share.

—GLORIA MEZIKOFSKY WAKEFIELD, MA

PREP: 25 MIN. • **BAKE:** 20 MIN. + STANDING
MAKES: 1 DOZEN

- 1 cup water
- ½ cup safflower oil
- ⅛ to ¼ teaspoon salt
- 1 cup matzo cake meal
- 7 large eggs

1. Preheat the oven to 450°. Generously grease 12 muffin cups. In a large saucepan, bring water, oil and salt to a rolling boil. Add cake meal all at once and beat until blended. Remove from heat; let stand 5 minutes.

2. Transfer mixture to a blender. Add two eggs; process, covered, until blended. Continue adding eggs, one at a time, and process until incorporated. Process for 2 minutes longer or until mixture is smooth.

3. Fill prepared muffin cups three-fourths full. Bake 18-22 minutes or until puffed, very firm and golden brown. Turn off oven (do not open oven door); leave popovers in oven for 10 minutes. Immediately remove popovers from pan to a wire rack. Serve hot.

NOTE *This recipe was tested with Manischewitz cake meal. Look for it in the baking aisle or kosher foods section.*

MARINA'S GOLDEN
CORN FRITTERS

PASSOVER POPOVERS

**BROCCOLI-MUSHROOM
BUBBLE BAKE**

**MONKEY BREAD
BISCUITS**

GARLIC LOAF

Broccoli-Mushroom Bubble Bake

I got bored with the same old breakfast casseroles served at our monthly moms' meeting, so I decided to create something new. Judging by the reactions of the other moms, this one's a keeper. It's perfect with a slow-cooked side dish.

—**SHANNON KOENE** BLACKSBURG, VA

PREP: 20 MIN. • **BAKE:** 25 MIN.
MAKES: 12 SERVINGS

- 1 teaspoon canola oil
- ½ pound fresh mushrooms, finely chopped
- 1 medium onion, finely chopped
- 1 tube (16.3 ounces) large refrigerated flaky biscuits
- 1 package (10 ounces) frozen broccoli with cheese sauce
- 3 large eggs
- 1 can (5 ounces) evaporated milk
- 1 teaspoon Italian seasoning
- ½ teaspoon garlic powder
- ½ teaspoon salt
- ¼ teaspoon pepper
- 1½ cups (6 ounces) shredded Colby-Monterey Jack cheese

1. Preheat oven to 350°. In a large skillet, heat oil over medium-high heat. Add mushrooms and onion; cook and stir for 4-6 minutes or until tender.
2. Cut each biscuit into eight pieces; place in a greased 13x9-in. baking dish. Top with mushroom mixture.
3. Cook broccoli with cheese sauce according to package directions. Spoon over mushroom mixture.
4. In a large bowl, whisk eggs, milk and seasonings; pour over the top. Sprinkle with cheese. Bake 25-30 minutes or until golden brown.

Monkey Bread Biscuits

Classic monkey bread is a sweetly spiced breakfast treat. I came up with an easy dinner version featuring garlic and Italian seasoning. You can serve it with nearly any main course.
—**DANA JOHNSON** SCOTTSDALE, AZ

START TO FINISH: 20 MIN.
MAKES: 1 DOZEN

- 1 tube (16.3 ounces) large refrigerated flaky biscuits
- 3 tablespoons butter, melted
- 1 garlic clove, minced
- ½ teaspoon Italian seasoning
- ¼ cup grated Parmesan cheese
  Additional Italian seasoning

1. Preheat oven to 425°. Separate biscuits; cut each into six pieces. In a large bowl, combine butter, garlic and Italian seasoning; add biscuit pieces and toss to coat.
2. Place four pieces in each of 12 greased muffin cups. Sprinkle with cheese and additional Italian seasoning. Bake 8-10 minutes or until golden brown. Serve warm.

⑤ INGREDIENTS READY IN ④

Garlic Loaf

This golden loaf has garlicky goodness in every bite. People go wild over its savory flavor. Try serving it with an herb-infused or lightly salted olive oil for dunking.
—**TASTE OF HOME** COOKING SCHOOL

PREP: 15 MIN. + RISING • **BAKE:** 20 MIN.
MAKES: 1 LOAF (24 PIECES)

- 2 loaves (1 pound each) frozen bread dough or 24 frozen unbaked white dinner rolls, thawed
- ½ cup finely chopped sweet onion
- ½ cup butter, melted

- 2 garlic cloves, minced
- 1 teaspoon dried parsley flakes
- ¼ teaspoon salt
  Herb-seasoned olive oil, optional

1. Divide dough into 24 pieces. In a small bowl, combine the onion, butter, garlic, parsley and salt. Dip each piece of dough into butter mixture; place in a 10-in. fluted tube pan coated with cooking spray. Cover and let rise in a warm place until doubled, about 1 hour.
2. Bake at 375° for 20-25 minutes or until golden brown. Serve warm with olive oil if desired.

Parmesan Breadsticks

These tender and flavorful breadsticks make a foolproof addition to any meal. You'll love the change-of-pace flavor that cumin and paprika offer.
—**LINDA FINCHMAN** SPENCER, WV

START TO FINISH: 15 MIN.
MAKES: 1 DOZEN

- ½ cup grated Parmesan cheese
- ¼ teaspoon paprika
- ⅛ teaspoon ground cumin
- 3 tablespoons butter, melted
- 1 tube (11 ounces) refrigerated breadsticks

1. In a shallow bowl, combine the cheese, paprika and cumin. Place butter in another shallow bowl. Separate dough into individual breadsticks. Dip in butter, then in cheese mixture. Twist two to three times and place on an ungreased baking sheet.
2. Bake at 375° for 10-12 minutes or until golden brown. Serve immediately.

EXPRESS *PREP* **READY IN** ④

Mexican Cheese Corn Bread

This moist and cheesy corn bread is the perfect side for chili and soups. It's great for soaking up every last bit of goodness in your bowl.

—SUSAN WESTERFIELD
ALBUQUERQUE, NM

START TO FINISH: 30 MIN.
MAKES: 9 SERVINGS

- 1 package (8½ ounces) corn bread/muffin mix
- 1 teaspoon dried minced onion
- ½ teaspoon ground cumin
- 2 large eggs
- ⅓ cup 2% milk
- 2 tablespoons butter, melted, divided
- ¾ cup shredded Mexican cheese blend, divided

1. In a small bowl, combine the muffin mix, onion and cumin. In another bowl, whisk the eggs, milk and 1 tablespoon butter; stir into the dry ingredients just until moistened. Fold in ½ cup cheese.
2. Transfer to a greased 8-in. square baking dish. Bake at 400° for 15 minutes. Brush with the remaining butter and sprinkle with the remaining cheese; bake 2-4 minutes longer or until cheese is melted and a toothpick inserted near the center comes out clean. Serve warm.

⑤ INGREDIENTS **EXPRESS** *PREP*
READY IN ④

Navajo Fry Bread

While taking a trip to the Grand Canyon, my family drove through the Navajo reservation and stopped at a little cafe for dinner. I complimented the young Navajo waiter on the delicious bread and he gave me the recipe. It is very easy to make.

—MILDRED STEPHENSON
HARTSELLE, AL

PREP: 5 MIN. + STANDING • **COOK:** 5 MIN.
MAKES: 2 SERVINGS

- 1 cup all-purpose flour
- 1 teaspoon baking powder
- ⅛ teaspoon salt
- ⅓ cup hot water
  Oil for deep-fat frying

1. In a small bowl, combine the flour, baking powder and salt; stir in hot water to form a soft dough. Cover and let stand for 30 minutes.
2. Divide the dough in half. On a lightly floured surface, roll each portion into a 6-in. circle.
3. In an electric skillet, heat 1 in. of oil to 375°. Fry bread in hot oil for 2-3 minutes on each side or until golden brown; drain bread on paper towels.

EXPRESS *PREP* **READY IN** ④

Ham and Swiss Biscuits

These can be made ahead and frozen. To reheat frozen biscuits, place them on an ungreased baking sheet in a 375° oven for 6-10 minutes or until heated through.

—TRISHA KRUSE EAGLE, ID

START TO FINISH: 20 MIN.
MAKES: 10 BISCUITS

- 2 cups biscuit/baking mix
- ¼ pound fully cooked ham, finely chopped
- ½ cup shredded Swiss cheese
- ⅔ cup 2% milk
- 1 large egg, beaten
- 1 tablespoon honey mustard
- 2 teaspoons dried minced onion

1. In a small bowl, combine the biscuit mix, ham and cheese. Combine the milk, egg, mustard and onion. Stir into biscuit mixture just until moistened. Drop dough by ¼ cupfuls 2 in. apart onto a greased baking sheet.
2. Bake at 425° for 10-12 minutes or until golden brown. Serve warm. Refrigerate leftovers.

▶ DID YOU KNOW?

Golden fry bread is a savory treat that can be enjoyed on its own, often topped with honey or jam. It's a delicious alternative to yeast bread, particularly when served alongside a piping hot bowl of soup.

**GRILLED CHEESE &
TOMATO FLATBREADS**

READY IN (4)

Grilled Cheese &
Tomato Flatbreads

This is a combination of grilled pizza and a cheesy flatbread recipe that I discovered years ago. It's a great way to jazz up a meal, or impress guests by serving it as an appetizer.

—**TINA MIRILOVICH** JOHNSTOWN, PA

PREP: 30 MIN. • **GRILL:** 5 MIN.
MAKES: 2 FLATBREADS
(12 SERVINGS EACH)

- 1 package (8 ounces) cream cheese, softened
- ⅔ cup grated Parmesan cheese, divided
- 2 tablespoons minced fresh parsley, divided
- 1 tablespoon minced chives
- 2 garlic cloves, minced
- ½ teaspoon minced fresh thyme
- ¼ teaspoon salt
- ¼ teaspoon pepper
- 1 tube (13.8 ounces) refrigerated pizza crust
- 2 tablespoons olive oil
- 3 medium tomatoes, thinly sliced

1. In a small bowl, beat the cream cheese, ⅓ cup Parmesan cheese, 1 tablespoon parsley, chives, garlic, thyme, salt and pepper until blended.

2. Unroll the pizza crust and cut in half. On a lightly floured surface, roll out each portion into a 12x6-in. rectangle; brush each side with oil. Grill, covered, over medium heat for 1-2 minutes or until bottoms are lightly browned. Remove from the grill.

3. Spread grilled sides with cheese mixture. Sprinkle with remaining Parmesan cheese; top with the tomatoes. Return to the grill. Cover and cook for 2-3 minutes or until crust is lightly browned and cheese is melted, rotating halfway through cooking to ensure an evenly browned crust. Sprinkle with remaining parsley.

HERBED PARMESAN BREAD

CHEDDAR CORN DOG MUFFINS

⑤INGREDIENTS *EXPRESS PREP*
READY IN ④

Herbed Parmesan Bread

I've been making my Parmesan bread for so many years, I can't remember where I got the recipe! Thanks to a convenient baking mix, a freshly made loaf gets into the oven fast.
—**LESLEY ARCHER** JALISCO, MEXICO

PREP: 10 MIN. • **BAKE:** 35 MIN. + COOLING
MAKES: 1 LOAF (12 SLICES)

- 3¾ **cups biscuit/baking mix**
- 1 **cup plus 2 tablespoons grated Parmesan cheese, divided**
- 1 **teaspoon Italian seasoning**
- ½ **teaspoon salt**
- 1 **large egg**
- 1 **can (5 ounces) evaporated milk**
- ¾ **cup water**

1. Preheat oven to 350°. In a large bowl, combine biscuit mix, 1 cup cheese, Italian seasoning and salt. In a small bowl, whisk the egg, milk and water. Stir into dry ingredients just until moistened. Transfer to a greased 8x4-in. loaf pan. Sprinkle with remaining cheese.

2. Bake 35-40 minutes or until a toothpick inserted in center comes out clean. Cool 10 minutes before removing from pan to a wire rack.

⑤INGREDIENTS *EXPRESS PREP*
READY IN ④

Cheddar Corn Dog Muffins

I wanted a change from hot dogs, so I made corn dog muffins. I added jalapenos to this kid friendly recipe and won my husband over, too!
—**BECKY TARALA** PALM COAST, FL

START TO FINISH: 25 MIN.
MAKES: 9 MUFFINS

- 1 **package (8½ ounces) corn bread/muffin mix**
- ⅔ **cup 2% milk**
- 1 **large egg, lightly beaten**
- 5 **turkey hot dogs, sliced**
- ½ **cup shredded sharp cheddar cheese**
- 2 **tablespoons finely chopped pickled jalapeno, optional**

1. Preheat oven to 400°. Line nine muffin cups with foil liners or grease nine nonstick muffin cups.

2. In a small bowl, combine muffin mix, milk and egg; stir in hot dogs, cheese and, if desired, jalapeno. Fill prepared muffin cups three-fourths full.

3. Bake 14-18 minutes or until a toothpick inserted in center comes out clean. Cool 5 minutes before removing from pan to a wire rack. Serve warm. Refrigerate leftovers.
FREEZE OPTION *Freeze cooled muffins in resealable plastic freezer bags. To use, microwave each muffin on high for 30-60 seconds or until heated through.*

TOP TIP

Not only are Cheddar Corn Dog Muffins great alongside soups and roasts, they also make satisfying after-school snacks, sleepover treats, game-day bites and comforting additions to backyard barbecues. Double the recipe for fun contributions to potlucks as well!

Grandma's Biscuits

Homemade biscuits add a warm and comforting touch to any meal. My grandmother makes these tender biscuits to go with her special seafood chowder.

—MELISSA BEYER UTICA, NY

START TO FINISH: 25 MIN.
MAKES: 10 BISCUITS

- 2 **cups all-purpose flour**
- 3 **teaspoons baking powder**
- 1 **teaspoon salt**
- ⅓ **cup shortening**
- ⅔ **cup 2% milk**
- 1 **large egg, lightly beaten**

1. Preheat oven to 450°. In a large bowl, whisk flour, baking powder and salt. Cut in shortening until mixture resembles coarse crumbs. Add milk; stir just until moistened.
2. Turn onto a lightly floured surface; knead gently 8-10 times. Pat dough into a 10x4-in. rectangle. Cut rectangle lengthwise in half; cut crosswise to make 10 squares.
3. Place biscuits 1 in. apart on an ungreased baking sheet; brush tops with egg. Bake 8-10 minutes or until golden brown. Serve warm.

Honey-Moon Rolls

I like to dress up plain crescent roll dough with cream cheese, honey and sliced almonds. Yum!

—ABBY RUTILA WHITE LAKE, MI

START TO FINISH: 30 MIN.
MAKES: 8 ROLLS

- 4 **ounces cream cheese, softened**
- 2 **tablespoons plus 2 teaspoons honey, divided**
- ¼ **cup sliced almonds**
- 1 **tube (8 ounces) refrigerated crescent rolls**
- ¼ **teaspoon ground cinnamon**

1. In a small bowl, beat cream cheese and 2 tablespoons honey until smooth; stir in almonds. Unroll crescent dough; separate into triangles.
2. Place 1 tablespoon of cream cheese mixture in the center of each triangle. Roll up and place point side down 2 in. apart on an ungreased baking sheet; curve ends to form a crescent. Sprinkle tops with cinnamon.
3. Bake at 375° for 12-14 minutes or until golden brown. Drizzle with remaining honey. Serve warm. Refrigerate leftovers.

GRANDMA'S BISCUITS

Cumin Roasted Tortillas

You'll discover a new favorite with these easy but zesty tortillas. They make a great snack, too.
—EMILY SEEFELDT RED WING, MN

START TO FINISH: 15 MIN.
MAKES: 8 SERVINGS

- ¼ cup olive oil
- 1 teaspoon dried oregano
- 1 teaspoon ground cumin
- ¼ teaspoon salt
- 8 flour tortillas (8 inches)

In a small bowl, combine the oil, oregano, cumin and salt; brush over both sides of tortillas. Fold tortillas into quarters; place on an ungreased baking sheet. Bake at 425° for 4-5 minutes or until tortillas are heated through. Serve immediately.

Romano Sticks

It's hard to munch just one of these yummy breadsticks. I can make them quickly using puff pastry.
—TIM AILPORT WEST LAKELAND, MN

START TO FINISH: 20 MIN.
MAKES: 20 PASTRY STICKS

- 1 package (17.3 ounces) frozen puff pastry, thawed
- 1 large egg, lightly beaten
- 1½ cups grated Romano cheese
- 1 tablespoon dried basil

1. Brush one side of each puff pastry sheet with egg; sprinkle with cheese and basil. Cut each sheet into ten 1-in. strips. Place 1 in. apart on greased baking sheets.
2. Bake at 400° for 10-13 minutes or until golden brown.

Zesty Jalapeno Corn Muffins

I make these tender corn muffins at least twice a month. My husband and relatives love the zippy flavor.
—SHARI DORE PORT SEVEN, ON

PREP: 20 MIN. • **BAKE:** 20 MIN.
MAKES: 1 DOZEN

- 2 packages (8½ ounces each) corn bread/muffin mix
- ¼ cup minced fresh cilantro
- 1 tablespoon grated lime peel
- 2 teaspoons ground cumin
- 2 large eggs
- ⅔ cup buttermilk
- 4 ounces cream cheese, cubed
- 2 jalapeno peppers, seeded and minced
- 4 green onions, finely chopped

1. In a large bowl, combine the muffin mixes, cilantro, lime peel and cumin. Whisk the eggs and buttermilk; stir into the dry ingredients just until moistened. Fold in the cream cheese, jalapenos and onions.
2. Fill greased or paper-lined muffin cups three-fourths full. Bake at 400° for 16-20 minutes or until a toothpick inserted into muffin comes out clean. Cool for 5 minutes before removing from pan to a wire rack. Serve warm.
NOTE *Wear disposable gloves when cutting hot peppers; the oils can burn skin. Avoid touching your face.*

Triple Tomato Flatbread

Tomatoes are the reason I have a vegetable garden, and I developed this recipe as a way to show off my garden's plum, sun-dried and cherry tomatoes. It's so easy, and will absolutely impress.
—RACHEL KIMBROW PORTLAND, OR

START TO FINISH: 20 MIN.
MAKES: 8 PIECES

- 1 tube (13.8 ounces) refrigerated pizza crust
  Cooking spray
- 3 plum tomatoes, finely chopped (about 2 cups)
- ½ cup soft sun-dried tomato halves (not packed in oil), julienned
- 2 tablespoons olive oil
- 1 tablespoon dried basil
- ¼ teaspoon salt
- ¼ teaspoon pepper
- 1 cup shredded Asiago cheese
- 2 cups yellow and/or red cherry tomatoes, halved

1. Unroll and press dough into a 15x10-in. rectangle. Transfer the dough to an 18x12-in. piece of heavy-duty foil coated with cooking spray; spritz dough with cooking spray. In a large bowl, toss plum tomatoes and sun-dried tomatoes with oil and seasonings.
2. Carefully invert dough onto grill rack; remove foil. Grill, covered, over medium heat for 2-3 minutes or until bottom is golden brown. Turn dough; grill 1-2 minutes longer or until second side begins to brown.
3. Remove from grill. Spoon plum tomato mixture over crust; top with cheese and cherry tomatoes. Return flatbread to grill. Grill, covered, 2-4 minutes or until the crust is golden brown and cheese is melted.

Cheese & Pesto Biscuits

Biscuits always liven up a meal, especially when they're golden brown and filled with pesto, garlic and cheese for extra flair.

—LIZ BELLVILLE JACKSONVILLE, NC

START TO FINISH: 25 MIN.
MAKES: 1 DOZEN

- 2 **cups all-purpose flour**
- 2 **teaspoons baking powder**
- ½ **teaspoon salt**
- ¼ **teaspoon baking soda**
- ⅓ **cup cold butter, cubed**
- 1 **cup (4 ounces) shredded Italian cheese blend**
- 1¼ **cups buttermilk**
- 1 **tablespoon prepared pesto**
- 1 **tablespoon butter, melted**
- 1 **garlic clove, minced**

1. Preheat oven to 450°. In a large bowl, whisk flour, baking powder, salt and baking soda. Cut in butter until mixture resembles coarse crumbs. Stir in cheese. In a small bowl, whisk buttermilk and pesto until blended; stir into flour mixture just until moistened.
2. Drop dough by ¼ cupfuls 2 in. apart onto an ungreased baking sheet. Bake 10-12 minutes or until golden brown.
3. Mix melted butter and garlic; brush over biscuits. Serve warm.

TRIPLE TOMATO FLATBREAD

CHEESE & PESTO BISCUITS

(5) INGREDIENTS *EXPRESS* PREP
READY IN (4)

Italian Puff Pastry Twists

Not only are these twists delicious, but they'll look pretty displayed on your table, too!

—*TASTE OF HOME* TEST KITCHEN

PREP: 10 MIN. • **BAKE:** 10 MIN./BATCH
MAKES: 2 DOZEN

- ¼ cup butter, melted
- 1 garlic clove, minced
- 1 teaspoon Italian seasoning
- 1 package (17.3 ounces) frozen puff pastry, thawed
- ¼ cup grated Parmesan cheese

1. In a small bowl, combine the butter, garlic and Italian seasoning; set aside.
2. On a lightly floured surface, roll each pastry sheet into a 12x10-in. rectangle; cut each widthwise into 1-in. strips.
3. Twist each strip two to three times; place on greased baking sheets. Brush with butter mixture; sprinkle with cheese. Bake at 400° for 8-12 minutes or until golden brown.

READY IN (4)

Chimichurri Monkey Bread

The herby goodness of my favorite sauce shines in this nostalgic bread recipe that comes together quickly thanks to refrigerated biscuits. Serve warm as an appetizer with marinara for dipping, or as a side to an Italian main course.

—**EDEN DRANGER** LOS ANGELES, CA

PREP: 20 MIN. • **BAKE:** 20 MIN.
MAKES: 12 SERVINGS

- ¼ cup minced fresh parsley
- ¼ cup olive oil
- 2 tablespoons minced fresh oregano
- 1 tablespoon white wine vinegar
- 2 garlic cloves
- ¾ teaspoon kosher salt

- ¼ teaspoon ground cumin
- ¼ teaspoon pepper
- ⅛ teaspoon crushed red pepper flakes
- 2 tubes (12 ounces each) refrigerated buttermilk biscuits

1. In a shallow bowl, combine the first nine ingredients. Cut each biscuit in half and shape into a ball. Roll in herb mixture.
2. Place biscuit pieces in a greased 10-in. fluted tube pan. Bake at 375° for 18-22 minutes or until golden brown. Cool for 5 minutes before inverting onto a serving plate.

READY IN (4)

Garlic Bread Spirals

These satisfying bites are wonderful for holiday meals, but they're so easy you'll want to bake them up all year long! They're ideal with slow-cooked comfort foods.

—**MARIE RIZZIO** INTERLOCHEN, MI

START TO FINISH: 25 MIN.
MAKES: 1 DOZEN

- ¼ cup butter, melted
- 2 green onions, finely chopped
- 3 tablespoons grated Parmesan cheese
- 2 tablespoons minced fresh parsley
- 3 garlic cloves, minced
- 1 tube (11 ounces) refrigerated crusty French loaf

1. In a small bowl, mix the first five ingredients. Unroll dough; spread butter mixture to within ½ in. of edges. Roll up jelly-roll style, starting with a long side. Cut into 12 slices; place in greased muffin cups, cut side down.
2. Bake at 400° for 10-12 minutes or until golden brown.

READY IN (4)

Home-Style Sausage Gravy and Biscuits

My mother-in-law introduced me to her hamburger gravy, and I modified it slightly. We have this hearty specialty nearly every weekend.

—**MICHELE BAPST** JACKSONVILLE, NC

START TO FINISH: 30 MIN.
MAKES: 8 SERVINGS

- 1 tube (16.3 ounces) large refrigerated flaky biscuits
- 1 pound bulk pork sausage
- 1 cup chopped sweet onion
- 2 tablespoons butter
- 1 envelope country gravy mix
- 1 tablespoon all-purpose flour
  Dash each garlic powder, Italian seasoning, onion powder and pepper
- 1½ cups 2% milk
- 1 cup reduced-sodium chicken broth

1. Bake biscuits according to package directions.
2. Meanwhile, in a large skillet, cook sausage and onion over medium heat until sausage is no longer pink; drain. Add butter; cook until melted. Stir in the gravy mix, flour and seasonings until blended. Gradually add milk and broth. Bring to a boil; cook and stir for 1 minute or until thickened. Serve with biscuits.

TOP TIP

I use canned chicken broth instead of bouillon cubes in recipes because it has less salt, but I always have some left over. So I pour the extra broth into an ice cube tray and freeze for future use. Then I can pull out as many cubes as I need.

—**MARALYN BERNI** SEBASTIAN, FL

GARLIC BREAD
SPIRALS

HOME-STYLE SAUSAGE
GRAVY AND BISCUITS

General Index *Recipes listed by food category and major ingredient*

APPETIZERS
(also see Dips; Fondue)

Barbecue Sausage Bites 14
Chunky Applesauce 11
Creamy Cranberry Meatballs 20
Marinated Chicken Wings 13
Party-Pleasing Beef Dish 15
Porky Picadillo Lettuce Wraps 11
Reuben Spread 12
Simmered Smoked Links 18
Slow-Cooker Candied Nuts 14
Slow-Cooker Spiced Mixed Nuts 19
Sweet & Salty Party Mix 23
Sweet & Spicy Chicken Wings 17

APPLES
Apple & Cheddar Salad 225
Apple Balsamic Chicken 126
Apple-Dijon Pork Roast 148
Apple Granola Dessert 204
Apple-Nut Bread Pudding 190
Apple-Pear Compote 193
Apple Pie Oatmeal Dessert 208
Butterscotch Apple Crisp 207
Caramel-Pecan Stuffed Apples 202
Chunky Applesauce 11
Cinnamon-Apple Brown Betty 186
Cranberry Apple Cider 22
Garlic-Apple Pork Roast 130
Glazed Cinnamon Apples 196
Hot Caramel Apples 188
Nutty Apple Butter 65
Slow Cooker Baked Apples 198
Warm Apple-Cranberry Dessert 201

BACON & CANADIAN BACON
Bacon-Ranch Spinach Dip 17
Easy Beans & Potatoes with Bacon 63
Sweet & Hot Baked Beans 59

BEANS
APPETIZER
Championship Bean Dip 15
MAIN DISHES
Beef 'n' Bean Torta 93
Ham and Bean Stew 135
Marty's Bean Burger Chili 160
Slow Cooker Chicken & Black Bean Soft
   Tacos 107
Sweet Sausage 'n' Beans 146
Three Beans and Sausage 145
Vegetarian Red Bean Chili 171
SALAD
Southwest Black Bean Pasta 224
SOUPS
Beef & Black Bean Soup 30

Beefy Cabbage Bean Stew 40
Chicken Bean Soup 34
Navy Bean Vegetable Soup 44
Slow-Cooked Cannellini Turkey Soup 46
Texas Black Bean Soup 49
SIDE
Sweet & Hot Baked Beans 59

BEEF
(also see Ground Beef)
APPETIZER
Creamy Chipped Beef Fondue 20
MAIN DISHES
Autumn Beef Stew 80
Barbecue Beef Brisket 98
Best Ever Roast Beef 90
Braised Beef Short Ribs 93
Brisket with Cranberry Gravy 86
Burgundy Beef 89
Chile Colorado Burritos 74
Chipotle Beef Chili 97
Chipotle Carne Guisada 80
Flavorful Beef in Gravy 98
Garlic-Sesame Beef 75
Hearty Busy-Day Stew 92
Home-Style Stew 79
Java Roast Beef 76
Melt-in-Your-Mouth Meat Loaf 94
Mexican Shredded Beef Wraps 84
No-Fuss Beef Roast 82
Pork and Beef Barbecue 154
Sassy Pot Roast 87
Shredded Beef au Jus 94
Slow-Cooked Beef Brisket 85
Slow-Cooked Coffee Pot Roast 82
Slow-Cooked Tex-Mex Flank Steak 86
Slow Cooker Pot Roast 85
Smoked Beef Brisket 97
Spring Herb Roast 79
Steak San Marino 94
Sweet and Sour Brisket 89
Sweet & Tangy Beef Roast 89
Tender Beef over Noodles 83
Zesty Orange Beef 99
SANDWICHES
Dilly Beef Sandwiches 98
Family-Favorite Italian Beef Sandwiches .. 83
Italian Beef 76
Simply Delicious Roast Beef Sandwiches . 97
Slow Cooker French Dip Sandwiches 80
SOUPS
Beef & Black Bean Soup 30
Beef Barley Soup 33
Big Red Soup 39
Savory Beef Soup 45
Slow-Cooker Vegetable Soup 30

BERRIES
Blueberry Cobbler 198
Blueberry Spinach Salad 227
Pear-Blueberry Granola 201
Slow Cooker Rhubarb Strawberry Sauce .. 206
Strawberry Rhubarb Sauce 195
Warm Strawberry Fondue 196

BEVERAGES
Cranberry Apple Cider 22
Hot Cider with Orange Twists 20
Peachy Spiced Cider 18
Spiced Apricot Cider 12
Spiced Fruit Punch 17
Viennese Coffee 24

BISCUITS & BISCUIT MIX
Cheese & Pesto Biscuits 243
Grandma's Biscuits 241
Ham and Swiss Biscuits 238
Home-Style Sausage Gravy and Biscuits .. 244
Monkey Bread Biscuits 237

BREADS, MUFFINS & ROLLS
(also see Biscuits & Biscuit Mix)
Cheddar Corn Dog Muffins 240
Chimichurri Monkey Bread 244
Garlic Bread Spirals 244
Garlic Loaf 237
Grilled Cheese & Tomato Flatbreads 239
Herbed Parmesan Bread 240
Honey-Moon Rolls 241
Italian Puff Pastry Twists 244
Mexican Cheese Corn Bread 238
Navajo Fry Bread 238
Parmesan Breadsticks 237
Parmesan-Herb Dinner Rolls 234
Passover Popovers 234
Romano Sticks 242
Savory Biscuit-Breadsticks 232
Sweet Onion Bread Skillet 233
Triple Tomato Flatbread 242
Zesty Jalapeno Corn Muffins 242

BROCCOLI
Broccoli-Mushroom Bubble Bake 237
Broccoli Side Dish 222
Broccoli with Orange Browned Butter 226
Cajun Spiced Broccoli 214
Slow-Cooked Broccoli 57
Slow Cooker Cheesy Broccoli Soup 38
Warm Broccoli Cheese Dip 24

CARROTS
Classy Carrots 224
Honey-Butter Peas and Carrots 59

Marmalade-Glazed Carrots 70
Spiced Carrots & Butternut Squash 60

CHEESE
APPETIZERS
Beer Cheese Fondue.................................11
Cheesy Pizza Fondue 24
Garlic Swiss Fondue................................22
Warm Broccoli Cheese Dip.....................24
BREADS
Cheddar Corn Dog Muffins....................240
Cheese & Pesto Biscuits 243
Grilled Cheese & Tomato Flatbreads.......239
Ham and Swiss Biscuits 238
Herbed Parmesan Bread 240
Mexican Cheese Corn Bread 238
Romano Sticks 242
MAIN DISHES
Buffalo Shrimp Mac & Cheese...............168
Carolina Cheese Shrimp and Grits...........158
Cheesy Tater Tot Dinner 183
Chili & Cheese Crustless Quiche 162
Easy Slow Cooker Mac & Cheese...........175
Ham 'n' Swiss Chicken 119
Slow Cooker Mac n Cheese 160
SALADS
Apple & Cheddar Salad 225
Pear & Blue Cheese Salad......................219
SIDE DISHES
Cheesy Creamed Corn............................66
Cheesy Spinach 69
Comforting Cheesy Potatoes 56
Garlic Green Beans with Gorgonzola 56
Grilled Romaine with Swiss 222
Sauteed Corn with Cheddar 214
Slow-Cooked Mac 'n' Cheese 64
SOUP
Slow Cooker Cheesy Broccoli Soup...........38

CHICKEN & CHICKEN SAUSAGE
APPETIZERS
Marinated Chicken Wings.......................13
Sweet & Spicy Chicken Wings.................17
MAIN DISHES
Apple Balsamic Chicken 126
Barbecue Cobb Salad 163
Busy-Day Chicken Fajitas 110
Busy Mom's Chicken Fajitas 120
Chicken a la King 116
Chicken Chili..128
Chicken Stew 115
Chicken Veggie Alfredo 109
Chili-Lime Chicken Tostadas...................126
Chunky Chicken Cacciatore....................118
Cranberry Chicken 105
Creamy Chicken Fettuccine....................106

Creamy Chicken Thighs & Noodles.........112
Creamy Garlic-Lemon Chicken...............102
Creamy Italian Chicken 110
Curry Chicken Stew 100
Fruited Chicken 124
Greek Dinner.......................................115
Greek Garlic Chicken............................123
Gulf Coast Jambalaya Rice....................170
Ham 'n' Swiss Chicken 119
Herbed Chicken and Tomatoes................106
Italian Shrimp 'n' Pasta 179
Meaty Slow-Cooked Jambalaya...............159
Mushroom Chicken Cacciatore...............110
Party-Time Wings 120
Pineapple Chicken 127
Posole Verde 171
Red Pepper Chicken 106
Rosemary Cashew Chicken 102
Saucy BBQ Chicken Thighs 101
Slow-Cooked Coconut Chicken 108
Slow-Cooked Jambalaya........................113
Slow Cooker Chicken & Black Bean
   Soft Tacos......................................107
Slow Cooker Chicken Cacciatore.............102
Slow Cooker Chicken Dinner 120
Slow Cooker Mushroom
   Chicken & Peas 118
Slow Cooker Roast Chicken....................111
Slow-Roasted Chicken with Vegetables.105
Snappy Southwest Chicken 113
Spring-Thyme Chicken Stew 123
Sunday Chicken Supper 114
Sweet and Tangy Chicken 124
Sweet-and-Sour Chicken 109
Sweet Pepper Chicken 119
Wine-Braised Chicken with
   Pearl Onions 125
Sandwiches
Carolina-Style Vinegar BBQ Chicken.......105
Chipotle Pulled Chicken 116
Polynesian Pull Chicken 129
Shredded Chicken Gyros 116
SOUPS & CHILI
Chicken Bean Soup...............................34
Chicken Vegetable Soup 33
Coconut-Lime Chicken Curry Soup...........28
Ginger Chicken Noodle Soup 46
Herbed Chicken & Spinach Soup..............40
Smoked Sausage Soup...........................37
Southwestern Chicken Soup....................50
Spicy Chicken Chili 37
Vegetable Chicken Soup 49
CHILI
Autumn Pumpkin Chili 180
Beer Brat Chili 152
Chicken Chili.......................................128
Chili & Cheese Crustless Quiche 162

Chipotle Beef Chili 97
Marty's Bean Burger Chili......................160
Pork Chili 142
Slow-Cooked Chunky Chili 87
Spicy Chicken Chili 37
Vegetarian Red Bean Chili 171

CHOCOLATE
Chocolate Bread Pudding......................205
Chocolate Peanut Clusters.....................200
Chocolate Peanut Drops 190
Chocolate Pecan Fondue 188
Chocolate Pudding Cake 191
Crunchy Candy Clusters 187
Gooey Peanut Butter-Chocolate Cake......197
Minty Hot Fudge Sundae Cake 210
Molten Mocha Cake..............................193

CORN
Cheesy Creamed Corn............................66
Corn Chowder......................................46
Green Chili Creamed Corn 59
Marina's Golden Corn Fritters 234
Mexican Cheese Corn Bread 238
Nebraska Creamed Corn 63
Sauteed Corn with Cheddar 214
Shoepeg Corn Side Dish 70

CORNISH HENS
Cornish Hens with Potatoes....................123

CRANBERRIES
Brisket with Cranberry Gravy...................86
Cranberry Apple Cider...........................22
Cranberry Chicken 105
Cranberry-Mustard Pork Loin 137
Cranberry Pork & Sweet Potatoes............145
Warm Apple-Cranberry Dessert...............201

DESSERTS
Apple Granola Dessert 204
Apple Pie Oatmeal Dessert 208
Burgundy Pears 188
Butterscotch Pears 202
Caramel-Pecan Stuffed Apples 202
Cherry & Spice Rice Pudding..................211
Chocolate Pecan Fondue 188
Chocolate Pudding Cake 191
Cinnamon-Apple Brown Betty 186
Classic Bananas Foster 193
Elvis' Pudding Cake..............................202
Fruit Compote Dessert...........................207
Fruit Dessert Topping............................194
Glazed Cinnamon Apples 196
Gooey Peanut Butter-Chocolate Cake......197
Molten Mocha Cake..............................193
Pumpkin Pie Pudding............................187

DESSERTS
(continued)

Slow Cooker Baked Apples 198
Slow Cooker Cherry Buckle 210
Tropical Compote Dessert 209
Warm Apple-Cranberry Dessert 201

DIPS
(also see Fondue)

Bacon-Ranch Spinach Dip 17
Buffalo Wing Dip 18
Butterscotch Dip 12
Championship Bean Dip 15
Creamy Artichoke Dip 17
Jalapeno Popper & Sausage Dip 20
Jalapeno Spinach Dip 23
Pepperoni Extreme Dip 11
Slow-Cooked Crab Dip 22
Taco Joe Dip 24
Warm Broccoli Cheese Dip 24

EXPRESS PREP
APPETIZERS

Barbecue Sausage Bites 14
Championship Bean Dip 15
Cheesy Pizza Fondue 24
Chunky Applesauce 11
Creamy Chipped Beef Fondue 20
Creamy Cranberry Meatballs 20
Garlic Swiss Fondue 22
Jalapeno Spinach Dip 23
Marinated Chicken Wings 13
Pepperoni Extreme Dip 11
Reuben Spread 12
Simmered Smoked Links 18
Slow-Cooker Candied Nuts 14
Taco Joe Dip 24

DESSERTS

Apple Granola Dessert 204
Apple-Nut Bread Pudding 190
Blueberry Cobbler 198
Burgundy Pears 188
Butterscotch Apple Crisp 207
Cherry & Spice Rice Pudding 211
Chocolate Bread Pudding 205
Chocolate Pecan Fondue 188
Chocolate Pudding Cake 191
Cinnamon-Raisin Banana Bread
    Pudding 208
Classic Bananas Foster 193
Elvis' Pudding Cake 202
Fruit Compote Dessert 207
Fruit Dessert Topping 194
Fruit Salsa 204
Molten Mocha Cake 193
Pumpkin Pie Pudding 187
Slow Cooker Cherry Buckle 210

Slow Cooker Rhubarb Strawberry Sauce 206
Strawberry Rhubarb Sauce 195
Warm Strawberry Fondue 196

MAIN DISHES

Beer Brat Chili 152
Burgundy Beef 89
Butter & Herb Turkey 124
Carolina-Style Vinegar BBQ Chicken 105
Chicken a la King 116
Chicken Chili 128
Chicken Stew 115
Chicken Veggie Alfredo 109
Chili-Lime Chicken Tostadas 126
Chunky Chicken Cacciatore 118
Country Pork Chop Supper 137
Country Ribs Dinner 142
Cranberry Chicken 105
Cranberry Pork & Sweet Potatoes 145
Creamy Chicken Thighs & Noodles 112
Easy Chili Verde 131
Fruited Chicken 124
Garlic-Apple Pork Roast 130
Green Chili Shredded Pork 148
Ham and Bean Stew 135
Ham 'n' Swiss Chicken 119
Ham Barbecue 152
Hearty Busy-Day Stew 92
Herbed Chicken and Tomatoes 106
Italian Shrimp 'n' Pasta 179
Java Roast Beef 76
Lemony Turkey Breast 108
No-Fuss Beef Roast 82
Pork Chop Dinner 138
Sausage Spanish Rice 149
Shredded Beef au Jus 94
Simple Poached Salmon 168
Slow Cook Lamb Chops 172
Slow-Cooked Beef Brisket 85
Slow-Cooked Coconut Chicken 108
Slow-Cooked Coffee Pot Roast 82
Slow-Cooked Ham with
    Pineapple Sauce 142
Slow Cooker Chicken Dinner 120
Slow Cooker Mushroom
    Chicken & Peas 118
Slow Cooker Salmon Loaf 183
Smoked Beef Brisket 97
Sweet & Tangy Beef Roast 89
Sweet and Tangy Chicken 124
Sweet Pepper Chicken 119
Sweet Sausage 'n' Beans 146
Tangy Venison Stroganoff 183
Tender Pork Roast 138
Tender Spareribs 132
Teriyaki Pork Roast 153
Vegetarian Red Bean Chili 171
Wild Rice Turkey Dinner 128

Wine-Braised Chicken with
    Pearl Onions 125
Zesty Ham 155

SIDE DISHES

Asparagus, Mushrooms and Peas 226
Broccoli Side Dish 222
Broccoli with Orange Browned Butter 226
Brussels Sprouts with Leeks 216
Cajun Spiced Broccoli 214
Cheesy Creamed Corn 66
Cheesy Spinach 69
Classy Carrots 224
Comforting Cheesy Potatoes 56
Creamed Spinach and Mushrooms 221
Curry Rice Pilaf 228
Dill Potato Wedges 222
Easy Lemon-Pepper Green Beans 218
Easy Spanish Rice 224
Fruited Rice Pilaf 214
Glazed Pearl Onions 228
Green Chili Creamed Corn 59
Grilled Romaine with Swiss 222
Lemon Date Couscous 221
Lemon Green Beans 224
Marmalade-Glazed Carrots 70
Mushroom Wild Rice 66
Nebraska Creamed Corn 63
Pea Pods and Peppers 214
Rosemary Polenta 216
Sauteed Corn with Cheddar 214
Scalloped Taters 69
Slow-Cooked Broccoli 57
Slow-Cooked Green Beans 68
Spinach & Feta Saute 228
Summertime Squash 218
Tarragon Asparagus 225
Walnut Zucchini Saute 221

FISH
(also see Seafood)

Simple Poached Salmon 168
Slow-Cooked Fish Stew 164
Slow Cooker Salmon Loaf 183
Trout Chowder 159

⑤ INGREDIENTS
APPETIZERS

Butterscotch Dip 12
Chunky Applesauce 11
Creamy Cranberry Meatballs 20
Simmered Smoked Links 18

DESSERTS

Blueberry Cobbler 198
Chocolate Peanut Drops 190
Crunchy Candy Clusters 187
Warm Strawberry Fondue 196

MAIN DISHES

Apple-Dijon Pork Roast 148
Brisket with Cranberry Gravy......................... 86
Carolina-Style Vinegar BBQ Chicken 105
Chile Colorado Burritos 74
Cranberry Pork & Sweet Potatoes 145
Easy Chili Verde 131
Garlic-Apple Pork Roast 130
Ham and Bean Stew 135
Home-Style Stew 79
Java Roast Beef 76
No-Fuss Beef Roast 82
Saucy Ranch Pork and Potatoes................ 138
Slow Cooker Kalua Pork & Cabbage....... 134
Super Easy Country-Style Ribs 151
Tender Pork Roast 138
Zesty Ham 155

SIDE DISHES

Broccoli Side Dish... 222
Broccoli with Orange Browned Butter .. 226
Brussels Sprouts with Leeks 216
Cajun Spiced Broccoli.................................... 214
Creamed Spinach and Mushrooms.......... 221
Dill Potato Wedges... 222
Easy Beans & Potatoes with Bacon.......... 63
Easy Lemon-Pepper Green Beans............. 218
Easy Spanish Rice 224
Fruited Rice Pilaf 214
Glazed Pearl Onions 228
Lemon Green Beans.. 224
Nebraska Creamed Corn 63
Rosemary Polenta... 216
Sauteed Corn with Cheddar 214
Slow-Cooked Green Beans............................ 68
Spinach & Feta Saute 228
Tarragon Asparagus....................................... 225
Walnut Zucchini Saute 221

FONDUE

Beer Cheese Fondue... 11
Cheesy Pizza Fondue......................................24
Chocolate Pecan Fondue 188
Creamy Chipped Beef Fondue 20
Garlic Swiss Fondue..22
Warm Strawberry Fondue............................ 196

FRUIT

(also see specific kinds)
Fruit Compote Dessert................................... 207
Fruit Dessert Topping.................................... 194
Fruit Salsa... 204
Fruited Chicken 124
Fruited Rice Pilaf 214
Spiced Fruit Punch 17

GREEN BEANS

Easy Beans & Potatoes with Bacon.............. 63
Easy Lemon-Pepper Green Beans............. 218
Garlic Green Beans with Gorgonzola 56
Lemon Green Beans.. 224
Slow-Cooked Green Beans............................ 68

GROUND BEEF
APPETIZER
Party-Pleasing Beef Dish 15
MAIN DISHES
Beef 'n' Bean Torta.. 93
Chunky Pasta Sauce....................................... 167
Deluxe Walking Nachos 172
Meat-Lover's Pizza Hot Dish 79
Mexican Beef-Stuffed Peppers..................... 76
Mushroom-Beef Spaghetti Sauce 90
Pasta e Fagioli 177
Potato Pizza Casserole...................................75
Slow-Cooked Chunky Chili 87
Slow-Cooked Meat Loaf 90
Slow Cooker Golombki....................................91
SANDWICH
Slow-Cooker Sloppy Joes 77
SOUPS & STEW
Beef Barley Lentil Soup.................................. 43
Beefy Cabbage Bean Stew............................ 40
Savory Beef & Veggie Soup 50

HAM

Ham and Bean Stew 135
Ham and Swiss Biscuits 238
Ham 'n' Swiss Chicken 119
Ham Barbecue 152
Hash Brown Egg Breakfast 132
Hash Browns with Ham................................ 156
Hearty Split Pea Soup.................................... 38
Light Ham Tetrazzini...................................... 140
Minestrone Soup...29
Pineapple-Dijon Ham Sandwiches 144
Slow-Cooked Ham with Pineapple Sauce.142
Slow-Cooked Split Pea Soup......................... 43
Slow Cooker BBQ Ham Sandwiches 156
Slow Cooker Ham & Eggs 168
Slow-Cooker Potato & Ham Soup................ 46
Zesty Ham 155

LAMB

Lamb with Orzo 167
Slow Cook Lamb Chops 172

MEATBALLS

Creamy Cranberry Meatballs 20
French Onion Soup with Meatballs................ 36
Hearty Veggie Meatball Soup...................... 30

MEATLESS MAIN DISHES

African Peanut Sweet Potato Stew 178
Breakfast-for-Dinner Bake 167
Chili & Cheese Crustless Quiche 162
Creamy Mushrooms & Potatoes................ 177
Easy Slow Cooker Mac & Cheese............... 175
Marty's Bean Burger Chili 160
Slow-Cooked Stuffed Peppers....................... 15
Slow Cooker Mac n Cheese 160
Vegetarian Red Bean Chili 171

MUSHROOMS

Asparagus, Mushrooms and Peas 226
Broccoli-Mushroom Bubble Bake 237
Creamed Spinach and Mushrooms........... 221
Mushroom-Beef Spaghetti Sauce 90
Mushroom Chicken Cacciatore 110
Mushroom Wild Rice 66
Slow Cooker Mushroom, Chicken & Peas 118
Slow Cooker Mushroom Rice Pilaf 55
Sweet Creamy Mushrooms & Potatoes... 177

NUTS & PEANUT BUTTER

African Peanut Sweet Potato Stew 178
Apple-Nut Bread Pudding 190
Butterscotch-Pecan Bread Pudding 198
Caramel-Pecan Stuffed Apples 202
Chocolate Peanut Clusters.......................... 200
Chocolate Peanut Drops 190
Chocolate Pecan Fondue 188
Crunchy Candy Clusters 187
Maple-Walnut Sweet Potatoes 54
Pecan-Coconut Sweet Potatoes 64
Rosemary Cashew Chicken......................... 102
Slow-Cooker Candied Nuts........................... 14
Slow-Cooker Spiced Mixed Nuts.................. 19
Sweet & Salty Party Mix 23
Walnut Zucchini Saute.................................. 221

ONIONS

Cucumber and Red Onion Salad.................. 226
Glazed Pearl Onions 228
Onion-Garlic Hash Browns............................ 61
Sweet Onion & Red Bell Pepper Topping...62
Sweet Onion Bread Skillet 233
Wine-Braised Chicken with Pearl Onions.125

PASTA & COUSCOUS
MAIN DISHES
Chicken Veggie Alfredo 109
Chunky Chicken Cacciatore.......................... 118
Creamy Chicken Fettuccine.......................... 106
Italian Shrimp 'n' Pasta................................ 179
Light Ham Tetrazzini...................................... 140
Meat-Lover's Pizza Hot Dish 79
Mushroom Chicken Cacciatore 110
Pasta e Fagioli 177
Rosemary Cashew Chicken......................... 102
Shrimp Marinara 160
Slow-Cooked Turkey Stroganoff............... 128

PASTA & COUSCOUS
(continued)
Slow Cooker Chicken Cacciatore 102
Tangy Venison Stroganoff...................... 183

SALADS
Greek Pasta Salad................................ 222
Pizza Salad 228
Southwest Black Bean Pasta................. 224
Spiral Pasta Salad................................ 218
Supreme Spaghetti Salad 221
Vermicelli Pasta Salad.......................... 219

SIDE DISH
Lemon Date Couscous 221

PEACHES
Old-Fashioned Peach Butter 70
Peachy Baby Back Ribs......................... 146
Peachy Pork Chops 152
Peachy Spiced Cider 18
Pork with Peach Picante Sauce.............. 140

PEARS
Apple-Pear Compote 193
Burgundy Pears 188
Butterscotch Pears 202
Pear & Blue Cheese Salad..................... 219
Pear-Blueberry Granola........................ 201

PEAS
Asparagus, Mushrooms and Peas 226
Hearty Split Pea Soup............................ 38
Honey-Butter Peas and Carrots 59
Pea Pods and Peppers.......................... 214
Slow-Cooked Split Pea Soup 43
Slow Cooker Mushroom Chicken & Peas..118

PEPPERS
Barbecue Brats & Peppers 151
Chipotle Beef Chili................................. 97
Chipotle Carne Guisada.......................... 80
Jalapeno Popper & Sausage Dip.............. 20
Jalapeno Spinach Dip 23
Mexican Beef-Stuffed Peppers................ 76
Pea Pods and Peppers.......................... 214
Red Pepper Chicken 106
Slow-Cooked Stuffed Peppers................. 15
Sweet Onion & Red Bell Pepper Topping...62
Zesty Jalapeno Corn Muffins 242

PORK
*(also see Bacon & Canadian Bacon; Ham;
Sausage)*

APPETIZER
Porky Picadillo Lettuce Wraps 11

MAIN DISHES
Apple-Dijon Pork Roast 148
Chunky Pasta Sauce............................. 167

Country Pork Chop Supper.................... 137
Country Ribs Dinner............................. 142
Cranberry Pork & Sweet Potatoes.......... 145
Cranberry-Mustard Pork Loin 137
Easy Chili Verde 131
Garlic-Apple Pork Roast 130
Green Chili Shredded Pork 148
Italian Shredded Pork Stew................... 156
Peachy Baby Back Ribs......................... 146
Peachy Pork Chops 152
Pork and Beef Barbecue 154
Pork Carnitas 155
Pork Chili 142
Pork Chops & Acorn Squash 139
Pork Chop Dinner................................ 138
Pork Chops with Sauerkraut.................. 134
Pork with Peach Picante Sauce.............. 140
Posole Verde 171
Saucy Ranch Pork and Potatoes............. 138
Slow Cooker Kalua Pork & Cabbage........ 134
Slow Cooker Tropical Pork Chops 154
Southwest Entree Salad 174
Super Easy Country-Style Ribs 151
Sweet & Sour Pork Wraps..................... 141
Tender Pork Roast............................... 138
Tender Spareribs 132
Teriyaki Pork Roast 153

SANDWICHES
Pulled Pork Sandwiches 146
Root Beer Pulled Pork Sandwiches 137

SOUP
Pork & Rice Noodle Soup 31

POTATOES
(also see Sweet Potatoes)

MAIN DISHES
African Peanut Sweet Potato Stew 178
Cheesy Tater Tot Dinner....................... 183
Cornish Hens with Potatoes.................. 123
Creamy Mushrooms & Potatoes............. 177
Hash Brown Egg Breakfast.................... 132
Hash Browns with Ham........................ 156
Potato Pizza Casserole.......................... 75
Potato Sausage Supper......................... 132
Saucy Ranch Pork and Potatoes............. 138
Spicy Hash Brown Supper..................... 180

SIDE DISHES
Comforting Cheesy Potatoes 56
Dill Potato Wedges............................... 222
Easy Beans & Potatoes with Bacon.......... 63
Onion-Garlic Hash Browns...................... 61
Parsley Smashed Potatoes...................... 68
Rich & Creamy Mashed Potatoes............. 54
Scalloped Taters................................... 69

SOUPS
Hearty Hash Brown Soup 40
Potato and Leek Soup............................ 43

Potato Minestrone 33
Slow-Cooker Potato & Ham Soup............. 46

READY IN ④

APPETIZERS
Bacon-Ranch Spinach Dip...................... 17
Barbecue Sausage Bites 14
Beer Cheese Fondue............................. 11
Buffalo Wing Dip 18
Butterscotch Dip 12
Championship Bean Dip 15
Creamy Artichoke Dip........................... 17
Creamy Chipped Beef Fondue................. 20
Creamy Cranberry Meatballs 20
Garlic Swiss Fondue............................. 22
Jalapeno Popper & Sausage Dip.............. 20
Jalapeno Spinach Dip 23
Marinated Chicken Wings 13
Pepperoni Extreme Dip 11
Porky Picadillo Lettuce Wraps 11
Reuben Spread 12
Slow-Cooked Crab Dip.......................... 22
Slow-Cooker Candied Nuts..................... 14
Slow-Cooker Spiced Mixed Nuts 19
Sweet & Salty Party Mix........................ 23
Warm Broccoli Cheese Dip..................... 24

DESSERTS
Apple-Nut Bread Pudding..................... 190
Apple-Pear Compote 193
Blueberry Cobbler 198
Burgundy Pears 188
Butterscotch Pears 202
Butterscotch-Pecan Bread Pudding........ 198
Caramel-Pecan Stuffed Apples 202
Cherry & Spice Rice Pudding................. 211
Chocolate Bread Pudding...................... 205
Chocolate Peanut Clusters 200
Chocolate Peanut Drops....................... 190
Chocolate Pecan Fondue 188
Cinnamon-Apple Brown Betty 186
Cinnamon-Raisin Banana...................... 208
Classic Bananas Foster......................... 193
Crunchy Candy Clusters 187
Elvis' Pudding Cake.............................. 202
Fruit Compote Dessert 207
Fruit Dessert Topping........................... 194
Fruit Salsa.. 204
Glazed Cinnamon Apples 196
Gooey Peanut Butter-Chocolate Cake..... 197
Molten Mocha Cake.............................. 193
Pear-Blueberry Granola........................ 201
Slow-Cooker Bread Pudding.................. 194
Slow Cooker Cherry Buckle.................... 210
Tropical Compote Dessert 209
Warm Apple-Cranberry Dessert............. 201
Warm Strawberry Fondue..................... 196

MAIN DISHES

Barbecue Cobb Salad 163
Buffalo Shrimp Mac & Cheese 168
Carolina Cheese Shrimp and Grits 158
Chili & Cheese Crustless Quiche 162
Chipotle Pulled Chicken 116
Creamy Chicken Fettuccine 106
Creamy Garlic-Lemon Chicken 102
Easy Slow Cooker Mac & Cheese 175
Greek Garlic Chicken 123
Gulf Coast Jambalaya Rice 170
Hash Brown Egg Breakfast 132
Meat-Lover's Pizza Hot Dish 79
Party-Time Wings 120
Polynesian Pull Chicken 129
Pork Chops with Sauerkraut 134
Shredded Chicken Gyros 116
Shrimp Marinara 160
Simple Poached Salmon 168
Slow-Cooked Stuffed Peppers 15
Slow Cooker Ham & Eggs 168
Slow Cooker Mac n Cheese 160
Slow Cooker Mushroom
    Chicken & Peas 118
Slow Cooker Tropical Pork Chops 154
Sweet-and-Sour Chicken 109
Tangy Venison Stroganoff 183

SIDE DISHES

Asparagus, Mushrooms and Peas 226
Broccoli Side Dish 222
Broccoli with Orange Browned Butter .. 226
Brussels Sprouts with Leeks 216
Cajun Spiced Broccoli 214
Cheesy Creamed Corn 66
Classy Carrots 224
Creamed Spinach and Mushrooms 221
Cucumber and Red Onion Salad 226
Curry Rice Pilaf 228
Dill Potato Wedges 222
Easy Lemon-Pepper Green Beans 218
Easy Spanish Rice 224
Fruited Rice Pilaf 214
Garlic Green Beans with Gorgonzola 56
Glazed Pearl Onions 228
Green Chili Creamed Corn 59
Grilled Romaine with Swiss 222
Lemon Date Couscous 221
Lemon Green Beans 224
Nebraska Creamed Corn 63
Onion-Garlic Hash Browns 61
Pea Pods and Peppers 214
Rich & Creamy Mashed Potatoes 54
Rosemary Polenta 216
Sauteed Corn with Cheddar 214
Savory Sausage Stuffing 60
Scalloped Taters 69
Shoepeg Corn Side Dish 70

Slow-Cooked Broccoli 57
Slow-Cooked Green Beans 68
Slow-Cooked Mac 'n' Cheese 64
Slow Cooker Mushroom Rice Pilaf 55
Spiced Acorn Squash 59
Spinach & Feta Saute 228
Summertime Squash 218
Tarragon Asparagus 225
Walnut Zucchini Saute 221

RICE

Butternut Squash with Whole Grain Pilaf ... 57
Cherry & Spice Rice Pudding 211
Curry Rice Pilaf 228
Easy Spanish Rice 224
Fruited Rice Pilaf 214
Gulf Coast Jambalaya Rice 170
Mushroom Wild Rice 66
Sausage Spanish Rice 149
Slow Cooker Mushroom Rice Pilaf 55
Wild Rice Turkey Dinner 128

SALADS

Apple & Cheddar Salad 225
Barbecue Cobb Salad 163
Blueberry Spinach Salad 227
Cucumber and Red Onion Salad 226
Easy Tossed Salad 222
Fiesta Side Salad 227
Greek Pasta Salad 222
Green Salad with Tangy Basil Vinaigrette . 216
Jeweled Endive Salad 221
Mixed Greens with Lemon Champagne
    Vinaigrette 214
Mixed Greens with Orange Juice
    Vinaigrette 217
Pear & Blue Cheese Salad 219
Pizza Salad 228
Potluck Antipasto Salad 217
Sesame Tossed Salad 228
Sicilian Salad 218
Southwest Black Bean Pasta 224
Southwest Entree Salad 174
Spiral Pasta Salad 218
Supreme Spaghetti Salad 221
Vermicelli Pasta Salad 219

SANDWICHES

Barbecue Brats & Peppers 151
Dilly Beef Sandwiches 98
Family-Favorite Italian Beef Sandwiches 83
Italian Beef 76
Italian Sausage Hoagies 131
Pineapple-Dijon Ham Sandwiches 144
Pulled Pork Sandwiches 146
Root Beer Pulled Pork Sandwiches 137
Simply Delicious Roast Beef Sandwiches 97

Slow Cooker BBQ Ham Sandwiches 156
Slow Cooker French Dip Sandwiches 80

SAUSAGE

(also see Chicken & Chicken Sausage)

APPETIZERS

Barbecue Sausage Bites 14
Jalapeno Popper & Sausage Dip 20
Simmered Smoked Links 18

MAIN DISHES

Beer Brat Chili 152
Eye-Opening Burritos 177
Gulf Coast Jambalaya Rice 170
Home-Style Sausage Gravy and Biscuits ... 244
Meat-Lover's Pizza Hot Dish 79
Potato Sausage Supper 132
Sausage Spanish Rice 149
Slow-Cooked Chunky Chili 87
Slow-Cooked Jambalaya 113
Slow Cooker Breakfast Casserole 151
Spicy Hash Brown Supper 180
Sweet Sausage 'n' Beans 146
Three Beans and Sausage 145

SANDWICHES

Barbecue Brats & Peppers 151
Italian Sausage Hoagies 131

SIDE DISH

Savory Sausage Stuffing 60

SOUPS & STEWS

Sauerkraut Sausage Soup 39
Smoked Sausage Soup 37

SEAFOOD

(also see Fish)

APPETIZER

Slow-Cooked Crab Dip 22

MAIN DISHES

Buffalo Shrimp Mac & Cheese 168
Carolina Cheese Shrimp and Grits 158
Gulf Coast Jambalaya Rice 170
Italian Shrimp 'n' Pasta 179
Meaty Slow-Cooked Jambalaya 159
Shrimp Marinara 160
Simple Poached Salmon 168
Slow-Cooked Fish Stew 164
Slow Cooker Salmon Loaf 183
Spicy Seafood Stew 180
Trout Chowder 159

SOUP

Maryland-Style Crab Soup 50
Shrimp Chowder 44

SIDE DISHES & CONDIMENTS

Asparagus, Mushrooms and Peas 226
Broccoli Side Dish 222
Broccoli with Orange Browned Butter 226
Brussels Sprouts with Leeks 216

SIDE DISHES & CONDIMENTS
(continued)

Butternut Squash with Whole Grain Pilaf...57
Cajun Spiced Broccoli..........................214
Cheesy Creamed Corn............................66
Cheesy Spinach....................................69
Classy Carrots.....................................224
Comforting Cheesy Potatoes 56
Creamed Spinach and Mushrooms...........221
Curry Rice Pilaf...................................228
Dill Potato Wedges...............................222
Easy Beans & Potatoes with Bacon...............63
Easy Lemon-Pepper Green Beans..............218
Easy Spanish Rice 224
Fruited Rice Pilaf.................................214
Garlic Green Beans with Gorgonzola 56
Glazed Pearl Onions 228
Green Chili Creamed Corn 59
Grilled Romaine with Swiss 222
Honey-Butter Peas and Carrots 59
Lemon Date Couscous 221
Lemon Green Beans...............................224
Maple-Walnut Sweet Potatoes 54
Marmalade-Glazed Carrots 70
Mushroom Wild Rice..............................66
Nebraska Creamed Corn 63
Nutty Apple Butter................................65
Old-Fashioned Peach Butter......................70
Onion-Garlic Hash Browns 61
Parsley Smashed Potatoes........................68
Pea Pods and Peppers.............................214
Pecan-Coconut Sweet Potatoes 64
Rich & Creamy Mashed Potatoes.................54
Rosemary Polenta..................................216
Sauteed Corn with Cheddar 214
Savory Sausage Stuffing...........................60
Scalloped Taters.....................................69
Shoepeg Corn Side Dish 70
Slow-Cooked Broccoli..............................57
Slow-Cooked Green Beans 68
Slow-Cooked Mac 'n' Cheese 64
Slow Cooker Mushroom Rice Pilaf 55
Spiced Acorn Squash...............................59
Spiced Carrots & Butternut Squash 60
Spinach & Feta Saute 228
Slow Cooker Rhubarb Strawberry Sauce....206
Strawberry Rhubarb Sauce 195
Summertime Squash 218
Sweet & Hot Baked Beans 59
Sweet Onion & Red Bell Pepper Topping...62
Sweet Potato Stuffing 66
Tarragon Asparagus................................225
Walnut Zucchini Saute 221

SOUPS
(also see Chili; Stews)
Beef & Black Bean Soup 30

Beef Barley Lentil Soup............................43
Beef Barley Soup 33
Big Red Soup...39
Chicken Bean Soup..................................34
Chicken Vegetable Soup 33
Coconut-Lime Chicken Curry Soup 28
Corn Chowder.......................................46
Curried Lentil Soup.................................50
French Onion Soup with Meatballs...............36
Ginger Chicken Noodle Soup 46
Healthy Tomato Soup..............................43
Hearty Hash Brown Soup 40
Hearty Minestrone 45
Hearty Split Pea Soup..............................38
Hearty Veggie Meatball Soup.....................30
Herbed Chicken & Spinach Soup.................40
Italian Cabbage Soup...............................48
Maryland-Style Crab Soup 50
Minestrone Soup....................................29
Navy Bean Vegetable Soup 44
Pepperoni Pizza Soup..............................29
Pork & Rice Noodle Soup 31
Potato and Leek Soup..............................43
Potato Minestrone 33
Sauerkraut Sausage Soup 39
Savory Beef & Veggie Soup 50
Savory Beef Soup....................................45
Shrimp Chowder....................................44
Slow-Cooked Cannellini Turkey Soup 46
Slow-Cooked Split Pea Soup 43
Slow Cooker Cheesy Broccoli Soup...............38
Slow Cooker Chicken Vegetable Soup 34
Slow-Cooker Potato & Ham Soup.................46
Slow-Cooker Vegetable Soup 30
Smoked Sausage Soup..............................37
Southwest Vegetarian Lentil Soup...............34
Southwestern Chicken Soup......................50
Spicy Chicken Chili.................................37
Texas Black Bean Soup.............................49
Vegetable Barley Soup..............................40
Vegetable Chicken Soup............................49

SPINACH
Bacon-Ranch Spinach Dip..........................17
Blueberry Spinach Salad 227
Cheesy Spinach......................................69
Creamed Spinach and Mushrooms...........221
Herbed Chicken & Spinach Soup.................40
Jalapeno Spinach Dip...............................23
Spinach & Feta Saute 228

SQUASH
Butternut Squash with Whole Grain Pilaf...57
Pork Chops & Acorn Squash 139
Smoked Sausage Soup..............................37
Spiced Acorn Squash...............................59
Spiced Carrots & Butternut Squash 60

Summertime Squash 218

STEWS
Autumn Beef Stew..................................80
Beefy Cabbage Bean Stew..........................40
Chicken Stew..115
Curry Chicken Stew...............................100
Hearty Busy-Day Stew.............................92
Home-Style Stew....................................79
Italian Shredded Pork Stew......................156
Spring-Thyme Chicken Stew 123

STUFFING
Savory Sausage Stuffing...........................60
Sweet Potato Stuffing 66

SWEET POTATOES
African Peanut Sweet Potato Stew 178
Cranberry Pork & Sweet Potatoes 145
Maple-Walnut Sweet Potatoes 54
Pecan-Coconut Sweet Potatoes 64
Sweet Potato Stuffing 66

TOMATOES
Grilled Cheese & Tomato Flatbreads..........239
Healthy Tomato Soup..............................43
Herbed Chicken and Tomatoes..................106
Triple Tomato Flatbread..........................242

TURKEY
MAIN DISHES
Autumn Pumpkin Chili...........................180
Butter & Herb Turkey.............................124
Lemony Turkey Breast............................108
Mandarin Turkey Tenderloin....................127
Slow-Cooked Turkey Stroganoff.................128
Wild Rice Turkey Dinner.........................128
SANDWICHES
Easy Turkey Sloppy Joes..........................101
Shredded Turkey Sandwiches....................112
SOUP
Slow-Cooked Cannellini Turkey Soup 46

VEGETABLES
Chicken Vegetable Soup 33
Chicken Veggie Alfredo 109
Hearty Veggie Meatball Soup.....................30
Navy Bean Vegetable Soup 44
Savory Beef & Veggie Soup 50
Slow Cooker Chicken Vegetable Soup 34
Slow-Cooker Vegetable Soup 30
Slow-Roasted Chicken with Vegetables 105
Vegetable Barley Soup..............................40
Vegetable Chicken Soup............................49

VENISON
Tangy Venison Stroganoff.........................183

Alphabetical Index

A

African Peanut Sweet Potato Stew 178
Apple & Cheddar Salad 225
Apple Balsamic Chicken 126
Apple-Dijon Pork Roast 148
Apple Granola Dessert 204
Apple-Nut Bread Pudding 190
Apple-Pear Compote 193
Apple Pie Oatmeal Dessert 208
Asparagus, Mushrooms and Peas 226
Autumn Beef Stew 80
Autumn Pumpkin Chili 180

B

Bacon-Ranch Spinach Dip 17
Barbecue Beef Brisket 98
Barbecue Brats & Peppers 151
Barbecue Cobb Salad 163
Barbecue Sausage Bites 14
Beef 'n' Bean Torta 93
Beef & Black Bean Soup 30
Beef Barley Lentil Soup 43
Beef Barley Soup 33
Beefy Cabbage Bean Stew 40
Beer Brat Chili 152
Beer Cheese Fondue 11
Best Ever Roast Beef 90
Big Red Soup 39
Blueberry Cobbler 198
Blueberry Spinach Salad 227
Braised Beef Short Ribs 93
Breakfast-for-Dinner Bake 167
Brisket with Cranberry Gravy 86
Broccoli-Mushroom Bubble Bake 237
Broccoli Side Dish 222
Broccoli with Orange Browned Butter 226
Brussels Sprouts with Leeks 216
Buffalo Shrimp Mac & Cheese 168
Buffalo Wing Dip 18
Burgundy Beef 89
Burgundy Pears 188
Busy-Day Chicken Fajitas 110
Busy Mom's Chicken Fajitas 120
Butter & Herb Turkey 124
Butternut Squash with Whole Grain Pilaf...57
Butterscotch Apple Crisp 207
Butterscotch Dip 12
Butterscotch Pears 202
Butterscotch-Pecan Bread Pudding 198

C

Cajun Spiced Broccoli 214
Caramel-Pecan Stuffed Apples 202
Carolina Cheese Shrimp and Grits 158

Carolina-Style Vinegar BBQ Chicken 105
Championship Bean Dip 15
Cheddar Corn Dog Muffins 240
Cheese & Pesto Biscuits 243
Cheesy Creamed Corn 66
Cheesy Pizza Fondue 24
Cheesy Spinach 69
Cheesy Tater Tot Dinner 183
Cherry & Spice Rice Pudding 211
Chicken a la King 116
Chicken Bean Soup 34
Chicken Chili 128
Chicken Stew 115
Chicken Vegetable Soup 33
Chicken Veggie Alfredo 109
Chile Colorado Burritos 74
Chili & Cheese Crustless Quiche 162
Chili-Lime Chicken Tostadas 126
Chimichurri Monkey Bread 244
Chipotle Beef Chili 97
Chipotle Carne Guisada 80
Chipotle Pulled Chicken 116
Chocolate Bread Pudding 205
Chocolate Peanut Clusters 200
Chocolate Peanut Drops 190
Chocolate Pecan Fondue 188
Chocolate Pudding Cake 191
Chunky Applesauce 11
Chunky Chicken Cacciatore 118
Chunky Pasta Sauce 167
Cinnamon-Apple Brown Betty 186
Cinnamon-Raisin Banana Bread
    Pudding 208
Classic Bananas Foster 193
Classy Carrots 224
Coconut-Lime Chicken Curry Soup 28
Comforting Cheesy Potatoes 56
Corn Chowder 46
Cornish Hens with Potatoes 123
Country Pork Chop Supper 137
Country Ribs Dinner 142
Cranberry Apple Cider 22
Cranberry Chicken 105
Cranberry-Mustard Pork Loin 137
Cranberry Pork & Sweet Potatoes 145
Creamed Spinach and Mushrooms 221
Creamy Artichoke Dip 17
Creamy Chicken Fettuccine 106
Creamy Chicken Thighs & Noodles 112
Creamy Chipped Beef Fondue 20
Creamy Cranberry Meatballs 20
Creamy Garlic-Lemon Chicken 102
Creamy Italian Chicken 110
Creamy Mushrooms & Potatoes 177

Crunchy Candy Clusters 187
Cucumber and Red Onion Salad 226
Cumin Roasted Tortillas 242
Curried Lentil Soup 50
Curry Chicken Stew 100
Curry Rice Pilaf 228

D

Deluxe Walking Nachos 172
Dill Potato Wedges 222
Dilly Beef Sandwiches 98

E

Easy Beans & Potatoes with Bacon 63
Easy Chili Verde 131
Easy Lemon-Pepper Green Beans 218
Easy Slow Cooker Mac & Cheese 175
Easy Spanish Rice 224
Easy Tossed Salad 222
Easy Turkey Sloppy Joes 101
Elvis' Pudding Cake 202
Eye-Opening Burritos 177

F

Family-Favorite Italian Beef
    Sandwiches 83
Fiesta Side Salad 227
Flavorful Beef in Gravy 98
French Onion Soup with Meatballs 36
Fruit Compote Dessert 207
Fruit Dessert Topping 194
Fruit Salsa 204
Fruited Chicken 124
Fruited Rice Pilaf 214

G

Garlic-Apple Pork Roast 130
Garlic Bread Spirals 244
Garlic Green Beans with Gorgonzola 56
Garlic Loaf 237
Garlic-Sesame Beef 75
Garlic Swiss Fondue 22
Ginger Chicken Noodle Soup 46
Glazed Cinnamon Apples 196
Glazed Pearl Onions 228
Gooey Peanut Butter-Chocolate Cake 197
Grandma's Biscuits 241
Greek Dinner 115
Greek Garlic Chicken 123
Greek Pasta Salad 222
Green Chili Shredded Pork 148
Green Chilli Creamed Corn 59
Green Salad with Tangy Basil
    Vinaigrette 216
Grilled Cheese & Tomato Flatbreads 239
Grilled Romaine with Swiss 222
Gulf Coast Jambalaya Rice 170

H

Ham and Bean Stew 135
Ham and Swiss Biscuits 238
Ham 'n' Swiss Chicken 119
Ham Barbecue 152
Hash Brown Egg Breakfast 132
Hash Browns with Ham 156
Healthy Tomato Soup 43
Hearty Beef Soup 45
Hearty Busy-Day Stew 92
Hearty Hash Brown Soup 40
Hearty Minestrone 45
Hearty Split Pea Soup 38
Hearty Veggie Meatball Soup 30
Herbed Chicken & Spinach Soup 41
Herbed Chicken and Tomatoes 106
Herbed Parmesan Bread 240
Home-Style Sausage Gravy and Biscuits .. 244
Home-Style Stew 79
Honey-Butter Peas and Carrots 59
Honey-Moon Rolls 241
Hot Caramel Apples 188
Hot Cider with Orange Twists 20

I

Italian Cabbage Soup 48
Italian Beef 76
Italian Puff Pastry Twists 244
Italian Sausage Hoagies 131
Italian Shredded Pork Stew 156
Italian Shrimp 'n' Pasta 179

J

Jalapeno Popper & Sausage Dip 20
Jalapeno Spinach Dip 23
Java Roast Beef 76
Jeweled Endive Salad 221

L

Lamb with Orzo 167
Lemon Date Couscous 221
Lemon Green Beans 224
Lemony Turkey Breast 108
Light Ham Tetrazzini 140

M

Mandarin Turkey Tenderloin 127
Maple-Walnut Sweet Potatoes 54
Marina's Golden Corn Fritters 234
Marinated Chicken Wings 13
Marmalade-Glazed Carrots 70
Marty's Bean Burger Chili 160
Maryland-Style Crab Soup 51
Meat-Lover's Pizza Hot Dish 79
Meaty Slow-Cooked Jambalaya 159
Melt-in-Your-Mouth Meat Loaf 94
Mexican Beef-Stuffed Peppers 76

Mexican Cheese Corn Bread 238
Mexican Shredded Beef Wraps 84
Minestrone Soup 29
Minty Hot Fudge Sundae Cake 210
Mixed Greens with Lemon Champagne
    Vinaigrette 214
Mixed Greens with Orange Juice
    Vinaigrette 217
Molten Mocha Cake 193
Monkey Bread Biscuits 237
Mushroom-Beef Spaghetti Sauce 90
Mushroom Chicken Cacciatore 110
Mushroom Wild Rice 66

N

Navajo Fry Bread 238
Navy Bean Vegetable Soup 44
Nebraska Creamed Corn 63
No-Fuss Beef Roast 82
Nutty Apple Butter 65

O

Old-Fashioned Peach Butter 70
Onion-Garlic Hash Browns 61

P

Parmesan Breadsticks 237
Parmesan-Herb Dinner Rolls 234
Parsley Smashed Potatoes 68
Party-Pleasing Beef Dish 15
Party-Time Wings 120
Passover Popovers 234
Pasta e Fagioli 177
Pea Pods and Peppers 214
Peachy Baby Back Ribs 146
Peachy Pork Chops 152
Peachy Spiced Cider 18
Pear & Blue Cheese Salad 219
Pear-Blueberry Granola 201
Pecan-Coconut Sweet Potatoes 64
Pepperoni Extreme Dip 11
Pepperoni Pizza Soup 29
Pineapple Chicken 127
Pineapple-Dijon Ham Sandwiches 144
Pizza Salad 228
Polynesian Pull Chicken 129
Pork & Rice Noodle Soup 31
Pork and Beef Barbecue 154
Pork Carnitas 155
Pork Chili 142
Pork Chop Dinner 138
Pork Chops & Acorn Squash 139
Pork Chops with Sauerkraut 134
Pork with Peach Picante Sauce 140
Porky Picadillo Lettuce Wraps 11
Posole Verde 171
Potato and Leek Soup 43

Potato Minestrone 33
Potato Pizza Casserole 75
Potato Sausage Supper 132
Potluck Antipasto Salad 217
Pulled Pork Sandwiches 146
Pumpkin Pie Pudding 187

R

Red Pepper Chicken 106
Reuben Spread 12
Rich & Creamy Mashed Potatoes 54
Romano Sticks 242
Root Beer Pulled Pork Sandwiches 137
Rosemary Cashew Chicken 102
Rosemary Polenta 216

S

Sassy Pot Roast 87
Saucy BBQ Chicken Thighs 101
Saucy Ranch Pork and Potatoes 138
Sauerkraut Sausage Soup 39
Sausage Spanish Rice 149
Sauteed Corn with Cheddar 214
Savory Beef & Veggie Soup 50
Savory Biscuit-Breadsticks 232
Savory Sausage Stuffing 60
Scalloped Taters 69
Sesame Tossed Salad 228
Shoepeg Corn Side Dish 70
Shredded Beef au Jus 94
Shredded Chicken Gyros 116
Shredded Turkey Sandwiches 112
Shrimp Chowder 44
Shrimp Marinara 160
Sicilian Salad 218
Simmered Smoked Links 18
Simple Poached Salmon 168
Simply Delicious Roast Beef Sandwiches 97
Slow Cook Lamb Chops 172
Slow-Cooked Beef Brisket 85
Slow-Cooked Broccoli 57
Slow-Cooked Cannellini Turkey Soup 46
Slow-Cooked Chunky Chili 87
Slow-Cooked Coconut Chicken 108
Slow-Cooked Coffee Pot Roast 82
Slow-Cooked Crab Dip 22
Slow-Cooked Fish Stew 174
Slow-Cooked Green Beans 68
Slow-Cooked Ham with Pineapple Sauce . 142
Slow-Cooked Jambalaya 113
Slow-Cooked Mac 'n' Cheese 64
Slow-Cooked Meat Loaf 90
Slow-Cooked Split Pea Soup 43
Slow-Cooked Stuffed Peppers 165
Slow-Cooked Tex-Mex Flank Steak 86
Slow-Cooked Turkey Stroganoff 128
Slow Cooker Baked Apples 198

Slow Cooker BBQ Ham Sandwiches 156
Slow-Cooker Bread Pudding 194
Slow Cooker Breakfast Casserole................. 151
Slow-Cooker Candied Nuts............................... 14
Slow Cooker Cheesy Broccoli Soup............... 38
Slow Cooker Cherry Buckle.......................... 210
Slow Cooker Chicken & Black Bean
   Soft Tacos 107
Slow Cooker Chicken Cacciatore 102
Slow Cooker Chicken Dinner 120
Slow Cooker Chicken Vegetable Soup 34
Slow Cooker French Dip Sandwiches 80
Slow Cooker Golombki.......................................91
Slow Cooker Ham & Eggs.............................. 168
Slow Cooker Kalua Pork & Cabbage........... 134
Slow Cooker Mac n Cheese 160
Slow Cooker Mushroom Chicken & Peas 118
Slow Cooker Mushroom Rice Pilaf 55
Slow-Cooker Potato & Ham Soup.................. 46
Slow Cooker Pot Roast.......................................85
Slow Cooker Rhubarb Strawberry
   Sauce 207
Slow Cooker Roast Chicken........................... 111
Slow Cooker Salmon Loaf............................ 183
Slow-Cooker Sloppy Joes.................................77
Slow-Cooker Spiced Mixed Nuts.................... 19
Slow Cooker Tropical Pork Chops 154
Slow-Cooker Vegetable Soup 30
Slow-Roasted Chicken with Vegetables.... 105
Smoked Beef Brisket...97
Smoked Sausage Soup....................................... 37
Snappy Southwest Chicken 113
Southwest Black Bean Pasta........................ 224

Southwest Entree Salad................................. 164
Southwest Vegetarian Lentil Soup............... 34
Southwestern Chicken Soup............................50
Spiced Acorn Squash...59
Spiced Apricot Cider...12
Spiced Carrots & Butternut Squash...............60
Spiced Fruit Punch...17
Spicy Chicken Chili.. 37
Spicy Hash Brown Supper 180
Spicy Seafood Stew 180
Spinach & Feta Saute 228
Spiral Pasta Salad... 218
Spring Herb Roast... 79
Spring-Thyme Chicken Stew 123
Steak San Marino 94
Strawberry Rhubarb Sauce 195
Summertime Squash 218
Sunday Chicken Supper 114
Super Easy Country-Style Ribs 151
Supreme Spaghetti Salad 221
Sweet & Hot Baked Beans................................59
Sweet & Salty Party Mix.................................... 23
Sweet and Sour Brisket 89
Sweet-and-Sour Chicken 109
Sweet & Sour Pork Wraps 141
Sweet & Spicy Chicken Wings.........................17
Sweet & Tangy Beef Roast............................... 89
Sweet and Tangy Chicken 124
Sweet Onion & Red Bell Pepper Topping...62
Sweet Onion Bread Skillet 233
Sweet Pepper Chicken 119
Sweet Potato Stuffing....................................... 66
Sweet Sausage 'n' Beans................................ 146

T
Taco Joe Dip 24
Tamale Cakes 233
Tangy Venison Stroganoff............................. 183
Tarragon Asparagus.. 225
Tender Beef over Noodles................................83
Tender Pork Roast 138
Tender Spareribs 132
Teriyaki Pork Roast 152
Texas Black Bean Soup.....................................49
Three Beans and Sausage 145
Triple Tomato Flatbread................................. 242
Tropical Compote Dessert 209
Trout Chowder 159

V
Vegetable Barley Soup 40
Vegetable Chicken Soup 49
Vegetarian Red Bean Chili 171
Vermicelli Pasta Salad 219
Viennese Coffee..24

W
Walnut Zucchini Saute.................................... 221
Warm Apple-Cranberry Dessert................... 201
Warm Broccoli Cheese Dip.............................24
Warm Strawberry Fondue.............................. 196
Wild Rice Turkey Dinner................................ 128
Wine-Braised Chicken with Pearl Onions. 125

Z
Zesty Ham 155
Zesty Jalapeno Corn Muffins 242
Zesty Orange Beef..99

COOK TIME INDEX

Slow-cooked main courses that fit your time frame

1 ½ Hours Cooking Time
Simple Poached Salmon 168

2 Hours Cooking Time
Slow Cooker BBQ Ham Sandwiches 156

2 ¾ Hours Cooking Time
Carolina Cheese Shrimp and Grits.............. 158

3 Hours Cooking Time
Barbecue Cobb Salad 163
Chili & Cheese Crustless Quiche 162
Chipotle Pulled Chicken 116
Creamy Chicken Fettuccine 106
Creamy Garlic-Lemon Chicken 102
Party-Time Wings 121
Pineapple-Dijon Ham Sandwiches 144

Pork Chops with Sauerkraut 134
Shredded Chicken Gyros.................................. 116
Slow-Cooked Stuffed Peppers...................... 165
Slow Cooker Ham & Eggs.............................. 168
Slow Cooker Mushroom Chicken & Peas 118
Slow-Cooker Sloppy Joes.................................77
Slow Cooker Tropical Pork Chops 154

3 ¼ Hours Cooking Time
Gulf Coast Jambalaya Rice............................ 170
Hash Browns with Ham.................................. 156
Meat-Lover's Pizza Hot Dish........................... 79
Polynesian Pull Chicken 129
Shrimp Marinara... 160
Sweet-and-Sour Chicken 109
Tangy Venison Stroganoff.............................. 183

3 ½ Hours Cooking Time
Buffalo Shrimp Mac & Cheese...................... 168
Greek Garlic Chicken...................................... 123
Hash Brown Egg Breakfast 132

3 ¾ Hours Cooking Time
Slow Cooker Mac n Cheese 160

4 Hours Cooking Time
Apple Balsamic Chicken 126
Apple-Dijon Pork Roast 148
Beef 'n' Bean Torta..93
Busy-Day Chicken Fajitas 110
Carolina-Style Vinegar BBQ Chicken 105
Cheesy Tater Tot Dinner 183
Chunky Chicken Cacciatore 118
Cranberry-Mustard Pork Loin 137
Creamy Italian Chicken 110
Curry Chicken Stew... 100
Easy Turkey Sloppy Joes 101
Eye-Opening Burritos...................................... 177

Ham 'n' Swiss Chicken....................119
Ham Barbecue....................152
Italian Sausage Hoagies....................131
Light Ham Tetrazzini....................140
Mushroom Chicken Cacciatore....................110
Pineapple Chicken....................127
Pork Chops & Acorn Squash....................139
Potato Pizza Casserole....................75
Rosemary Cashew Chicken....................102
Saucy Ranch Pork and Potatoes....................138
Slow-Cooked Chunky Chili....................87
Slow-Cooked Coconut Chicken....................108
Slow Cooker Roast Chicken....................110
Slow Cooker Salmon Loaf....................183
Spring Herb Roast....................79
Sweet Pepper Chicken....................119
Sweet Sausage 'n' Beans....................146

4 ¼ Hours Cooking Time
Slow Cooker Chicken & Black Bean Soft
    Tacos....................107

4 ½ Hours Cooking Time
Chicken Stew....................115
Mandarin Turkey Tenderloin....................127

4 ¾ Hours Cooking Time
Spicy Seafood Stew....................180

5 Hours Cooking Time
Beer Brat Chili....................152
Busy Mom's Chicken Fajitas....................120
Butter & Herb Turkey....................124
Chicken Chili....................128
Chili-Lime Chicken Tostadas....................126
Country Pork Chop Supper....................137
Cranberry Chicken....................105
Easy Chili Verde....................131
Garlic-Sesame Beef....................75
Greek Dinner....................115
Herbed Chicken and Tomatoes....................106
Lemony Turkey Breast....................108
Mexican Beef-Stuffed Peppers....................76
Peachy Pork Chops....................152
Saucy BBQ Chicken Thighs....................101
Sausage Spanish Rice....................149
Slow-Cooked Meat Loaf....................90
Spicy Chicken Chili....................37
Spicy Hash Brown Supper....................180
Super Easy Country-Style Ribs....................151
Vegetarian Red Bean Chili....................171
Zesty Orange Beef....................98

5 ¼ Cooking Time
Melt-in-Your-Mouth Meat Loaf....................94

5 ½ Hours Cooking Time
Pork with Peach Picante Sauce....................140
Slow Cook Lamb Chops....................172

Tender Beef Over Noodles....................83
Tender Spareribs....................132

6 Hours Cooking Time
African Peanut Sweet Potato Stew....................178
Barbecue Beef Brisket....................98
Barbecue Brats & Peppers....................151
Beefy Cabbage Bean Stew....................40
Braised Beef Short Ribs....................93
Chicken Veggie Alfredo....................109
Chipotle Beef Chili....................97
Chipotle Carne Guisada....................80
Chunky Pasta Sauce....................167
Cornish Hens with Potatoes....................123
Cranberry Pork & Sweet Potatoes....................145
Deluxe Walking Nachos....................172
Green Chili Shredded Pork....................148
Home-Style Stew....................79
Mexican Shredded Beef Wraps....................84
Mushroom-Beef Spaghetti Sauce....................90
No-Fuss Beef Roast....................82
Peachy Baby Back Ribs....................146
Pork and Beef Barbecue....................154
Pork Chili....................142
Pork Chop Dinner....................138
Potato Sausage Supper....................132
Red Pepper Chicken....................106
Shredded Beef au Jus....................94
Slow-Cooked Ham with Pineapple Sauce....................142
Slow-Cooked Tex-Mex Flank Steak....................86
Slow-Cooked Turkey Stroganoff....................128
Slow Cooker Chicken Cacciatore....................102
Slow Cooker Golombki....................91
Slow Cooker Pot Roast....................85
Slow-Roasted Chicken with Vegetables....................105
Snappy Southwest Chicken....................113
Southwest Entree Salad....................174
Sunday Chicken Supper....................114
Sweet & Sour Pork Wraps....................141
Wild Rice Turkey Dinner....................128
Zesty Ham....................155

6 ¼ Hours Cooking Time
Chile Colorado Burritos....................74
Country Ribs Dinner....................142
Slow-Cooked Jambalaya....................113

6 ½ Hours Cooking Time
Slow-Cooked Fish Stew....................164

7 Hours Cooking Time
Autumn Pumpkin Chili....................180
Best Ever Roast Beef....................90
Breakfast-for-Dinner Bake....................167
Creamy Chicken Thighs & Noodles....................112
Flavorful Beef in Gravy....................98
Ham and Bean Stew....................135

Marty's Bean Burger Chili....................160
Posole Verde....................171
Pulled Pork Sandwiches....................146
Shredded Turkey Sandwiches....................112
Slow Cooker Breakfast Casserole....................151
Spring-Thyme Chicken Stew....................123
Steak San Marino....................94
Sweet & Tangy Beef Roast....................89
Teriyaki Pork Roast....................152
Wine-Braised Chicken with
    Pearl Onions....................125

7 ¼ Hours Cooking Time
Meaty Slow-Cooked Jambalaya....................159

7 ½ Hours Cooking Time
Chicken a la King....................116
Hearty Busy-Day Stew....................92
Italian Shrimp 'n' Pasta....................179
Pasta e Fagioli....................177

8 Hours Cooking Time
Autumn Beef Stew....................80
Brisket with Cranberry Gravy....................86
Dilly Beef Sandwiches....................98
Family-Favorite Italian Beef Sandwiches....................83
Garlic-Apple Pork Roast....................130
Italian Shredded Pork Stew....................156
Java Roast Beef....................76
Lamb with Orzo....................167
Sassy Pot Roast....................87
Simply Delicious Roast Beef Sandwiches....................97
Slow Cooker Chicken Dinner....................120
Slow Cooker French Dip Sandwiches....................80
Smoked Beef Brisket....................97
Sweet and Sour Brisket....................89
Sweet and Tangy Chicken....................124
Tender Pork Roast....................138

8 ¼ Hours Cooking Time
Burgundy Beef....................89

8 ½ Hours Cooking Time
Root Beer Pulled Pork Sandwiches....................137
Slow-Cooked Beef Brisket....................85

9 Hours Cooking Time
Pork Carnitas....................155
Slow Cooker Kalua Pork & Cabbage....................134

9 ½ Hours Cooking Time
Slow-Cooked Coffee Pot Roast....................82

10 Hours Cooking Time
Italian Beef....................76